THE BLUES

THE BLUES

DAY-TO-DAY LIFE AT
STAMFORD BRIDGE

RICHARD LERMAN AND DAVID BROWN

MAINSTREAM
PUBLISHING

EDINBURGH AND LONDON

First published in Great Britain in 1998 by
MAINSTREAM PUBLISHING COMPANY (EDINBURGH) LTD
7 Albany Street
Edinburgh EH1 3UG

ISBN 1 84018 035 8

A catalogue record for this book is available from the British Library

Typeset in Times
Printed and bound in Great Britain by Butler & Tanner Ltd

Chelsea fans knew it all along, but their club is somewhat unique in the history of football. Whilst most clubs owe their very existence to either cricket clubs or the church, forming themselves into a football club in order to enjoy some form of recreation during the winter months, Chelsea were formed to take advantage of an existing ground. Mr HA Mears owned the Stamford Bridge ground and in 1904 invited Fulham to rent the premises from him for the purposes of football. Fulham preferred to remain at Craven Cottage and Mr Mears was faced with the choice of selling the land to the Great Western Railway company or developing the ground himself. Encouraged by Frederick Parker, Mr Mears opted for the latter choice and formed Chelsea FC in 1905. The whole history of Chelsea might have turned out completely different had he then been successful with an application to join the Southern League, but the backward thinking of this august body drove him and Chelsea into the arms of the Football League, with Chelsea joining the Second Division in 1905. Had Chelsea joined the Southern League, would they have risen above the status of Fulham? It is a debatable point, but within ten years Chelsea had reached the FA Cup final for the first time in their history and forty years later won the League title; Fulham still wait to welcome either trophy at Craven Cottage.

The usual football club history book is laid-out chronologically from past to present, developing chapter by chapter the story of the journey to prominence (or in some cases oblivion) and the characters that shaped the destiny of the club and the team.

Alternatively, a player by player analysis or a Who's Who will attempt to list, in alphabetical order, all or sometimes just the key participants who have taken part in the building of the organisation or the events on the field.

We believe that *The Blues* introduces a third, and new, concept to the study of football clubs.

Simply, by using a diary format, we have attempted to catalogue the important events, the landmarks along the way for both the club and its players and the highs and lows as they occurred on a day-to-day basis from formation to the present.

Obviously in a topic as large as the one we have attempted to cover there will be a debate about what material should be included and what should be left out. It would not have been practical to have included details on every player that has ever worn the blue shirt of Chelsea. We have had to establish criteria that only those who have played a minimum number of games, or have been recognised for some other aspect of their career, be included. If, as we suspect, this has lead to the omission of many fine players who for one reason or another did not make it into these pages, we apologise to them, their families and their supporters.

It has not been our policy to be contentious, we have desired to present a factual account of the history of this great club and, in so doing, some subjective decisions have had to be made. However, if any reader should consider we have made a glaring omission or a factual inaccuracy, we should be glad to address these matters with correspondence via our publisher, so that we might include any changes in a future edition of this book.

Finally, it has been our privilege to work on this subject matter. As can be seen from the text the last couple of years has seen Chelsea return to its rightful place among football's elite, with success in both domestic cups and European glory invoking memories of those heady days of the late 1960s and early 1970s. We suspect the wait for further glory at Stamford Bridge will not take as long next time around!

This is the first time that Richard Lerman and David Brown have worked together. This book, and three other titles from the same partnership, form part of a series on football that Mainstream Publishing are issuing where the material is organised in diary format.

Richard Lerman is married with three sons (all keen football enthusiasts) and lives in North London.

David Brown is married with two daughters (who care more for music than football) and lives in Kent.

Both men travel the length and breadth of Great Britain and Europe in pursuit of their obsession with football and are avid collectors of football memorabilia and statistics.

ACKNOWLEDGEMENTS

Richard Lerman and David Brown would like to thank the following who have helped us in the research and for providing us with the material to make this book possible: Robert Stein, Steve Johnson, Andy Kelly and Andrew Miller. We would also like to thank the many readers of *Boot Magazine*, which specialises in football memorabilia (6 Denmark Road, London, N8 0DZ), who have provided us with material for this publication.

Last but not least, we would very much like to thank Graham Betts for his efforts in organising this project, together with all the staff at Mainstream Publishing.

The phtographs in this book were supplied by Wellard Huxley Promotions, Bob Bond and John Allan (proprietor of the *Football Card Collector Magazine*, PO Box 21709, London, E14 6SR).

1886   Harold Halse born in Stratford in East London. After a remarkable two seasons with Southend United, during which he scored 200 goals, Harold was snapped up by Manchester United for £350 in March 1908. Although he didn't score with the same regularity at Old Trafford, he was one of the most dangerous forwards of his age and would go on to score six goals in the FA Charity Shield match against Swindon. He won a League championship and FA Cup winners' medal whilst at United, and was sold to Aston Villa for £1,200 in 1912, adding a second FA Cup winners' medal at the end of his first season at Villa Park. His third appearance in the final came in 1915 when he was playing for Chelsea, although this time he had to settle for a runners-up medal. At the end of the First World War he returned to Chelsea, subsequently moving on to Charlton in 1921, retiring in 1923 and then scouting for the club for a further two years.

1889   Angus Douglas was born in Lochmaben, Dumfries. He was signed by Chelsea from Dumfries in May 1908 after spells with local junior clubs Castlemilk and Lochmaben. A tricky winger, he quickly established himself as a crowd favourite at Stamford Bridge and it was, therefore, a surprise when he was sold to Newcastle United for £1,100 in October 1913 after amassing just over 100 appearances for the Blues in which he scored a dozen League goals. He also gained a Scottish international cap.

1938	Liverpool	A	League Division 1	2–2
1944	Brentford	H	Football League South	0–3
1948	Blackburn Rovers	A	League Division 1	1–1

William Dickson made his League debut for Chelsea.

1949	Birmingham City	H	League Division 1	2–0
1955	Bolton Wanderers	A	League Division 1	5–2
1957	Manchester United	A	League Division 1	0–3

John Sillett played his first game for the Blues.

1966	Blackpool	A	League Division 1	2–1
1972	Derby County	A	League Division 1	0–1
1974	Sheffield United	A	League Division 1	2–1
1976	Bristol Rovers	H	FA Cup 3rd round	1–1
1977	Hereford United	H	League Division 2	5–1
1980	Luton Town	A	League Division 2	3–3
1983	Shrewsbury Town	A	League Division 2	0–2
1985	Nottingham Forest	H	League Division 1	1–0
1987	Queens Park Rangers	H	League Division 1	3–1
1988	Luton Town	H	League Division 1	3–0
1990	Aston Villa	H	League Division 1	0–3
1991	Everton	H	League Division 1	1–2
1992	Manchester City	H	League Division 1	1–1
1994	Swindon Town	A	Premier League	3–1
1997	Liverpool	H	Premier League	1–0

JANUARY 2

1909	Liverpool	H	League Division 1	3–0
1911	Stockport County	A	League Division 2	2–2
1915	Tottenham Hotspur	H	League Division 1	1–1
1926	Bradford City	A	League Division 2	2–4
1932	Middlesbrough	H	League Division 1	4–0
1937	Birmingham City	A	League Division 1	0–0
1943	Fulham	A	Football League South	1–3
1954	Charlton Athletic	A	League Division 1	1–1
1960	Leicester City	H	League Division 1	2–2

1962 Peter Rhoades-Brown, one of a dying breed of footballers with double-barrelled names, was born in Hampton. He joined Chelsea as a schoolboy progressing via an apprenticeship to professional in July 1979. Although he mustered over 100 appearances he never became an integral member of the first team and moved on to Oxford United in January 1984 for a fee of £85,000. He retired from football six years later.

1965	Leicester City	H	League Division 1	4–1
1971	Crystal Palace	A	FA Cup 3rd round	2–2
1978	West Bromwich Albion	H	League Division 1	2–2
1984	Middlesbrough	A	League Division 2	1–2
1988	Tottenham Hotspur	A	League Division 1	0–1
1989	Oxford United	A	League Division 2	3–2
1996	Queens Park Rangers	A	Premier League	2–1

JANUARY 3

1904 Robert Edmond Gregg was born in Ferryhil. Arrived at Stamford Bridge after an illustrious career that had lead him from Darlington to Birmingham City via Sheffield Wednesday. However he failed to reproduce earlier form after the Blues had secured his services in September 1933 and made just 51 appearances before leaving for non-League football with Boston United in June 1938.

1914	Oldham Athletic	H	League Division 1	2–1
1920	Manchester United	A	League Division 1	2–0
1925	Oldham Athletic	H	League Division 2	4–1
1931	Manchester United	A	League Division 1	0–1
1942	Millwall	H	London War League	3–3
1948	Derby County	A	League Division 1	1–5
1953	Portsmouth	A	League Division 1	0–2
1959	Wolverhampton Wanderers	A	League Division 1	2–1
1965	Northampton Town	H	FA Cup 3rd round	4–1
1970	Birmingham City	H	FA Cup 3rd round	3–0
1973	Norwich City	A	League Cup semi-final	0–1
1976	Bristol Rovers	A	FA Cup 3rd round replay	1–0
1981	Southampton	A	FA Cup 3rd round	1–3

1983	Leicester City	A	League Division 2	0–3
1987	Luton Town	A	League Division 1	0–1
1994	Everton	H	Premier League	4–2

JANUARY 4

| 1908 | Sheffield United | A | League Division 1 | 3–0 |

1909 William Barraclough was born in Hull. Joined Chelsea in October 1934 from Wolverhampton Wanderers after an initial period with Hull City where he was an amateur. A tricky winger, Barraclough played a total of 81 games scoring 11 goals before departing in 1937 for Colchester Town.

1913	Sheffield United	A	League Division 1	3–3
1919	Fulham	H	London Combination League	3–0
1930	Oldham Athletic	H	League Division 2	1–1
1936	Grimsby Town	H	League Division 1	0–2
1941	Aldershot	A	London Cup 'A' Competition	0–1
1947	Liverpool	H	League Division 1	3–1

First appearance of Sydney Bathgate.

1958	Doncaster Rovers	A	FA Cup 3rd round	2–0
1964	Tottenham Hotspur	A	FA Cup 3rd round	1–1
1969	Carlisle United	H	FA Cup 3rd round	2–0
1975	Sheffield Wednesday	H	FA Cup 3rd round	3–2
1986	Shrewsbury Town	A	FA Cup 3rd round	1–0
1992	Hull City	A	FA Cup 3rd round	2–0
1997	West Bromwich Albion	H	FA Cup 3rd round	3–0
1998	Manchester United	H	FA Cup 3rd round	3–5

JANUARY 5

1907	Blackpool	H	League Division 2	3–0
1918	Crystal Palace	A	London Combination League	0–0
1924	Arsenal	H	League Division 1	0–0
1929	Blackpool	H	League Division 2	2–3
1935	Leicester City	A	League Division 1	0–1
1946	Leicester City	H	FA Cup 3rd round	1–1

After many appearances as a wartime guest, John Harris made his formal debut for the club. Also making their first appearances for the club were Len Goulden, Alexander Harold Machin, Tommy Lawton, Reg Williams and Daniel Winter.

1952	Fulham	A	League Division 1	2–1
1957	Leyton Orient	A	FA Cup 3rd round	2–0
1963	Tranmere Rovers	A	FA Cup 3rd round	2–2

1965 Vincent Peter Jones was born in Watford. The most celebrated former hod-carrier in football, Vinny came to prominence with Wimbledon who signed him from non-League Wealdstone. He was an integral part of the team that won the FA Cup with victory over Liverpool in 1988 and surprised many when he was transferred to Leeds United for £650,000 in June 1989. There he stayed for just over a year before joining neighbours, Sheffield United where he remained for an 11-month spell coming to Chelsea for £575,000 in August 1991. He was appreciated by the crowd for his robust, if unsophisticated, performances and appeared 52 times before closing the circle with a move back to Wimbledon in September 1992. Chelsea received £700,000 for 'Jonah', a small profit accruing to them in the transaction. He later moved on again, when on transfer deadline day 1998 he took a chance to move into a player-coaching role with Queens Park Rangers.

| 1972 | Tottenham Hotspur | A | League Cup semi-final | 2–2 |

Although Chelsea had won the first leg with a late goal, Spurs were confident of overturning the deficit and winning through to Wembley, even if extra time was required. With some five minutes or so left to play, the score was 2–1 on the night and 3–3 on aggregate. Then Chelsea were awarded a free kick out near the touchline; there appeared to be no immediate danger, as a low cross was fired into the Spurs penalty area. Cyril Knowles, guarding the near post, had the ball covered and could have chosen to kick the ball with either foot into the crowd for safety. Somehow, he changed his mind over which foot to use whilst the ball was in mid-flight and missed it altogether. Jennings, unable to see the ball until it was too late, could not prevent it going into the net to bring Chelsea level on the night and into the final. So much for confidence! Chelsea, not Spurs, would go to Wembley!

1974	Queens Park Rangers	H	FA Cup 3rd round	0–0
1985	Wigan Athletic	H	FA Cup 3rd round	2–2
1991	Oxford United	H	FA Cup 3rd round	1–3

JANUARY 6

1884 Goalkeeper Robert 'Pom-Pom' Whiting was born in West Ham. He joined Chelsea in 1906 and was a regular for barely a season and a half during which time he helped the club to gain promotion to the First Division for the first time and made a total of 54 appearances. After losing his place in the team to Jack Whiteley he moved to non-League Brighton and Hove Albion where he remained until the outbreak of the First World War.

1906	Blackpool	H	League Division 2	6–0
1912	Leeds City	H	League Division 2	4–2
1917	Portsmouth	A	London Combination League	1–2
1923	Liverpool	A	League Division 1	0–1

1928 Derek William Saunders was born in Ware. After a distinguished career with amateurs Walthamstow Avenue where Saunders was part of the 1952 FA Amateur Cup winning team and an Amateur international for England, he signed for Chelsea in July 1953. He certainly did not fail to adjust to the higher standard of football and was ever present in the Blues side that won the 1954–55 League Championship as well as later being made team captain. He retired as a player in May 1959 and joined the coaching staff.

| 1934 | Wolverhampton Wanderers | A | League Division 1 | 1–1 |
| 1940 | Fulham | H | Football League South B | 1–1 |

1943 Terence Frederick Venables was born in Bethnal Green. An international for England Schoolboys, Venables signed as a professional for the club in August 1960 and quickly developed into a first team regular, playing an important part in the promotion push during season 1962–63. After 237 appearances and 31 goals for Chelsea he was transferred to Tottenham Hotspur for £80,000 in May 1966. Later moved on to Queens Park Rangers and then Crystal Palace as a player before heading in the reverse direction as a manager where he sandwiched a brief but successful spell in charge at Barcelona in between managerial positions with QPR and Spurs. Following periods in charge of the England and Australian National teams and an involvement at Portsmouth he has returned to management with Crystal Palace. As a player Venables was capped at 5 different international levels and won a League Cup winners' medal in 1966 and an FA Cup winners' medal in 1967. At management level his only winning achievement of note is the capture of the Spanish League title with Barcelona in what many might regard as a two-horse race.

1945	Charlton Athletic	H	Football League South	4–0
1962	Liverpool	A	FA Cup 3rd round	3–4
1968	Southampton	A	League Division 1	5–3
1971	Crystal Palace	H	FA Cup 3rd round replay	2–0
1990	Crewe Alexandra	H	FA Cup 3rd round	1–1
1993	Crystal Palace	A	League Cup 5th round	1–3

JANUARY 7

1911	Barnsley	A	League Division 2	2–3
1922	West Bromwich Albion	A	FA Cup 1st round	2–4
1928	Blackpool	A	League Division 2	4–2
1933	Huddersfield Town	H	League Division 1	0–1

Allan Craig made his debut.

1939	Arsenal	H	FA Cup 3rd round	2–1
1950	Brentford	A	FA Cup 3rd round	1–0
1956	Hartlepool United	A	FA Cup 3rd round	1–0
1961	Crewe Alexandra	H	FA Cup 3rd round	1–2
1967	Southampton	H	League Division 1	4–1
1978	Liverpool	H	FA Cup 3rd round	4–2
1984	Blackburn Rovers	A	FA Cup 3rd round	0–1
1989	Barnsley	A	FA Cup 3rd round	0–4
1995	Charlton Athletic	H	FA Cup 3rd round	3–0
1996	Newcastle United	H	FA Cup 3rd round	1–1
1998	Ipswich Town	A	League Cup 5th round	2–2

JANUARY 8

| 1910 | Liverpool | A | League Division 1 | 1–5 |

Jimmy Stewart, better known for sharing his name with the actor, scored a hat-trick for Liverpool.

| 1916 | Queens Park Rangers | H | London Combination League (Part One) | 5–1 |

1921	Reading	A	FA Cup 1st round	0–0
1927	Luton Town	H	FA Cup 3rd round	4–0
1938	Everton	H	FA Cup 3rd round	0–1
1944	Arsenal	H	Football League South	2–0
1949	Bristol City	A	FA Cup 3rd round	3–1
1955	Walsall	H	FA Cup 3rd round	2–0
1964	Tottenham Hotspur	H	FA Cup 3rd round replay	2–0
1966	Tottenham Hotspur	H	League Division 1	2–1
1972	Huddersfield Town	H	League Division 1	2–2
1977	Southampton	A	FA Cup 3rd round	1–1
1983	Huddersfield Town	A	FA Cup 3rd round	1–1
1994	Barnet	A	FA Cup 3rd round	0–0

JANUARY 9

1909	Bury	A	League Division 1 (Abandoned)	1–4
1915	Swindon Town	H	FA Cup 1st round	1–1
1926	Plymouth Argyle	A	FA Cup 3rd round	2–1
1932	Tranmere Rovers	A	FA Cup 3rd round	2–2
1937	Middlesbrough	H	League Division 1	1–0
1943	West Ham United	H	Football League South	1–3
1951	Rochdale	A	FA Cup 3rd round	3–2
1954	West Bromwich Albion	A	FA Cup 3rd round	0–1
1960	Bradford Park Avenue	H	FA Cup 3rd round	5–1
1971	Manchester United	H	League Division 1	1–2
1980	Death of John Priestley.			
1988	Derby County	A	FA Cup 3rd round	3–1
1993	Man City	H	Premier League	2–4

JANUARY 10

1910	Preston North End	A	League Division 1	0–2
1914	Millwall	A	FA Cup 3rd round	0–0
1920	Bolton Wanderers	A	FA Cup 1st round	1–0
1925	Birmingham City	A	FA Cup 1st round	0–2
1931	West Ham United	A	FA Cup 3rd round	3–1
1942	Arsenal	H	London War League	1–5
1946	Leicester City	A	FA Cup 3rd round	2–0
1946	Leicester City	A	FA Cup 3rd round	2–0
1948	Barrow	H	FA Cup 3rd round	5–0
1953	Derby County	A	FA Cup 3rd round	4–4
1970	Leeds United	H	League Division 1	2–5
1976	Oldham Athletic	H	League Division 2	0–3
1981	Sheffield Wednesday	A	League Division 2	0–0
1987	Aston Villa	A	FA Cup 3rd round	2–2
1989	Nottingham Forest	H	Simod Cup 3rd round	1–4

| 1990 | Crewe Alexandra | A | FA Cup 3rd round replay | 2–0 |
| 1998 | Coventry City | H | Premier League | 3–1 |

JANUARY 11

| 1908 | Worksop Town | H | FA Cup 1st round | 9–1 |

The Blues' biggest victory in the FA Cup was achieved with the assistance of George Hilsdon's six goals! In netting a double hat-trick Hilsdon surpassed the five-goal tally he had achieved on his debut on the opening day of the previous season.

1913	Southend United	H	FA Cup 1st round	5–2
1919	Brentford	A	London Combination League	1–1
1930	Arsenal	A	FA Cup 3rd round	0–2
1936	Norwich City	A	FA Cup 3rd round	1–1
1941	Aldershot	H	London Cup 'A' Competition	5–1
1947	Arsenal	H	FA Cup 3rd round	1–1
1958	Everton	H	League Division 1	3–1
1964	Liverpool	A	League Division 1	1–2
1969	Man City	A	League Division 1	1–4
1975	Luton Town	A	League Division 1	1–1
1986	Luton Town	H	League Division 1	1–0
1992	Tottenham Hotspur	H	League Division 1	2–0
1997	Nottingham Forest	A	Premier League	0–2

JANUARY 12

1892 Goalkeeper Benjamin Howard Baker was born in Liverpool. An amateur all his career, he played for Chelsea in a five-year spell between 1921 and 1926 during which time he made 93 appearances for the Blues as they enjoyed success against the best professional teams in the land. Before coming to the Bridge, Baker had played for a variety of clubs including Old Marlburians, Liverpool, Balmoral, Preston North End, Corinthians and Everton. After Chelsea he returned to Everton before linking up with Oldham Athletic.

1907	Lincoln City	A	FA Cup 1st round	2–2
1918	Brentford	H	London Combination League	4–1
1921	Reading	H	FA Cup 1st round replay	2–2
1924	Southampton	H	FA Cup 1st round	1–1
1929	Everton	H	FA Cup 3rd round	2–0
1935	Luton Town	H	FA Cup 3rd round	1–1
1946	Leicester City	A	Football League South	7–1
1952	Chester	H	FA Cup 3rd round	2–2
1957	Cardiff City	H	League Division 1	1–2
1974	Coventry City	A	League Division 1	2–2
1977	Southampton	H	FA Cup 3rd round replay	0–3
1980	Newcastle United	H	League Division 2	4–0
1983	Huddersfield Town	H	FA Cup 3rd round replay	2–0
1991	Queens Park Rangers	H	League Division 1	2–0

JANUARY 13

1912	Sheffield United	H	FA Cup 1st round	1–0
1917	Millwall	H	London Combination League	4–0
1923	Rotherham County	H	FA Cup 1st round	1–0
1932	Tranmere Rovers	H	FA Cup 3rd round replay	5–3
1934	West Bromwich Albion	H	FA Cup 3rd round	1–1
1940	Portsmouth	A	Football League South B	2–1
1945	Clapton Orient	A	Football League South	6–2
1951	Newcastle United	H	League Division 1	3–1
1962	Fulham	A	League Division 1	4–3
1971	Crystal Palace	A	League Division 1	0–0
1973	Brighton & Hove Albion	A	FA Cup 3rd round	2–0
1976	Hereford United	A	Friendly	2–1
1988	Swindon Town	A	Simod Cup 3rd round	0–4

A record defeat in this competition previously known as the Full Members' Cup and subsequently as the ZDS Trophy.

| 1993 | Middlesbrough | A | FA Cup 3rd round | 1–2 |
| 1996 | Everton | A | Premier League | 1–1 |

JANUARY 14

1911	Leyton	H	FA Cup 1st round	0–0
1914	Millwall	H	FA Cup 3rd round replay	0–1
1922	Arsenal	A	League Division 1	0–1
1928	Wolverhampton Wanderers	A	FA Cup 3rd round	1–2
1933	Brighton & Hove Albion	A	FA Cup 3rd round	1–2
1939	Middlesbrough	H	League Division 1	4–2
1950	Manchester United	A	League Division 1	0–1
1953	Derby County	H	FA Cup 3rd round replay	1–0
1956	Sunderland	H	League Division 1	2–3
1961	Bolton Wanderers	H	League Division 1	1–1
1967	Sunderland	A	League Division 1	0–2
1978	Coventry City	A	League Division 1	1–5
1980	Wigan Athletic	H	FA Cup 3rd round	0–1
1981	DS79 Dordrecht, Holland	A	Friendly	4–2
1984	Derby County	A	League Division 2	2–1

The much-travelled Mickey Thomas begun his Chelsea career.

| 1989 | Crystal Palace | H | League Division 2 | 1–0 |

Dave Beasant made his Chelsea debut.

| 1990 | Sheffield Wednesday | A | League Division 1 | 1–1 |
| 1995 | Sheffield Wednesday | H | Premier League | 1–1 |

JANUARY 15

| 1910 | Hull City | H | FA Cup 1st round | 2–1 |
| 1916 | Arsenal | A | London Combination League (Part One) | 6–0 |

1917 Benjamin Warren died in Mickleover, Derbyshire. After a wonderful football career Warren was certified insane and died after spending time in a lunatic asylum.

1921	Man City	H	League Division 1	2–1
1927	Middlesbrough	A	League Division 2	0–0
1936	Norwich City	H	FA Cup 3rd round replay	3–1
1938	West Bromwich Albion	H	League Division 1	2–2
1947	Arsenal	A	FA Cup 3rd round replay	1–1
1972	Blackpool	A	FA Cup 3rd round	1–0
1974	Queens Park Rangers	A	FA Cup 3rd round replay	0–1
1979	Manchester United	A	FA Cup 3rd round	0–3
1983	Cambridge United	H	League Division 2	6–0
1994	Norwich City	A	Premier League	1–1

JANUARY 16

1907	Lincoln City	H	FA Cup 1st round replay	0–1
1909	Hull City	A	FA Cup 1st round	1–1
1915	Swindon Town	A	FA Cup 1st round replay	5–2

'One eye' Bob Thomson scored a hat-trick for Chelsea.

1921	Reading	H	FA Cup 1st round 2nd replay	3–1
1924	Southampton	A	FA Cup 1st round replay	0–2
1926	Port Vale	H	League Division 2	3–1
1932	Huddersfield Town	A	League Division 1	1–2
1935	Luton Town	A	FA Cup 3rd round replay	0–2
1937	Leeds United	H	FA Cup 3rd round	4–0
1943	Aldershot	A	Football League South	1–1
1952	Chester	A	FA Cup 3rd round replay	3–2
1954	Sheffield United	A	League Division 1	3–1
1960	Burnley	A	League Division 1	1–2
1965	Fulham	A	League Division 1	2–1
1971	Everton	A	League Division 1	0–3
1982	Bolton Wanderers	A	League Division 2	2–2
1988	Sheffield Wednesday	H	League Division 1	2–1
1991	Tottenham Hotspur	H	League Cup 5th round	0–0
1993	Nottingham Forest	A	Premier League	0–3

JANUARY 17

1914	Manchester United	A	League Division 1	1–0
1920	Manchester United	H	League Division 1	1–0
1925	Sheffield Wednesday	A	League Division 2	1–2

George Rodger made his first appearance after joining Chelsea from junior club,

Kilsyth Rangers. He went on to complete his time at the Bridge with 122 games (2 goals) before a knee injury put paid to his career.

1931	West Ham United	H	League Division 1	2–1
1934	West Bromwich Albion	A	FA Cup 3rd round replay	1–0
1942	Queens Park Rangers	H	London War League	3–1
1948	Huddersfield Town	H	League Division 1	2–4

Roy Bentley made his debut for Chelsea.

| 1953 | Bolton Wanderers | H | League Division 1 | 1–0 |
| 1959 | Portsmouth | H | League Division 1 | 2–2 |

1969 Samuel Irving died.

1970	Arsenal	A	League Division 1	3–0
1976	Nottingham Forest	A	League Division 2	3–1
1981	Queens Park Rangers	A	League Division 2	0–1
1996	Newcastle United	A	FA Cup 3rd round replay	2–2

JANUARY 18

1908	Nottingham Forest	H	League Division 1	0–4
1913	Newcastle United	H	League Division 1	1–0
1919	West Ham United	H	London Combination League	0–0
1922	Bolton Wanderers	H	League Division 1	0–3
1930	Millwall	A	League Division 2	0–0
1936	Leeds United	A	League Division 1	0–2
1947	Leeds United	A	League Division 1	1–2
1958	Newcastle United	H	League Division 1	2–1
1964	Aston Villa	H	League Division 1	1–0
1969	Liverpool	H	League Division 1	1–2
1975	Leeds United	H	League Division 1	0–2
1982	Hull City	H	FA Cup 3rd round	0–0
1986	West Bromwich Albion	A	League Division 1	3–0
1992	Wimbledon	A	League Division 1	2–1
1997	Derby County	H	Premier League	3–1
1998	Everton	A	Premier League	1–3

JANUARY 19

1883 Samuel Downing was born in Wilesden. Given his professional start by Queens Park Rangers from where he joined Chelsea in April 1909. Stayed for five seasons making just short of 150 appearances (10 goals) before moving to Croydon Common where he finished his career.

1911	Leyton	A	FA Cup 1st round replay	2–0
1918	Arsenal	A	London Combination League	1–4
1924	Huddersfield Town	A	League Division 1	1–0
1929	Middlesbrough	A	League Division 2	5–4
1935	Sunderland	H	League Division 1	2–2
1946	Leicester City	H	Football League South	4–0

1952	Huddersfield Town	A	League Division 1	0–1
1957	Birmingham City	A	League Division 1	1–0
1959	Newcastle United	A	FA Cup 3rd round	4–1
1974	Derby County	H	League Division 1	1–1
1985	Arsenal	H	League Division 1	1–1
1991	Sunderland	A	League Division 1	0–1
1994	Barnet	H	FA Cup 3rd round replay	4–0

JANUARY 20

1906	Bradford City	H	League Division 2	4–2
1909	Hull City	H	FA Cup 1st round replay	1–0
1912	Wolverhampton Wanderers	A	League Division 2	1–3
1917	Watford	A	London Combination League	3–0
1923	Newcastle United	H	League Division 1	3–0
1934	Sheffield United	H	League Division 1	5–0
1940	Queens Park Rangers	H	Football League South B	0–0
1945	Portsmouth	H	Football League South	1–1
1947	Arsenal	White Hart Lane		
			FA Cup 3rd round 2nd replay	2–0
1951	West Bromwich Albion	A	League Division 1	1–1
1962	Sheffield United	A	League Division 1	1–3
1965	Aston Villa	A	League Cup semi-final	3–2

John Boyle made the first of his many appearances for the Blues.

1968	Stoke City	A	League Division 1	1–0
1973	Arsenal	H	League Division 1	0–1
1990	Charlton Athletic	H	League Division 1	3–1
1996	Nottingham Forest	H	Premier League	1–0

JANUARY 21

1911	Leicester Fosse	H	League Division 2	2–0
1922	Bolton Wanderers	A	League Division 1	2–0
1928	Fulham	H	League Division 2	2–1
1933	Sheffield United	A	League Division 1	1–4
1939	Fulham	H	FA Cup 4th round	3–0
1950	Fulham	H	League Division 1	0–0
1956	Aston Villa	A	League Division 1	4–1
1961	West Ham United	A	League Division 1	1–3
1967	Aston Villa	H	League Division 1	3–1
1978	Ipswich Town	H	League Division 1	5–3
1979	Man City	A	League Division 1	3–2
1982	Hull City	A	FA Cup 3rd round replay	2–0
1984	Sheffield Wednesday	H	League Division 2	3–2
1987	Aston Villa	H	FA Cup 3rd round replay	2–1

| 1989 | Blackburn Rovers | A | League Division 2 | 1–1 |
| 1992 | Southampton | A | ZDS Cup Southern final | 0–2 |

An inglorious defeat in a competition that Chelsea had previously excelled in. They were favourites to win the Trophy overall.

| 1995 | Ipswich Town | A | Premier League | 2–2 |

JANUARY 22

1910	Aston Villa	H	League Division 1	0–0
1916	Fulham	H	London Combination League (Part One)	1–1
1921	Man City	A	League Division 1	0–1
1938	Birmingham City	A	League Division 1	1–1
1944	Charlton Athletic	H	Football League South	5–2
1949	Everton	A	League Division 1	1–2
1954	Huddersfield Town	H	League Division 1	2–2
1955	Man City	H	League Division 1	0–2
1963	Hibernian, Malta	A	Friendly	1–0
1966	Liverpool	A	FA Cup 3rd round	2–1

1968 Frank Leboeuf was born in France. He made an immediate impact when introduced to the Chelsea defence following a £2,500,000 move from Strasbourg in July 1996 and has risen to cult status with the fans at the Bridge based on his intelligent use of the ball and obvious passing ability. At the heart of all three recent cup successes, he has won medals for the FA Cup in 1997, Coca-Cola League Cup and European Cup-Winners' Cup in 1998. To complete matters he made an imperious showing in the 1998 World Cup final in Paris in 1998 when, in front of the host nation's fans, he helped France defeat Brazil and lift the ultimate prize in international football.

1972	Manchester United	A	League Division 1	1–0
1977	Orient	H	League Division 2	1–1
1983	Wolverhampton Wanderers	A	League Division 2	1–2
1986	Queens Park Rangers	A	League Cup 5th round	1–1
1994	Aston Villa	H	Premier League	1–1

JANUARY 23

1909	Sheffield United	H	League Division 1	1–1
1915	Middlesbrough	H	League Division 1	2–2
1926	Barnsley	A	League Division 2	3–2
1932	West Ham United	H	FA Cup 4th round	3–1
1937	West Bromwich Albion	A	League Division 1	0–2
1943	Southampton	H	Football League South	3–1
1960	Leeds United	H	League Division 1	1–3
1965	Leeds United	A	League Division 1	2–2
1971	Man City	H	FA Cup 4th round	0–3
1981	Brighton & Hove Albion	A	Friendly	2–2

1982	Wrexham	H	FA Cup 4th round	0–0
1988	Portsmouth	A	League Division 1	3–0
1990	Ipswich Town	A	ZDS Cup Southern semi-final	3–2

Kerry Dixon grabbed a goal and Kevin Wilson two as Chelsea secured a place in the Southern final against Crystal Palace.

| 1991 | Tottenham Hotspur | A | League Cup 5th round replay | 3–0 |

JANUARY 24

1914	Burnley	H	League Division 1	0–0
1920	Bradford City	A	League Division 1	1–3
1925	Clapton Orient	H	League Division 2	1–1
1931	Arsenal	H	FA Cup 4th round	2–1
1940	Brentford	H	Football League South B	3–2
1948	Man City	A	FA Cup 4th round	0–2
1953	Aston Villa	A	League Division 1	1–1
1959	Aston Villa	H	FA Cup 4th round	1–2
1970	Burnley	H	FA Cup 4th round	2–2
1976	York City	A	FA Cup 4th round	2–0
1987	Norwich City	A	League Division 1	2–2

Steve Clarke played his first game for Chelsea.

JANUARY 25

1908	Manchester United	A	League Division 1	0–1
1913	Oldham Athletic	A	League Division 1	2–3
1919	Tottenham Hotspur	A	London Combination League	1–1
1930	Southampton	H	League Division 2	2–0
1936	Plymouth Argyle	H	FA Cup 4th round	4–1
1941	Brentford	H	London Cup 'A' Competition	0–1
1947	Derby County	H	FA Cup 4th round	2–2
1958	Darlington	H	FA Cup 4th round	3–3
1964	Huddersfield Town	H	FA Cup 4th round	1–2
1969	Preston North End	A	FA Cup 4th round	0–0
1975	Birmingham City	H	FA Cup 4th round	0–1
1980	Stoke City	H	Friendly	0–1
1995	Nottingham Forest	H	Premier League	0–2

JANUARY 26

1907	West Bromwich Albion	H	League Division 2	2–0
1918	West Ham United	H	London Combination League	2–2
1924	Huddersfield Town	H	League Division 1	0–1
1946	West Ham United	H	FA Cup 4th round	2–0
1946	West Ham United	H	FA Cup 4th round	2–0
1952	Wolverhampton Wanderers	H	League Division 1	0–1

1957	Tottenham Hotspur	A	FA Cup 4th round	0–4
1963	Malta League	A	Friendly	4–0
1982	Wrexham	A	FA Cup 4th round replay	1–1
1985	Wigan Athletic	A	FA Cup 3rd round replay	5–0

Kerry Dixon scored four goals (including a penalty) whilst David Speedie scored the other.

1986	Liverpool	H	FA Cup 4th round	1–2
1992	Everton	H	FA Cup 4th round	1–0
1997	Liverpool	H	FA Cup 4th round	4–2

JANUARY 27

1906	West Bromwich Albion	A	League Division 2	1–1
1912	Leicester Fosse	H	League Division 2	2–1
1917	Clapton Orient	H	London Combination League	1–0
1923	Newcastle United	A	League Division 1	0–0
1929	Birmingham City	H	FA Cup 4th round	1–0
1934	Nottingham Forest	H	FA Cup 4th round	1–1
1945	Tottenham Hotspur	H	Football League South	1–2
1951	Exeter City	A	FA Cup 4th round	1–1
1968	Ipswich Town	H	FA Cup 3rd round	3–0
1970	Burnley	A	FA Cup 4th round replay	3–1
1973	West Ham United	A	League Division 1	1–3
1974	Stoke City	A	League Division 1	0–1
1990	Bristol City	A	FA Cup 4th round	1–3
1993	Queens Park Rangers	A	Premier League	1–1

JANUARY 28

| 1911 | Wolverhampton Wanderers | A | League Division 2 | 0–0 |

1922 Reginald Williams was born in Watford. He played for his local side as an amateur and joined Chelsea from the Hornets in October 1945. He remained at Stamford Bridge until 1951 when he finally conceded defeat in his constant battle against injury and retired. By this time he had made 74 appearances and scored 17 goals.

1928	Clapton Orient	H	League Division 2	1–0
1933	Wolverhampton Wanderers	H	League Division 1	3–1
1939	Manchester United	H	League Division 1	0–1
1950	Newcastle United	H	FA Cup 4th round	3–1

1952 Kenneth Swain was born in Birkenhead. He joined Chelsea in August 1973 from Wycombe Wanderers and was a regular in the side during his five-year stay at the Bridge, amassing 132 appearances and scoring 29 goals. He was allowed to leave in December 1978 in a £100,000 transfer to Aston Villa as much for fiscal as tactical reasons, and went on to carve out a fine career when converted from a wing position to full-back. At Villa he won both a League Championship medal and also a

European Cup winners' medal. Later moved to Nottingham Forest, Portsmouth, West Bromwich Albion (on loan) and Crewe Alexandra where he was player-coach.

1956	Burnley	A	FA Cup 4th round	1–1
1961	Bristol Rovers	A	Friendly	1–3
1967	Huddersfield Town	A	FA Cup 3rd round	2–1
1985	Sheffield Wednesday	H	League Cup 5th round	1–1
1995	Millwall	A	FA Cup 4th round	0–0
1998	Arsenal	A	League Cup semi-final	1–2

JANUARY 29

1921	Swindon Town	A	FA Cup 2nd round	2–0
1927	Accrington Stanley	H	FA Cup 4th round	7–2
1935	Tottenham Hotspur	A	League Division 1	3–1
1938	Middlesbrough	H	League Division 1	0–1
1944	Aldershot	H	Football League South	8–0

1948 David Hay was born in Paisley. Started his career with Celtic from where he joined Chelsea in August 1974 for £225,000 to begin a stay that would be cut short by injury and premature retirement. Nevertheless, he made 120 appearances in a Chelsea shirt before being forced to hang up his boots. Managed several Scottish clubs in a secondary career.

1949	Everton	H	FA Cup 4th round	2–0
1955	Bristol Rovers	A	FA Cup 4th round	3–1
1958	Darlington	A	FA Cup 4th round replay	1–4
1966	Burnley	A	League Division 1	2–1

1966 Keith Dublin was born in Wycombe. Came to the club as an apprentice in July 1982 and signed professional forms in January 1984 making his debut in May of the same-year. Finished with a total appearance record of 68 games and a move to Brighton and Hove Albion for £3,500 in August 1987. Later with Watford and Southend United.

1969	Preston North End	H	FA Cup 4th round replay (abandoned)	2–0
1972	Everton	H	League Division 1	4–0
1983	Derby County	A	FA Cup 4th round	1–2
1986	Queens Park Rangers	H	League Cup 5th round replay	0–2
1992	Southampton	H	ZDS Cup Southern final	1–3
1994	Sheffield Wednesday	H	FA Cup 4th round	1–1
1996	QPR	A	FA Cup 4th round	2–1

JANUARY 30

1909	Aston Villa	A	League Division 1	0–0
1915	Woolwich Arsenal	H	FA Cup 2nd round	1–0
1926	Crystal Palace	A	FA Cup 4th round	1–2
1929	Barnsley	A	League Division 2	1–0
1932	Aston Villa	A	League Division 1	3–1
1937	Millwall	A	FA Cup 4th round	0–3

1943	Crystal Palace	A	Football League South	2–0
1946	West Ham United	A	FA Cup 4th round	0–1
1946	West Ham United	A	FA Cup 4th round	0–1
1947	Derby County	A	FA Cup 4th round replay	0–1
1960	Aston Villa	H	FA Cup 4th round	1–2
1963	Tranmere Rovers	H	FA Cup 3rd round replay	3–1
1965	West Ham United	A	FA Cup 4th round	1–0
1971	West Bromwich Albion	H	League Division 1	4–1
1982	Shrewsbury Town	H	League Division 2	3–1
1985	Sheffield Wednesday	A	League Cup 5th round replay	4–4

Paul Canoville scored just 11 seconds into the second half of this match.

1988	Manchester United	A	FA Cup 4th round	0–2
1993	Sheffield Wednesday	H	Premier League	0–2

JANUARY 31

1920	Swindon Town	H	FA Cup 2nd round	4–0
1931	Liverpool	H	League Division 1	2–2
1934	Nottingham Forest	A	FA Cup 4th round replay	3–0
1942	Brighton & H.A.	A	London War League	2–8
1948	Bolton Wanderers	A	League Division 1	1–2
1951	Exeter City	H	FA Cup 4th round replay	2–0
1953	West Bromwich Albion	A	FA Cup 4th round	1–1
1959	Aston Villa	A	League Division 1	1–3
1970	Sunderland	H	League Division 1	3–1
1976	West Bromwich Albion	H	League Division 2	1–2
1978	Burnley	H	FA Cup 4th round	6–2

All six goals came from different scorers as Droy, Wicks, Wilkins R, Langley, Swain and Walker each hit the net.

1981	Shrewsbury Town	H	League Division 2	3–0
1998	Barnsley	H	Premier League	2–0

FEBRUARY 1

1908	Manchester United	A	FA Cup 2nd round	0–1
1913	Sheffield Wednesday	H	FA Cup 2nd round	1–1
1919	Clapton Orient	H	London Combination League	3–3
1930	Tottenham Hotspur	A	League Division 2	3–3

1933 Richard Peter Sillett was born in Southampton. Son of former Southampton player Charles Sillett and elder brother of John Sillett who joined the club at the same time, Peter was purchased from the Saints at a cost of £12,000 in May 1953. He won a League Championship medal in 1954–55 and took part in just under 300 games for the Blues before moving on a free transfer into non-League football.

1936	Sunderland	A	League Division 1	3–3
1941	Queens Park Rangers	A	London Cup 'A' Competition	2–5
1947	Charlton Athletic	A	League Division 1	3–2

1956	Burnley	H	FA Cup 4th round replay	1–1
1958	Burnley	A	League Division 1	1–2
1964	Tottenham Hotspur	A	League Division 1	2–1
1969	Southampton	A	League Division 1	0–5

Debuts made by John Dempsey and Alan Hudson.

| 1975 | Leicester City | A | League Division 1 | 1–1 |

Steve Finnieston played his first senior game for the club.

1982	Wrexham	A	FA Cup 4th round 2nd replay	2–1
1986	Leicester City	H	League Division 1	2–2
1987	Watford	A	FA Cup 4th round	0–1
1992	Liverpool	A	League Division 1	2–1
1997	Tottenham Hotspur	A	Premier League	2–1

FEBRUARY 2

1903 Hugh Kilpatrick Gallacher was born in Bellshill, Lanarkshire. One of the great names in the history of the English Football League he came to Chelsea in May 1930 for a fee of £10,000 joining from Newcastle United having previously established his reputation with Airdrieonians. A Scottish international who won 20 caps, he played 144 games and scored 81 goals in his time at Stamford Bridge before moving to Derby County for £3,000 in November 1934. Later moved down the League for spells at Notts County, Grimsby Town and Gateshead before retiring in 1939. Committed suicide in 1957.

| 1907 | Leicester Fosse | A | League Division 2 | 1–1 |
| 1918 | Fulham | A | London Combination League | 2–0 |

1928 Thomas Charles Harmer was born in Hackney. He joined Tottenham Hotspur as an amateur in 1945 and signed professional forms in August 1948. Unfortunately, he had a small frame (he was 5' 6" tall and weighed under 9 stone) which often counted against him in the hustle and bustle of League football. However, at Spurs Tommy, known affectionately as 'Harmer The Charmer', made 205 appearances in the League and 17 in the FA Cup. Then, in October 1960, he was allowed to leave the club and signed with Watford, although he was back in the capital by September 1962 when he joined Chelsea (where he made 9 appearances) eventually becoming coach at Stamford Bridge until released in June 1967.

| 1929 | Bristol City | H | League Division 2 | 3–0 |
| 1935 | Preston North End | H | League Division 1 | 0–0 |

1940 Marvin Hinton was born in Norwood. Bought from Charlton Athletic in August 1963 for £30,000 he served Chelsea for 13 years in which time he amassed over 300 appearances for the club. He won an FA Cup winners' medal in 1970 and a Football League Cup winners' medal in 1966. Continued in non-League football when his Chelsea career came to an end.

1946	Coventry City	A	Football League South	0–2
1952	Tranmere Rovers	H	FA Cup 4th round	4–0
1957	West Bromwich Albion	H	League Division 1	2–4
1971	Santos, Brazil	A	Friendly	0–1

1974	Leeds United	A	League Division 1	1–1
1980	Shrewsbury Town	H	League Division 2	2–4
1985	Leicester City	A	League Division 1	1–1
1991	Arsenal	H	League Division 1	2–1

FEBRUARY 3

1912	Bradford City	A	FA Cup 2nd round	0–2
1917	Fulham	A	London Combination League	0–2
1923	Southampton	H	FA Cup 2nd round	0–0
1934	Leicester City	H	League Division 1 (abandoned)	1–1
1937	Manchester City	H	League Division 1	4–4
1945	Luton Town	A	Football League South Cup Group 4	1–0
1951	Stoke City	H	League Division 1	1–1
1962	West Ham United	H	League Division 1	0–1
1968	Nottingham Forest	H	League Division 1	1–0
1969	Preston North End	H	FA Cup 4th round replay	2–1
1973	Ipswich Town	H	FA Cup 4th round	2–0
1979	Birmingham City	H	League Division 1	2–1

League debut of Eamonn Bannon.

| 1990 | Coventry City | A | League Division 1 | 2–3 |

FEBRUARY 4

1911	Chesterfield Town	A	FA Cup 2nd round	4–1
1920	Bradford City	H	League Division 1	1–0
1922	Oldham Athletic	A	League Division 1	3–0
1928	West Bromwich Albion	A	League Division 2	0–3
1931	Bolton Wanderers	A	League Division 1	1–1
1933	Newcastle United	A	League Division 1	0–2
1939	Stoke City	A	League Division 1	1–6
1950	Stoke City	H	League Division 1	2–2
1953	West Bromwich Albion	H	FA Cup 4th round replay	0–0
1956	Wolverhampton Wanderers	H	League Division 1	2–3
1961	Fulham	H	League Division 1	2–1
1967	Arsenal	A	League Division 1	1–2
1984	Huddersfield Town	H	League Division 2	3–1
1985	Millwall	H	FA Cup 4th round	2–3
1989	Walsall	A	League Division 2	7–0

Gordon 'Juke Box' Durie scored five of the goals as Chelsea romped home.

| 1995 | Coventry City | A | Premier League | 2–2 |
| 1996 | Middlesbrough | H | Premier League | 5–0 |

FEBRUARY 5

| 1906 | Leicester Fosse | H | League Division 2 | 3–3 |

1910	Tottenham Hotspur	H	FA Cup 2nd round	0–1
1913	Sheffield Wednesday	A	FA Cup 2nd round replay	0–6
1916	Queens Park Rangers	A	London Combination League (Part Two)	3–0

1916 Goalkeeper Harry Edward Medhurst was born in Byfleet. Signed from West Ham United in December 1946 as part of the deal that took Joe Payne in the opposite direction. He made 157 appearances for the Blues and then departed for Brighton and Hove Albion in November 1952, only to return to the Bridge six months later in the capacity of assistant coach.

1921	Newcastle United	H	League Division 1	2–0
1927	Bradford City	H	League Division 2	5–2
1938	Stoke City	A	League Division 1	1–2
1944	Luton Town	A	Football League South	5–3
1949	Preston North End	H	League Division 1	5–3

Frank Rawlinson Mitchell, a native of Goulburn, Australia, played his first game for Chelsea. He gained experience with Coventry City and Birmingham City before joining the Blues in January 1949 to commence a period in which he made 85 appearances (1 goal). He lost his place to Bill Dickson and took a move to Watford in August 1952 (for £7,000) where he stayed for five years until retiring.

| 1955 | Aston Villa | A | League Division 1 | 2–3 |

1960 Michael Hazard was born in Sunderland. He cost £310,000 when signed from Tottenham Hotspur in September 1985 for which Chelsea got just under 100 senior games before moving him on to Portsmouth in January 1990; the club recouped £100,000 of its initial outlay. Later went to Swindon Town and then back to Spurs where unbelievably he got a call-up to the England squad.

1966	Fulham	H	League Division 1	2–1
1972	Bolton Wanderers	H	FA Cup 4th round	3–0
1977	Carlisle United	A	League Division 2	1–0
1983	Derby County	H	League Division 2	1–3
1994	Everton	A	Premier League	2–4

FEBRUARY 6

1909	Blackburn Rovers	A	FA Cup 2nd round	1–2
1915	Aston Villa	H	League Division 1	3–1
1926	Fulham	A	League Division 2	3–0
1932	Leicester City	H	League Division 1	1–0
1937	Portsmouth	A	League Division 1	1–4
1943	Tottenham Hotspur	H	Football League South	0–1
1954	Aston Villa	A	League Division 1	2–2
1956	Burnley	Birmingham		
			FA Cup 4th round 2nd replay	2–2
1960	West Ham United	A	League Division 1	2–4

El Tel, then plain Terry Venables, made his League debut.

| 1965 | Arsenal | H | League Division 1 | 2–1 |
| 1971 | Newcastle United | A | League Division 1 | 1–0 |

1982	Watford	A	League Division 2	0–1
1985	Sheffield Wednesday	H	League Cup 5th round 2nd replay	2–1
1988	Nottingham Forest	H	League Division 1	4–3
1993	Oldham Athletic	A	Premier League	1–3

FEBRUARY 7

1904 Allen Craig was born in Paisley. Signed from Motherwell in January 1933 at a cost of £4,000 and remained on the club's books until released in May 1939. A Scottish international (3 caps) who played over 200 games at the centre of Chelsea's defence.

1914	Preston North End	A	League Division 1	3–3
1920	Bolton Wanderers	A	League Division 1	2–1
1923	Southampton	A	FA Cup 2nd round replay	0–1
1925	Southampton	H	League Division 2	1–0

Robert Turnbull made his debut.

1931	Middlesbrough	A	League Division 1	2–2
1942	Brentford	H	London War League	1–1
1953	Sunderland	H	League Division 1	3–2
1959	West Ham United	H	League Division 1	3–2

Debut of Barry Bridges and a 17-year-old Bobby Tambling who, in front of a crowd of 52,000, scored one of the goals that defeated London rivals West Ham.

1970	Crystal Palace	A	FA Cup 5th round	4–1
1976	Oxford United	A	League Division 2	1–1
1981	Cambridge United	H	League Division 2	3–0
1987	Sheffield Wednesday	H	League Division 1	2–0

FEBRUARY 8

| 1908 | Bolton Wanderers | A | League Division 1 | 2–1 |

1909 Samuel Weaver was born in Pilsley, Derbyshire. He had made his name with Hull City and Newcastle United prior to joining Chelsea in August 1936 for just over £4,000. He was made team captain for the season 1938–39 but the Second World War put paid to what had looked to be a promising career at the Bridge and he left to join Stockport County in December 1945. He retired from football two years later. An English international (3 caps), he made 125 appearances for the Blues.

1911	Clapton Orient	H	League Division 2	1–0
1913	Sunderland	A	League Division 1	0–4
1919	Arsenal	H	London Combination League	1–2
1922	Cardiff City	A	League Division 1	0–2
1930	West Bromwich Albion	H	League Division 2	2–0
1934	Aston Villa	A	League Division 1	0–2
1936	Birmingham City	H	League Division 1	0–0
1941	Crystal Palace	A	London Cup 'A' Competition	3–3
1947	Grimsby Town	H	League Division 1	0–0
1958	Preston North End	H	League Division 1	0–2

1958 Thomas Langley was born in Lambeth. An England schoolboy international, Tommy was quickly promoted through the Chelsea youth system and made his First team debut at the age of only 16 years 9 months, some four months before signing as a professional. Although he amassed just over 150 appearances and scored 43 goals in a five-year spell before being transferred to Queens Park Rangers in August 1980 for £425,000, he left behind a feeling of a potential talent that had gone unfulfilled. Had a string of clubs thereafter including Crystal Palace, AEK Athens, Coventry City, Wolverhampton Wanderers, Aldershot and Exeter City.

1964	Wolverhampton Wanderers	H	League Division 1	2–3
1972	Charlton Athletic	A	Testimonial	4–2
1975	Birmingham City	H	League Division 1	2–1
1986	Oxford United	H	League Division 1	1–4
1992	Crystal Palace	H	League Division 1	1–1
1995	Millwall	H	FA Cup 4th round replay	1–1
1998	Arsenal	A	Premier League	0–2

FEBRUARY 9

1907	Nottingham Forest	H	League Division 2	0–2
1918	Clapton Orient	H	London Combination League	3–0
1921	Newcastle United	A	League Division 1	0–1
1924	Notts County	H	League Division 1	0–6

The worst defeat in a relegation season.

1929	Nottingham Forest	A	League Division 2	0–3
1935	Grimsby Town	A	League Division 1	1–3
1946	Aston Villa	H	FA Cup 5th round	0–1
1946	Aston Villa	H	FA Cup 5th round	0–1
1952	Sunderland	A	League Division 1	1–4
1953	West Brom	Highbury	FA Cup 4th round 2nd replay	1–1
1957	Portsmouth	A	League Division 1	2–2
1963	Swansea Town	A	League Division 2	0–2
1966	AC Milan	A	Fairs Cup 3rd round	1–2
1974	Manchester City	H	League Division 1	1–0
1980	Watford	A	League Division 2	3–2
1991	Manchester City	A	League Division 1	1–2
1994	Sheffield Wednesday	A	FA Cup 4th round replay	3–1

FEBRUARY 10

1900 Sidney Macdonald Bishop was born in Stepney. He came to Chelsea in June 1928 and finished his career at the club playing over 100 games (scoring 6 goals) before retiring in May 1933.

1906	Hull City	A	League Division 2	3–4
1912	Grimsby Town	H	League Division 2	4–1
1914	Bolton Wanderers	A	League Division 1	1–1

1917	Queens Park Rangers	H	London Combination League	3–0
1923	Everton	A	League Division 1	1–3
1926	Clapton Orient	H	League Division 2	1–3

1926 Danny Blanchflower was born in Belfast. Began his professional career with Glentoran and was transferred to Barnsley in 1949 for £6,500 and six months later won the first of his 56 caps for Northern Ireland. Aston Villa paid £15,000 for his signature in 1951 and three years later sold him to Spurs for £30,000. His stylish midfield play was one of the keys to their double-winning side of 1961, a team that then went on to retain the FA Cup and, in 1963, lift the European Cup-Winners' Cup. Troubled by knee injury for some time Blanchflower retired in 1964 and immediately launched into a career in journalism, broken only by spells in charge at Chelsea in 1978 and as Northern Ireland's manager. Footballer of the Year in both 1958 and 1961, he died in 1993.

1940	Charlton Athletic	A	Football League South C	3–3
1945	Watford	H	Football League South Cup Group 4	3–1
1951	Fulham	H	FA Cup 5th round	1–1
1962	Blackburn Rovers	A	League Division 1	0–3
1965	Aston Villa	H	League Cup semi-final	1–1
1968	Coventry City	A	League Division 1	1–2
1973	Sheffield United	H	League Division 1	4–2
1987	Oxford United	H	League Division 1	4–0
1990	Tottenham Hotspur	H	League Division 1	1–2
1993	Liverpool	H	Premier League	0–0
1996	Coventry	A	Premier League	0–1

FEBRUARY 11

1922	Oldham Athletic	H	League Division 1	1–0
1928	Bristol City	H	League Division 2	5–2
1933	Aston Villa	H	League Division 1	0–1
1939	Sheffield Wednesday	H	FA Cup 5th round	1–1
1950	Chesterfield	A	FA Cup 5th round	1–1
1953	West Bromwich Albion	A	FA Cup 4th round 3rd replay	4–0
1956	Manchester City	A	League Division 1	2–2
1961	Blackpool	H	League Division 1	2–2
1967	Manchester City	H	League Division 1	0–0
1970	Derby County	A	League Division 1	2–2
1978	Manchester United	H	League Division 1	2–2
1980	International XI	H	Testimonial	5–3

The match was played for John Dempsey and raised over £17,000.

1984	Cambridge United	A	League Division 2	1–0
1989	Swindon Town	H	League Division 2	3–2
1995	Tottenham Hotspur	H	Premier League	1–1

FEBRUARY 12

1910	Bolton Wanderers	A	League Division 1	2–5

1916	Crystal Palace	H	London Combination League (Part Two)	0–1
1921	West Bromwich Albion	H	League Division 1	3–0
1927	Fulham	A	League Division 2	2–1
1934	Tottenham Hotspur	A	League Division 1	1–2
1938	Portsmouth	H	League Division 1	3–1
1944	Crystal Palace	A	Football League South	0–1
1946	Aston Villa	A	FA Cup 5th round	0–1
1946	Aston Villa	A	FA Cup 5th round	0–1
1949	West Bromwich Albion	A	FA Cup 5th round	0–3
1955	Newcastle United	H	League Division 1	4–3
1966	Leeds United	H	FA Cup 4th round	1–0
1968	Liverpool	H	League Division 1	3–1
1969	Stoke City	H	FA Cup 5th round	3–2
1977	Millwall	H	League Division 2	1–1
1983	Grimsby Town	A	League Division 2	1–2
1992	Southampton	H	League Division 1	1–1
1994	Oldham Athletic	A	Premier League	1–2

1998 One of the most controversial events of Chelsea's modern history took place when the Board announced that, after failing to agree a framework for a new contract, manager Ruud Gullit had been relieved of his position and that Gianluca Vialli would thus assume the post. Although it transpired that the nub of the problem between Gullit and the club centred around the former manager's wage expectations, the full story would remain known only to Mr Bates. The timing of the decision did appear to be somewhat bizarre, however, as the club sat tucked in behind Manchester United in the Premiership looking to mount an end-of-season Championship challenge and in the semi-final of the Coca-Cola Cup and latter stages of the European Cup-Winners' Cup. However, as the dust settles, the Board might claim that their decision was vindicated in the light of two successful Cup campaigns enjoyed in 1997–98.

FEBRUARY 13

1901 William Ferguson was born in Muirkirk. Joined the club from Queen of the South in October 1921 and remained on the staff for 12 years during which time Chelsea suffered relegation in 1924 and gained promotion back to Division 1 six years later. Clocked up nearly 300 appearances and scored 11 goals over his time at the Bridge.

1909	Sunderland	A	League Division 1	2–1
1915	Liverpool	A	League Division 1	3–3
1926	Hull City	A	League Division 2	1–0
1932	Sheffield Wednesday	A	FA Cup 5th round	1–1
1937	Preston North End	H	League Division 1	0–0
1939	Sheffield Wednesday	A	FA Cup 5th round replay	0–0
1943	Clapton Orient	A	Football League South	1–3
1954	Wolverhampton Wanderers	H	League Division 1	4–2

1956	Burnley	White Hart Lane		
			FA Cup 4th round 3rd replay	0–0
1960	Fulham	H	League Division 1	4–2
1965	Blackburn Rovers	A	League Division 1	3–0
1971	Wolverhampton Wanderers	A	League Division 1	0–1

Mickey Droy made his first start for Chelsea.

1982	Liverpool	H	FA Cup 5th round	2–0
1985	Sunderland	A	League Cup semi-final	0–2
1988	Manchester United	A	League Division 1	1–3
1993	Aston Villa	H	Premier League	0–1

FEBRUARY 14

1896 Andrew Nesbit Wilson was born in Newmains, Lanarkshire. Purchased from Middlesbrough at a cost of £6,500 in November 1923, he established his place in Chelsea folklore with over 250 appearances and 62 goals over an eight-year period. He was a Scottish international although all of his 12 caps had been won prior to his arrival in London. He transferred to Queens Park Rangers in October 1931 and played out the last of his career in France with Nimes, retiring in 1934.

1914	Newcastle United	H	League Division 1	0–1
1920	Bolton Wanderers	H	League Division 1	2–3
1923	Everton	H	League Division 1	3–1
1925	Fulham	A	League Division 2	2–1
1931	Blackburn Rovers	H	FA Cup 5th round	3–0
1942	Crystal Palace	A	London War League	2–3
1948	Wolverhampton Wanderers	H	League Division 1	1–1
1951	Fulham	A	FA Cup 5th round replay	0–3
1953	Birmingham City	H	FA Cup 5th round	0–4
1976	Crystal Palace	H	FA Cup 5th round	2–3
1981	West Ham United	A	League Division 2	0–4
1987	Coventry City	A	League Division 1	0–3

FEBRUARY 15

1908	Birmingham City	H	League Division 1	2–2
1913	Woolwich Arsenal	H	League Division 1	1–1
1919	Crystal Palace	H	London Combination League	0–2
1941	Portsmouth	H	Football League War Cup South 1st round	3–1
1947	Stoke City	A	League Division 1	1–6
1950	Chesterfield	H	FA Cup 5th round replay	3–0
1956	Burnley	White Hart Lane		
			FA Cup 4th round 4th replay	2–0
1958	Sheffield Wednesday	A	League Division 1	3–2
1969	Leeds United	A	League Division 1	0–1

1975	Sheffield United	A	League Division 1	1–2
1977	Notts County	A	League Division 2	1–2
1992	Sheffield United	H	FA Cup 5th round	1–0

FEBRUARY 16

1907	Lincoln City	A	League Division 2	5–0
1918	Millwall	A	London Combination League	4–0
1924	Everton	A	League Division 1	0–2
1929	Portsmouth	H	FA Cup 5th round	1–1
1946	Luton Town	H	Football League South	2–1
1952	Middlesbrough	H	League Division 1	5–0

Roy Bentley hit two goals and Seamus D'Arcy a hat-trick.

1960	Sittingbourne	A	Friendly	8–3
1962	Blackpool	H	League Division 1	1–0
1963	Cardiff City	A	League Division 2	0–1
1965	Germany XI	A	Friendly	1–0
1966	AC Milan	H	Fairs Cup 3rd round	2–1
1974	Aberdeen	A	Friendly	1–2
1980	Cambridge United	H	League Division 2	1–1
1985	Newcastle United	H	League Division 1	1–0
1991	Wimbledon	H	League Division 1	0–0
1997	Leicester City	A	FA Cup 5th round	2–2

FEBRUARY 17

1906	Lincoln City	H	League Division 2	4–2
1912	Nottingham Forest	A	League Division 2	3–2
1917	Arsenal	A	London Combination League	0–3
1923	Arsenal	H	League Division 1	0–0
1932	Sheffield Wednesday	H	FA Cup 5th round replay	2–0
1934	Stoke City	A	FA Cup 5th round	1–3
1940	Southampton	H	Football League South C	5–1
1945	Crystal Palace	A	Football League South Cup Group 4	1–1
1951	Everton	A	League Division 1	0–3
1968	Norwich City	H	FA Cup 4th round	1–0
1971	Nottingham Forest	H	League Division 1	2–0
1973	Leeds United	A	League Division 1	1–1
1976	Thomas Law died.			
1982	Cardiff City	H	League Division 2	1–0
1990	Nottingham Forest	A	League Division 1	1–1
1996	West Ham United	H	Premier League	1–2

FEBRUARY 18

| 1911 | Blackpool | A | League Division 2 | 2–0 |

1929 Leslie Stubbs was born in Great Wakering. Began his senior career at Southend

United and moved to Chelsea for £10,000 in November 1952 where he managed to make 122 appearances and score 35 goals over the course of six years. He was a part of the side that won the League Championship in 1954–55. He returned to Southend United in November 1958 in a deal that was worth £12,000 and also included Alan Dicks.

1931	Huddersfield Town	H	League Division 1	1–2
1939	Arsenal	A	League Division 1	0–1
1950	Burnley	A	League Division 1	2–1
1953	Wolverhampton Wanderers	A	League Division 1	2–2
1956	Everton	A	FA Cup 5th round	0–1
1961	Everton	A	League Division 1	1–1
1967	Brighton & Hove Albion	A	FA Cup 4th round	1–1
1976	Hull City	H	League Division 2	0–0
1978	Orient	A	FA Cup 5th round	0–0
1989	Plymouth Argyle	A	League Division 2	1–0
1991	Luton Town	H	ZDS Cup 3rd round	1–1
1998	Arsenal	H	League Cup semi-final	3–1

Gianluca Vialli's first game in charge of the team had the necessary motivational effect to inspire the Blues to reach their second cup final within a year. Trailing by two goals to one from the first leg at Highbury when Mark Hughes had scored a late away goal to swing the initiative towards Chelsea, the same player scored the opener in the return game early in the first half. After Arsenal's Vieira had been sent off just after the start of the second period further goals from Di Matteo and Petrescu ensured the trip to Wembley.

FEBRUARY 19

1910	Middlesbrough	H	League Division 1	2–1
1916	West Ham United	A	London Combination League (Part Two)	0–2
1921	Plymouth Argyle	A	FA Cup 3rd round	0–0
1927	Burnley	H	FA Cup 5th round	2–1
1936	Fulham	H	FA Cup 5th round	0–0
1938	Arsenal	A	League Division 1	0–2
1944	Southampton	H	Football League South Cup Group B	3–2
1949	Burnley	A	League Division 1	0–3
1955	Notts County	A	FA Cup 5th round	0–1
1966	Arsenal	H	League Division 1	0–0
1972	Leicester City	H	League Division 1	2–1
1977	Plymouth Argyle	H	League Division 2	2–2
1983	Leeds United	A	League Division 2	3–3
1994	Oxford United	A	FA Cup 5th round	2–1
1997	AC Milan	A	Friendly	0–2

1915	Manchester City	A	FA Cup 3rd round	1–0
1926	Darlington	H	League Division 2	5–2
1928	Stoke City	A	League Division 2	0–1
1929	Portsmouth	A	FA Cup 5th round replay	0–1
1932	Grimsby Town	H	League Division 1	4–1
1935	Everton	H	League Division 1	3–0
1937	Sheffield Wednesday	A	League Division 1	1–1
1939	Sheffield Wednesday	Highbury	FA Cup 5th round 2nd replay	3–1

1940 Jimmy Greaves was born in East Ham. Perhaps the most prolific goalscorer of his and any other era, Greaves was a schoolboy phenomenon, scoring over 100 goals in a single season for Chelsea Juniors and a first team regular by the time he was 17, scoring on his debut against Spurs. Thereafter Greaves scored on every debut match; for England Youth, England Under-23, England full, AC Milan (whom he joined in 1960 for £80,000), Spurs (who paid £99,999 to bring him back home to England) and West Ham (joining in 1970). In the four seasons he spent at the Bridge he finished as leading scorer and totalled 132 goals from just 169 games. He holds the Chelsea record for the most goals scored in a single season, with an accumulated 41. In all he scored 357 League goals (all of which were scored in the First Division), and 44 goals for England (he is England's third top goalscorer behind Bobby Charlton and Gary Lineker, although Greaves played only 57 matches). Alf Ramsey's decision to leave him out of the 1966 World Cup final – a bout of hepatitis the season before the World Cup robbed him of a yard or two of pace – is still debated.

After retiring as a player (although he made a brief comeback with non-League Barnet in the 1970s) he slipped into well-publicised alcoholism before emerging with a successful career in journalism and broadcasting, forming a partnership with former Liverpool and Scotland striker Ian St John.

| 1943 | Reading | H | Football League South | 2–0 |

1947 Seven years after the birth of Greaves another Chelsea Legend entered the world as Peter Leslie Osgood was born in Windsor. He joined Chelsea as an amateur in September 1964 having played in Junior football with local clubs, made his debut nine months later (scoring twice in the game). After he had grabbed his chance, he then established himself as one of the first names on the team sheet for a period of nine years. Unfortunately after a disagreement with manager Dave Sexton he was allowed to leave the club and joined Southampton in March 1974 for £275,000. After a spell in the USA with Philadelphia Fury he rejoined Chelsea for £25,000 in December 1978 and played out the remainder of his career at the Bridge. His Chelsea combined record finished with 289 League, 34 FA Cup, 30 League Cup, 15 Fairs Cup and 11 European Cup-Winners' Cup appearances in which he amassed 140 goals. He won 4 international caps for England and medals for the FA Cup in 1970 and the European Cup-Winners' Cup in 1971.

| 1954 | Sunderland | A | League Division 1 | 2–1 |
| 1957 | Tottenham Hotspur | A | League Division 1 | 4–3 |

1960 David Robert Speedie was born in Glenrothes. It would be perhaps unfair to make comparisons with the two other strikers born on this day and it is difficult, in any case, to judge how stars of the past might perform in a game that has become much faster and perhaps more demanding of athletic skills. What one can say, however, is that Speedie never gave less than 100 per cent effort, was never afraid to put himself where the ball was (even amongst the flying boots) and had a very short fuse. All qualities that endeared him to the fans. He was a Scottish international, won a Second Division championship medal in 1984 and a Full Members Cup medal in 1986. Chelsea signed him from Darlington for £65,000 in May 1982 and sold him to Coventry City for £750,000 in July 1987. In this time he played over 200 games and netted 64 times for the club.

1965	Tottenham Hotspur	H	FA Cup 5th round	1–0
1971	Stoke City	A	League Division 1	2–1
1974	Basingstoke	A	Friendly	4–0
1982	Norwich City	A	League Division 2	1–2

FEBRUARY 21

1920	Leicester City	H	FA Cup 3rd round	3–0
1925	Stockport County	A	League Division 2	0–4
1931	Sheffield United	A	League Division 1	0–4
1934	Liverpool	H	League Division 1	2–0
1942	Fulham	H	London War League	1–5
1948	Aston Villa	A	League Division 1	0–3
1953	Charlton Athletic	H	League Division 1	0–1
1959	Burnley	H	League Division 1	1–3
1970	Queens Park Rangers	A	FA Cup 6th round	4–2
1976	Notts County	A	League Division 2	2–3

Ray Lewington played his first match for the club.

1979	Coventry City	H	League Division 1	1–3
1981	Watford	H	League Division 2	0–1
1987	Manchester United	H	League Division 1	1–1
1990	Crystal Palace	A	ZDS Cup Southern final	2–0
1993	Blackburn Rovers	A	Premier League	0–2
1996	Grimsby Town	A	FA Cup 5th round	0–0
1998	Leicester City	A	Premier League	0–2

FEBRUARY 22

1913	Bradford City	A	League Division 1	2–2
1919	Millwall	H	London Combination League	3–2
1930	Notts County	H	League Division 2	3–1

1933 Robert Albert Smith was born in Lingdale, Yorkshire. Bobby joined Chelsea as an amateur in 1948 and was upgraded to the professional ranks in May 1950. He made his debut at the age of 17 and hit 30 goals in 86 games for the first team, but he was seldom a regular for the centre-forward slot, that honour being held by Roy Bentley. In December 1955 Spurs paid £16,000 to take him to White Hart Lane where the club were engaged in a desperate battle against relegation. It was largely his goals that enabled them to build a side good enough to win the double in 1961. Although only 5' 10" he used every ounce of his 12 stone 11 pounds weight to intimidate opponents, not only for his own benefit but also to create space and chances for his team mates. He was also extremely skilful and able to forge good goalscoring opportunities purely by his positional sense. He was rewarded with a total of 15 caps, scoring 13 goals. In May 1964 he was transferred to Brighton for £5,000 and scored 18 goals to help them win the Fourth Division championship in his only season with the club, for he was sacked before the following season over some newspaper comments. He then drifted into the non-League game before retiring.

1936	Everton	H	League Division 1	2–2
1940	Bournemouth	H	Football League South B	4–3
1941	Portsmouth	A	Football League War Cup South 1st round	4–1
1956	Charlton Athletic	H	League Division 1	3–1
1958	Aston Villa	A	League Division 1	3–1
1964	Ipswich Town	H	League Division 1	4–0
1965	Nottingham Forest	H	League Division 1	0–1
1966	Sunderland	H	League Division 1	3–2
1967	Brighton & Hove Albion	H	FA Cup 4th round replay	4–0
1969	Sunderland	H	League Division 1	5–1
1975	Newcastle United	H	League Division 1	3–2
1992	Nottingham Forest	A	League Division 1	1–1
1997	Manchester United	H	Premier League	1–1

FEBRUARY 23

1907	Burton United	H	League Division 2	1–0
1918	Tottenham Hotspur	H	London Combination League	3–0
1924	Everton	H	League Division 1	1–1
1929	Clapton Orient	A	League Division 2	0–1
1935	Huddersfield Town	A	League Division 1	0–3
1946	Aston Villa	H	Football League South	2–2
1952	Leeds United	A	FA Cup 5th round	1–1
1957	Bolton Wanderers	H	League Division 1	2–2
1974	Queens Park Rangers	H	League Division 1	3–3
1980	Bristol Rovers	A	League Division 2	0–3
1985	Coventry City	A	League Division 1	0–1

FEBRUARY 24

1906	Chesterfield	A	League Division 2	2–0
1912	Burnley	H	League Division 2	0–2

1916 Hugh John Billington was born in Ampthill and did not join Chelsea until the age of 32. Up until then his career had been spent entirely at Luton Town to whom the Blues paid £8,000 to secure his services in March 1948. He made 90 senior appearances, scoring 32 goals, before moving on to Worcester City at the beginning of season 1951–52.

1917	Millwall	H	London Combination League	0–2
1921	Plymouth Argyle	H	FA Cup 3rd round replay	0–0
1923	Arsenal	A	League Division 1	1–3
1934	Middlesbrough	A	League Division 1	2–2

Debut of William Mitchell.

John O'Hare also made his first appearance out of a total of 108 compiled in the seasons leading up to the Second World War.

1936	Fulham	A	FA Cup 5th round replay	2–3
1940	Tottenham Hotspur	H	Football League South C	0–2
1945	Luton Town	H	Football League South Cup Group 4	4–1
1951	Sheffield Wednesday	A	League Division 1	2–2
1960	West Bromwich Albion	H	League Division 1	2–2
1962	Sheffield Wednesday	H	League Division 1	1–0

Debut of Ron 'Chopper' Harris.

1973	Sheffield Wednesday	A	FA Cup 5th round	2–1
1979	Bolton Wanderers	A	League Division 1	1–2
1990	Manchester United	H	League Division 1	1–0
1991	Sheffield Wednesday	H	League Cup semi-final	0–2
1996	Southampton	A	Premier League	3–2

FEBRUARY 25

1911	Wolverhampton Wanderers	A	FA Cup 3rd round	2–0
1922	Cardiff City	H	League Division 1	1–0
1928	Southampton	H	League Division 2	0–2
1933	Bolton Wanderers	H	League Division 1	1–1
1939	Brentford	H	League Division 1	1–3
1950	Manchester City	A	League Division 1	1–1
1956	Tottenham Hotspur	A	League Division 1	0–4
1961	Sheffield Wednesday	A	League Division 1	0–1
1967	Burnley	A	League Division 1	2–1
1970	Newcastle United	H	League Division 1	0–0
1976	Portsmouth	H	League Division 2	2–0
1978	Leeds United	A	League Division 1	0–2
1984	Carlisle United	H	League Division 2	0–0
1989	Oldham Athletic	H	League Division 2	2–2
1995	West Ham United	A	Premier League	2–1

FEBRUARY 26

1908 James Peter O'Dowd was born in Halifax. An English international he was a classy centre-half who had gained experience at Bradford, Blackburn Rovers and Burnley from where he linked up with the Blues following a £5,250 transfer in November

1931. He played 87 games for the club before departing to France to join Valenciennes in September 1934 following a disagreement with Chelsea's management. He returned to the UK in 1937 to end his career at Torquay United.

1910 Victor Robert Woodley was born in Chippenham. An English international goalkeeper (he won 19 caps), he joined Chelsea from non-League Windsor and Eton in May 1931 and remained on the club's books until the end of World War Two. He made 272 appearances in regular football and over 100 more during the war. Laid a serious claim on the title of the Blues all-time greatest goalie before quitting for Bath City from where Derby County retrieved him to solve a goalkeeping crisis and allowed him the opportunity of rounding off his career with an FA Cup final victory at Wembley against Charlton Athletic in 1946.

1910	Blackburn Rovers	H	League Division 1	3–1
1921	Everton	H	League Division 1	0–1
1927	South Shields	H	League Division 2	4–1
1938	Blackpool	H	League Division 1	1–3
1944	Watford	A	Football League South Cup Group B	3–0
1949	Stoke City	H	League Division 1	2–2
1955	Huddersfield Town	H	League Division 1	4–1
1966	Everton	A	League Division 1	1–2
1972	Orient	A	FA Cup 5th round	2–3
1974	Ipswich Town	A	League Division 1	1–1
1977	Bolton Wanderers	A	League Division 2	2–2
1983	Blackburn Rovers	H	League Division 2	2–0
1992	Manchester United	A	League Division 1	1–1
1997	Leicester City	H	FA Cup 5th round replay	1–0

FEBRUARY 27

1909	Blackburn Rovers	H	League Division 1	1–1
1915	Oldham Athletic	A	League Division 1	0–0
1926	South Shields	H	League Division 2	0–0
1932	Liverpool	A	FA Cup 6th round	2–0
1937	Manchester United	H	League Division 1	4–2
1943	Millwall	A	Football League South	0–3
1952	Leeds United	H	FA Cup 5th round replay	1–1
1954	Sheffield Wednesday	H	League Division 1	0–1
1959	Robert McRoberts died in Birkenhead.			
1960	Sheffield Wednesday	A	League Division 1	1–1
1965	Stoke City	A	League Division 1	2–0
1971	Southampton	A	League Division 1	0–0
1978	Orient	H	FA Cup 5th round replay	1–2
1982	Wrexham	A	League Division 2	0–1
1988	Newcastle United	H	League Division 1	2–2
1991	Sheffield Wednesday	A	League Cup semi-final	1–3
1994	Tottenham Hotspur	H	Premier League	4–3

FEBRUARY 28

1914	Aston Villa	H	League Division 1	0–3
1920	Blackburn Rovers	H	League Division 1	2–1

Buchanan Sharp played his first game for Chelsea.

1921	Plymouth Argyle	Bristol	FA Cup 3rd round 2nd replay	2–1
1925	Portsmouth	H	League Division 2	2–3
1931	Birmingham City	A	FA Cup 6th round	2–2
1942	Tottenham Hotspur	A	London War League	0–2
1948	Liverpool	H	League Division 1	3–1
1951	Blackpool	H	League Division 1	0–2
1953	Preston North End	A	League Division 1	1–2
1970	Coventry City	A	League Division 1	3–0
1976	Blackburn Rovers	H	League Division 2	3–1
1981	Preston North End	A	League Division 2	0–1
1987	Nottingham Forest	A	League Division 1	1–0
1989	Hull City	H	League Division 2	2–1
1995	Club Brugge	A	Cup-Winners' Cup 3rd round	0–1
1996	Grimsby Town	H	FA Cup 5th round replay	4–1
1998	Manchester United	H	Premier League	0–1

FEBRUARY 29

1908	Sunderland	H	League Division 1	2–1
1964	Sheffield Wednesday	A	League Division 1	2–3
1992	Sheffield Wednesday	H	League Division 1	0–3

MARCH 1

1884 Andrew Ormiston was born in Paisley. Joined from Lincoln City in the close season of 1909 and remained for nine years when he re-signed for the Imps. He made 102 appearances for Chelsea during this time.

1913	Manchester City	H	League Division 1	2–1
1915	Bradford Park Avenue	H	League Division 1	0–1
1919	Fulham	A	London Combination League	2–6
1924	West Bromwich Albion	A	League Division 1	2–2

Debut of William Brown.

1930	Reading	A	League Division 2	1–3
1933	Middlesbrough	A	League Division 1	1–2

Debut of George Bennett Gibson who had signed for Chelsea the previous month having been transferred from Bolton Wanderers. A Scot born in Hamilton who got his start with local club Academical, moved to Dundee and then south to Bolton. Appeared 141 times for the Blues with 24 goals but was not retained after the 1937–38 season.

1941	Brentford	A	Football League War Cup South 2nd round	2–2
1947	Arsenal	A	League Division 1	2–1

1952	West Bromwich Albion	A	League Division 1	1–0
1969	West Bromwich Albion	H	FA Cup 6th round	1–2
1975	Liverpool	A	League Division 1	2–2
1980	Cardiff City	H	League Division 2	1–0

Colin Lee played his first game for the club.

| 1993 | Arsenal | H | Premier League | 1–0 |
| 1997 | Derby County | A | Premier League | 2–3 |

MARCH 2

1907	Grimsby Town	A	League Division 2	1–2
1912	Clapton Orient	H	League Division 2	3–0
1918	Crystal Palace	H	London Combination League	2–0
1929	Oldham Athletic	H	League Division 2	2–3

1930 Charles Richard Thomson was born in Perth. A goalkeeper, 'Chick' joined from Clyde for £5,000 in October 1952 and shared the net-minding duties with Bill Robertson for the duration of his Chelsea career which lasted five years and encompassed the League Championship winning season 1954–55. After 59 games, he was transferred to Nottingham Forest in August 1957 where he achieved an FA Cup-winning performance in 1959.

1932	Sunderland	H	League Division 1	2–2
1940	Brentford	A	Football League South C	1–1
1946	Tottenham Hotspur	A	Friendly	2–4
1957	Wolverhampton Wanderers	A	League Division 1	1–3
1963	Huddersfield Town	H	League Division 2	1–2
1966	AC Milan	A	Fairs Cup 3rd round play-off	1–1
1968	Manchester United	A	League Division 1	3–1
1974	West Ham United	A	League Division 1	0–3
1985	Ipswich Town	A	League Division 1	0–2
1991	Tottenham Hotspur	A	League Division 1	1–1
1996	Wimbledon	A	Premier League	1–1

MARCH 3

1906	Burslem Port Vale	H	League Division 2	7–0
1917	Brentford	A	London Combination League	0–3
1923	Cardiff City	H	League Division 1	1–1
1928	Hull City	A	League Division 2	2–0

Samuel Irving made his debut.

1934	Blackburn Rovers	H	League Division 1	3–0
1945	Watford	A	Football League South Cup Group 4	2–0
1951	Tottenham Hotspur	A	League Division 1	1–2
1952	Leeds United	Villa Park	FA Cup 5th round 2nd replay	5–1
1956	Manchester United	H	League Division 1	2–4
1973	Birmingham City	H	League Division 1	0–0

| 1979 | Liverpool | H | League Division 1 | 0–0 |

Petar Borota kept goal for Chelsea for the first time and managed to shut out the opposition.

1984	Oldham Athletic	H	League Division 2	3–0
1987	Blackburn Rovers	A	Full Members Cup quarter-final	0–3
1990	Southampton	A	League Division 1	3–2

MARCH 4

1907	Stockport County	H	League Division 2	2–0
1911	Lincoln City	A	League Division 2	0–0
1916	Fulham	A	London Combination League (Part Two)	1–0
1922	West Bromwich Albion	A	League Division 1	2–2
1931	Birmingham City	H	FA Cup 6th round replay	0–3
1936	Middlesbrough	A	League Division 1	1–4
1939	Grimsby Town	H	FA Cup 6th round	0–1
1944	West Ham United	H	Football League South Cup Group B	4–0
1950	Manchester United	H	FA Cup 6th round	2–0

1954 Gary Stanley was born in Burton upon Trent. He was brought to Chelsea's attention by former manager, Frank Upton, whilst playing for Derbyshire schools and quickly established himself in the Blues' junior sides. He was awarded a full professional contract in March 1971 and went on to play 120 games for the club over an eight-year period. However, partly because of Chelsea's financial plight at the time, he was allowed to leave in 1979 for Fort Lauderdale Strikers in the USA, where he stayed for only a short period before returning in a £300,000 deal to Everton. Later moved to Swansea City, Portsmouth and, finally, Bristol City.

1955 Joseph Patrick Jones was born in Llandudno. Having spent time at Liverpool sandwiched between two periods with Wrexham his reputation was already well established before he joined the Blues in October 1982 at a cost of £34,500. He enjoyed a tremendous rapport with the supporters at Stamford Bridge who recognised his unfailing devotion to the cause although it was recognised that he lacked finesse and some of the finer skills of the game. He made approaching 100 appearances before moving on to Huddersfield Town for £35,000 in August 1985 from where he returned once again to Wrexham.

| 1959 | Bolton Wanderers | A | League Division 1 | 0–6 |
| 1961 | Birmingham City | H | League Division 1 | 3–2 |

1962 Paul Canoville was born in Hillingdon. Signed for Chelsea in December 1981 and made over 100 appearances in his time at Stamford Bridge, although a large percentage came as substitute. Scored 15 goals for the Blues. He was sold to Reading for £50,000 in August 1986.

1964	Stoke City	A	League Division 1	0–2
1967	Fulham	H	League Division 1	0–0
1972	Stoke City	Wembley	League Cup final	1–2
1978	Liverpool	H	League Division 1	3–1
1985	Sunderland	H	League Cup semi-final	2–3

MARCH 5

1910	Nottingham Forest	A	League Division 1	0–0
1921	Cardiff City	A	FA Cup 4th round	0–1
1924	Notts County	A	League Division 1	0–0
1927	Cardiff City	H	FA Cup 6th round	0–0
1932	Blackburn Rovers	A	League Division 1	2–2
1949	Liverpool	H	League Division 1	2–1

1952 Petar Borota was born in Belgrade. A Yugoslavian international goalkeeper (he picked up 14 caps) who joined Chelsea in March 1979 from Partizan Belgrade for a fee of £70,000. Despite his highly eccentric style he nevertheless made in excess of 100 appearances for the club before moving on to Brentford, eventually ending his career in Portuguese football.

1955	Aston Villa	A	League Division 1	2–3
1960	Luton Town	H	League Division 1	3–0
1966	Shrewsbury Town	H	FA Cup 5th round	3–2
1969	Stoke City	H	League Division 1	1–0
1977	Blackpool	H	League Division 2	2–2
1983	Charlton Athletic	A	League Division 2	2–5
1988	Coventry City	H	League Division 1	1–0
1994	Manchester United	A	Premier League	1–0
1995	Crystal Palace	H	Premier League	0–0
1997	Blackburn Rovers	H	Premier League	1–1
1998	Real Betis	A	Cup-Winners' Cup 3rd round	1–2

MARCH 6

1911	Glossop North End	H	League Division 2	2–0
1915	Newcastle United	H	FA Cup 4th round	1–1
1920	Bradford Park Avenue	H	FA Cup 4th round	4–1
1926	Preston North End	A	League Division 2	1–3
1935	Birmingham City	H	League Division 1	2–2
1937	Derby County	A	League Division 1	1–1
1940	Aldershot	A	Football League South B	1–5
1943	Tottenham Hotspur	A	Football League Cup South Group 3	0–2
1948	Middlesbrough	A	League Division 1	0–0
1954	Middlesbrough	A	League Division 1	3–3
1963	Charlton Athletic	A	FA Cup 4th round	3–0
1965	Peterborough United	H	FA Cup 6th round	5–1
1971	Blackpool	H	League Division 1	2–0
1973	Wolverhampton Wanderers	H	League Division 1	0–2
1976	Plymouth Argyle	A	League Division 2	3–0
1982	Tottenham Hotspur	H	FA Cup 6th round	2–3

MARCH 7

1908	Woolwich Arsenal	A	League Division 1	0–0
1910	Sheffield United	A	League Division 1	0–0
1914	Middlesbrough	A	League Division 1	0–2
1925	Hull City	A	League Division 2	0–1
1931	Blackpool	A	League Division 1	1–2
1936	Sheffield Wednesday	H	League Division 1	1–2

1941 Graham Moore was born in Hengoed. A Welsh international before Tommy Docherty brought him to the Bridge from Cardiff City in December 1961 for a fee of £35,000, he made 72 appearances in the course of a two-year stay (scoring 14 goals) then moved for the same price to Manchester United. Later played for Northampton Town, Charlton Athletic and Doncaster Rovers.

1942	Portsmouth	H	London War League	3–4
1953	Burnley	H	League Division 1	0–2
1959	Luton Town	H	League Division 1	3–3
1964	Fulham	H	League Division 1	1–2
1970	Nottingham Forest	H	League Division 1	1–1
1981	Bolton Wanderers	H	League Division 2	2–0
1987	Arsenal	H	League Division 1	1–0

MARCH 8

1913	West Bromwich Albion	A	League Division 1	1–0
1915	Sheffield United	A	League Division 1	1–1
1919	Brentford	H	London Combination League	1–4
1930	Charlton Athletic	H	League Division 2	1–1
1939	Derby County	A	League Division 1	1–0
1941	Brentford	H	Football League War Cup Sth 2nd round	3–1
1947	Blackpool	H	League Division 1	1–4
1950	Charlton Athletic	H	League Division 1	1–3
1952	Sheffield United	A	FA Cup 6th round	1–0
1958	Arsenal	A	League Division 1	4–5

Two goals by Greaves and one apiece for Tindall and Block were not enough as Chelsea notched four away goals but still narrowly lost a nine-goal thriller!

1969	West Bromwich Albion	A	League Division 1	3–0
1975	Derby County	H	League Division 1	1–2
1980	Fulham	A	League Division 2	2–1
1986	Manchester City	H	League Division 1	1–0
1995	Manchester City	A	Premier League	2–1
1997	Portsmouth	A	FA Cup 6th round	4–1
1998	Aston Villa	H	Premier League	0–1

MARCH 9

1907	Burslem Port Vale	H	League Division 2	2–1
1912	Bristol City	A	League Division 2	1–1

1918	Brentford	A	London Combination League	1–0
1927	Cardiff City	A	FA Cup 6th round replay	2–3
1929	Southampton	A	League Division 2	2–1
1935	Stoke City	A	League Division 1	1–0
1938	Brentford	A	League Division 1	1–1
1940	Portsmouth	H	Football League South C	4–1
1946	Arsenal	A	Football League South	2–1
1955	West Bromwich Albion	A	League Division 1	4–2
1957	Manchester City	H	League Division 1	4–2
1962	Birmingham City	H	League Division 1	1–1
1963	Middlesbrough	A	League Division 2	0–1
1968	Sheffield Wednesday	A	FA Cup 5th round	2–2
1974	Norwich City	A	League Division 1	2–2
1982	Leicester City	H	League Division 2	4–1
1985	Southampton	H	League Division 1	0–2
1991	Manchester United	H	League Division 1	3–2
1992	Sunderland	H	FA Cup 6th round	1–1
1996	Wimbledon	H	FA Cup 6th round	2–2

MARCH 10

1906	Barnsley	A	League Division 2	2–1
1923	Cardiff City	A	League Division 1	1–6

The worst defeat in a campaign that saw Chelsea finish in 19th place in the League

1928	Preston North End	H	League Division 2	2–1
1934	Newcastle United	A	League Division 1	2–2
1945	Crystal Palace	H	Football League South Cup Group 4	2–0
1956	Burnley	A	League Division 1	0–5
1965	Tottenham Hotspur	H	League Division 1	3–1
1969	Coventry City	H	League Division 1	2–1
1971	RFC Bruges, Belgium	A	Cup-Winners' Cup 3rd round	0–2
1973	West Bromwich Albion	A	League Division 1	1–1
1979	Norwich City	A	League Division 1	0–2
1984	Newcastle United	A	League Division 2	1–1
1990	Norwich City	H	League Division 1	0–0
1993	Everton	H	Premier League	2–1

MARCH 11

1916	Luton Town	H	London Combination League (Part Two)	11–1
1920	Blackburn Rovers	A	League Division 1	1–3
1922	West Bromwich Albion	H	League Division 1	1–1
1933	Blackpool	H	League Division 1	1–0
1936	West Bromwich Albion	H	League Division 1	2–2
1939	Grimsby Town	H	League Division 1	5–1

1944	Southampton	A	Football League South Cup Group B	5–1
1950	Everton	A	League Division 1	1–1
1958	Wolverhampton Wanderers	H	League Division 1	1–2

Melvyn Scott made his first senior appearance.

1961	Burnley	A	League Division 1	4–4
1967	Sheffield United	H	FA Cup 5th round	2–0
1972	Liverpool	H	League Division 1	0–0
1978	Derby County	A	League Division 1	1–1
1980	Birmingham City	A	League Division 2	1–5
1989	Watford	H	League Division 2	2–2
1992	Norwich City	A	League Division 1	1–0
1995	Leeds United	H	Premier League	0–3
1998	Crystal Palace	H	Premier League	6–2

MARCH 12

1910	Sunderland	H	League Division 1	1–4
1921	Sunderland	H	League Division 1	3–1
1924	West Bromwich Albion	H	League Division 1	0–0
1927	Oldham Athletic	A	League Division 2	2–1
1930	Bradford Park Avenue	A	League Division 2	3–1
1932	Newcastle United	Huddersfield		
			FA Cup semi-final	1–2
1938	Bolton Wanderers	H	League Division 1	0–0
1949	Blackpool	A	League Division 1	1–2
1952	Newcastle United	H	League Division 1	1–0
1955	Blackpool	H	League Division 1	0–0
1960	Everton	A	League Division 1	1–6
1966	Manchester United	H	League Division 1	2–0

Joe Kirkup began his Chelsea career in this match.

1968	Sheffield Wednesday	H	FA Cup 5th round replay	2–0

1969 Gareth Hall was born in Croydon. A Welsh international who signed from apprentice to professional status in April 1986. He made over 150 appearances for the Blues before a £300,000 transfer took him to Sunderland in December 1995. Joined Swindon Town in the summer of 1998.

1977	Cardiff City	A	League Division 2	3–1
1982	Barnsley	A	League Division 2	1–2
1983	Carlisle United	H	League Division 2	4–2
1988	Everton	A	League Division 1	1–4
1990	Crystal Palace	H	ZDS Cup Southern final	2–0
1996	Manchester City	H	Premier League	1–1
1997	West Ham United	A	Premier League	2–3

MARCH 13

1909	Manchester United	H	League Division 1	1–1
1911	Swindon Town	H	FA Cup 4th round	3–1
1915	Newcastle United	A	FA Cup 4th round replay	1–0
1920	Notts County	A	League Division 1	1–0
1926	Oldham Athletic	H	League Division 2	3–0
1929	Notts County	A	League Division 2	3–4
1937	Wolverhampton Wanderers	H	League Division 1	0–1
1943	Millwall	H	Football League Cup South Group 3	5–2
1948	Charlton Athletic	H	League Division 1	3–0

Debut of Hugh Billington. Also first game for William Marshall Hughes who, after time spent at Birmingham City and Luton Town, joined the Blues for £12,000 just prior to this match. A Welsh international (10 caps) he managed 105 games for the club over a three-year period before dropping to non-League football.

1965	Manchester United	A	League Division 1	0–4
1971	Tottenham Hotspur	A	League Division 1	1–2
1974	Burnley	H	League Division 1	3–0
1976	Southampton	H	League Division 2	1–1
1994	Wolverhampton Wanderers	H	FA Cup 6th round	1–0

MARCH 14

1908	Sheffield Wednesday	H	League Division 1	3–1
1914	Sheffield United	H	League Division 1	2–0
1921	West Bromwich Albion	A	League Division 1	1–1
1925	Blackpool	H	League Division 2	3–0
1928	Grimsby Town	H	League Division 2	4–0
1931	Blackburn Rovers	H	League Division 1	3–2
1936	Bolton Wanderers	A	League Division 1	3–2
1942	Clapton Orient	A	London War League	3–0
1953	Tottenham Hotspur	A	League Division 1	3–2

Debut of Frank Blunstone.

1959	Leicester City	A	League Division 1	3–0
1960	Boston United	A	Friendly	4–1
1964	Arsenal	A	League Division 1	4–2
1970	Watford	White Hart Lane	FA Cup semi-final	5–1
1972	Nottingham Forest	A	League Division 1	1–2
1979	West Bromwich Albion	A	League Division 1	0–1
1981	Bristol Rovers	A	League Division 2	0–1
1987	Manchester City	A	League Division 1	2–1
1992	Coventry City	H	League Division 1	0–1
1995	Club Brugge	H	Cup-Winners' Cup 3rd round	2–0

| 1998 | West Ham United | A | Premier League | 1–2 |

MARCH 15

1913	Everton	H	League Division 1	1–3
1919	West Ham United	A	London Combination League	3–3
1924	Birmingham City	H	League Division 1	1–1
1930	Hull City	A	League Division 2	3–1
1939	Blackpool	H	League Division 1	1–1
1941	Queens Park Rangers	A	Football League War Cup Sth 3rd round	0–2

1946 John Thomas Dempsey was born in Hampstead. Started with Fulham and joined the Blues in January 1969 for £70,000 where he remained for nine years eventually leaving for Philadelphia Fury (in March 1978). He was the cornerstone of the defence during the two winning Cup campaigns of 1970 (FA Cup) and 1971 (Cup-Winners' Cup) in which he scored in the replay against Real Madrid in Athens. He made over 200 appearances and scored 7 goals.

1947	Brentford	A	League Division 1	2–0
1952	Bolton Wanderers	A	League Division 1	0–3
1958	Blackpool	H	League Division 1	1–4
1965	Leicester City	H	League Cup final	3–2
1966	TSV 1860 Munich	A	Fairs Cup 4th round	2–2
1969	Manchester United	H	League Division 1	3–2
1975	Wolverhampton Wanderers	A	League Division 1	1–7
1980	Burnley	H	League Division 2	2–1
1983	Hacken BK, Sweden	H	Friendly	3–1
1989	Brighton & Hove Albion	A	League Division 2	1–0
1993	Crystal Palace	A	Premier League	1–1

MARCH 16

1907	Burnley	A	League Division 2	1–1
1912	Birmingham City	H	League Division 2	0–2
1918	Arsenal	H	London Combination League	4–2
1927	Port Vale	H	League Division 2	2–0
1929	Wolverhampton Wanderers	H	League Division 2	0–2
1932	Portsmouth	H	League Division 1	0–0
1935	Leeds United	H	League Division 1	7–1

Chelsea debut of Harry Burgess in a record-winning performance in the top division. James Bambrick scored four goals to help establish the feat in what was sweet revenge for a 5–2 reverse at Elland Road earlier in the season.

1940	Millwall	A	Football League South C	3–2
1946	Arsenal	H	Football League South	1–2
1957	Charlton Athletic	A	League Division 1	1–3

1963	Manchester United	A	FA Cup 5th round	1–2
1968	Leicester City	H	League Division 1	4–1
1974	Newcastle United	H	League Division 1	1–0

Kenny Swain's first game for the club.

1982	Crystal Palace	H	League Division 2	1–2
1984	Blackburn Rovers	H	League Division 2	2–1
1985	Watford	A	League Division 1	3–1
1986	Everton	A	League Division 1	1–1
1991	Sheffield United	A	League Division 1	0–1
1994	Wimbledon	H	Premier League	2–0
1996	Liverpool	A	Premier League	0–2
1997	Sunderland	H	Premier League	6–2

MARCH 17

1906	Clapton Orient	H	League Division 2	6–1
1915	Newcastle United	A	League Division 1	0–2
1917	Watford	H	London Combination League	2–2
1920	Notts County	H	League Division 1	2–0
1923	West Bromwich Albion	A	League Division 1	0–0
1928	Swansea Town	A	League Division 2	0–0
1934	Sheffield Wednesday	H	League Division 1	0–1
1945	West Ham United	White Hart Lane	Fooball League South Cup semi-final	2–1

1945 Patrick Martin Mulligan was born in Dublin. Paddy had played for Irish clubs Home Farm and Shamrock Rovers prior to moving to London in October 1969 for £17,500 in what was at the time a record deal for a Republic of Ireland player. He appeared 78 times for the Blues, was loaned to Boston Beacons in the USA, and then sold to Crystal Palace for £75,000 in September 1972 where he remained for three years before finishing his career with West Bromwich Albion.

| 1951 | Sunderland | A | League Division 1 | 1–1 |
| 1954 | West Bromwich Albion | H | League Division 1 | 5–0 |

1956 Death of Charles Freeman in Fulham.

1962	Everton	A	League Division 1	0–4
1970	Stoke City	H	League Division 1	1–0
1973	Arsenal	H	FA Cup 6th round	2–2
1979	Queens Park Rangers	H	League Division 1	1–3
1983	Barnet	A	Friendly	5–2
1990	Arsenal	A	League Division 1	1–0

MARCH 18

1911	Birmingham City	A	League Division 2	1–2
1914	Liverpool	A	League Division 1	0–3
1916	Crystal Palace	A	London Combination League (Part Two)	2–4
1922	Manchester City	H	League Division 1	0–0

1933	Birmingham City	A	League Division 1	0–0

Jack Horton made his debut.

1939	Sunderland	A	League Division 1	2–3
1944	Watford	H	Football League South Cup Group B	1–1
1950	Arsenal	White Hart Lane		
			FA Cup semi-final	2–2
1961	Preston North End	H	League Division 1	1–1
1967	Tottenham Hotspur	A	League Division 1	1–1

Ian 'Chico' Hamilton became the youngest player ever to appear in a senior competitive match for the club. He was 16 years 4 months and 18 days old. He also scored the Chelsea goal in this game. Only later, in January 1968, did he sign professional forms but his career did not take off and in total he played only five times for the Blues before being sold in August 1968 for £5,000 to Southend United. Later with Aston Villa, Sheffield United, Minnesota Kicks and San Jose Earthquake.

1972	Manchester City	A	League Division 1	0–1
1975	Queens Park Rangers	A	League Division 1	0–1
1978	Newcastle United	H	League Division 1	2–2
1980	Norwich City	A	Friendly	0–2

Played for the Norfolk Invitation Cup.

1989	Manchester City	A	League Division 2	3–2
1992	Sunderland	A	FA Cup 6th round replay	1–2
1995	Blackburn Rovers	A	Premier League	1–2

MARCH 19

1907	Bradford City	A	League Division 2	3–6
1910	Everton	A	League Division 1	2–2
1921	Sunderland	A	League Division 1	0–1
1927	Grimsby Town	H	League Division 2	2–0
1932	Derby County	A	League Division 1	0–1
1938	Sunderland	A	League Division 1	1–1
1949	Sheffield United	H	League Division 1	1–0
1955	Charlton Athletic	A	League Division 1	2–0
1957	Sparta Prague	H	Friendly	2–0
1960	Blackpool	H	League Division 1	2–3
1966	Newcastle United	A	League Division 1	1–0
1977	Bristol Rovers	H	League Division 2	2–0

1977 Peter Houseman and his wife, Sally, were killed in a car crash only hours after he had played in a League game for Oxford United.

1982	Rotherham United	H	League Division 2	1–4
1983	Crystal Palace	A	League Division 2	0–0
1986	Queens Park Rangers	H	League Division 1	1–1
1988	Oxford United	H	League Division 1	2–1
1994	Liverpool	A	Premier League	1–2

| 1997 | Southampton | H | Premier League | 1–0 |
| 1998 | Real Betis | H | Cup-Winners' Cup 3rd round | 3–1 |

MARCH 20

1909	Everton	A	League Division 1	2–3
1911	Huddersfield Town	H	League Division 2	2–0
1912	Gainsborough Trinity	A	League Division 2	2–0
1915	Blackburn Rovers	H	League Division 1	1–3
1919	Queens Park Rangers	H	London Victory Cup 2nd round	2–0
1920	Sheffield Wednesday	H	League Division 1	1–1
1926	Stockport County	A	League Division 2	0–0
1937	Sunderland	A	League Division 1	3–2
1943	Reading	A	Football League Cup South Group 3	2–7
1948	Arsenal	A	League Division 1	2–0
1954	Liverpool	A	League Division 1	1–1

1959 Dave Beasant was born in Willesden. He came to prominence with Wimbledon for whom he played just under 400 games, followed by a brief spell at Newcastle United before being signed for £725,000 in January 1989, a club record fee at the time. Despite many rather eccentric performances and some heavy criticism from the team's management, he played over 150 games in goal for the Blues before making a permanent move to Southampton (in November 1993) for £300,000 after loan spells with Grimsby Town and Wolverhampton Wanderers. He was ousted from the Saints first team by a succession of keepers including Neil Moss, Chris Woods, Maik Taylor and Paul Jones and finally left to join old boss Dave 'Harry' Bassett at Nottingham Forest.

1966 Death of Robert Lawrence Abrams in Southport.

| 1968 | Leeds United | H | League Division 1 | 0–0 |

1969 Gareth David Hall was born in Croydon. Joined as an apprentice in August 1984 and quickly progressed to the first team. Won his first full international cap for Wales at the age of nineteen but struggled to command a regular berth in the defence and moved on to Sunderland for £300,000 in December 1995. Made over 150 appearances during his time at the Bridge.

1971	Huddersfield Town	H	League Division 1	0–0
1973	Arsenal	A	FA Cup 6th round replay	1–2
1976	Bristol Rovers	H	League Division 2	0–0
1993	Tottenham Hotspur	H	Premier League	1–1
1996	Wimbledon	A	FA Cup 6th round replay	3–1

MARCH 21

1908	Bristol City	A	League Division 1	0–0
1913	Aston Villa	H	League Division 1	1–2
1914	Derby County	A	League Division 1	1–0
1925	Derby County	A	League Division 2	0–1
1927	Preston North End	A	League Division 2	2–0

1931	Manchester City	A	League Division 1	0–2
1936	Aston Villa	H	League Division 1	1–0
1942	Crystal Palace	H	London War Cup Group 4	3–3
1953	Sheffield Wednesday	H	League Division 1	1–0
1956	Birmingham City	H	League Division 1	1–2
1959	Preston North End	H	League Division 1	3–1
1964	West Bromwich Albion	H	League Division 1	3–1
1966	Leicester City	A	League Division 1	1–1
1970	Manchester United	H	League Division 1	2–1
1978	Bristol City	A	League Division 1	0–3
1981	Blackburn Rovers	H	League Division 2	0–0
1987	West Ham United	H	League Division 1	1–0
1989	Sunderland	A	League Division 2	2–1
1990	Manchester City	A	League Division 1	1–1
1992	Sheffield United	H	League Division 1	1–2

1997 Danny Granville joined Chelsea from Cambridge United for a fee of £300,000. A promising left back his path into the first team was blocked by two internationals, Graham Le Saux and Celestine Babayaro, for much of his brief stay at the club. He appeared in the Cup-Winners' Cup final as a deputy for the injured Le Saux and thus claimed a medal but departed in the 1998 close season to Leeds United for a fee of £1.5 million.

MARCH 22

1909	Sheffield Wednesday	A	League Division 1	1–5
1913	Sheffield Wednesday	A	League Division 1	2–3
1919	Tottenham Hotspur	H	London Combination League	1–2
1924	Birmingham City	A	League Division 1	0–1
1930	Stoke City	H	League Division 2	3–2
1940	Fulham	H	Football League South C	1–4
1941	Queens Park Rangers	H	Football League War Cup South 3rd round	2–4
1947	Sunderland	H	League Division 1	2–1
1950	Arsenal	White Hart Lane	FA Cup semi-final replay	0–1
1952	Stoke City	H	League Division 1	1–0
1958	Leicester City	A	League Division 1	2–3
1965	Sheffield United	H	League Division 1	3–0
1969	Tottenham Hotspur	A	League Division 1	0–1
1975	Middlesbrough	H	League Division 1	1–2
1980	Orient	H	League Division 2	1–0
1986	Southampton	A	League Division 1	1–0
1995	Queens Park Rangers	A	Premier League	0–1
1997	Middlesbrough	A	Premier League	0–1

MARCH 23

1907	Leeds City	H	League Division 2	2–0
1912	Huddersfield Town	A	League Division 2	3–1
1918	West Ham United	A	London Combination League	2–2

1920 Thomas Benjamin Jones was born in Frodsham. Signed from Tranmere Rovers in November 1947 he struggled to win a regular first team spot and ended with only 62 appearances (13 goals) by the time that he was transferred to Accrington Stanley in July 1953.

1929	Preston North End	A	League Division 2	0–3
1935	West Bromwich Albion	A	League Division 1	2–2
1940	Arsenal	A	Football League South C	0–3
1946	Luton Town	A	Football League South	1–3
1951	Burnley	A	League Division 1	1–2

Sidney Tickridge made his debut for the Blues.

1953	Liverpool	H	League Division 1	3–0
1955	Cardiff City	A	League Division 1	1–0
1957	Sunderland	H	League Division 1	0–2
1963	Newcastle United	A	League Division 2	0–2
1964	Manchester United	A	League Division 1	1–1
1968	West Ham United	A	League Division 1	1–0
1974	Everton	A	League Division 1	1–1
1976	West Ham United	H	Testimonial	1–0
1986	Manchester City	Wembley	Full Members Cup final	5–4
1991	Southampton	H	League Division 1	0–2
1996	Queens Park Rangers	H	Premier League	1–1

MARCH 24

1906	Burnley	A	League Division 2	0–2
1913	Liverpool	A	League Division 1	2–1
1917	Luton Town	A	London Combination League	2–0
1928	Manchester City	H	League Division 2	0–1
1934	Derby County	A	League Division 1	0–1
1951	Charlton Athletic	H	League Division 1	2–3
1954	Newcastle United	H	League Division 1	1–2
1956	West Bromwich Albion	A	League Division 1	0–3
1962	Arsenal	H	League Division 1	2–3
1967	Blackpool	H	League Division 1	0–2
1971	RFC Bruges, Belgium	H	Cup-Winners' Cup 3rd round	4–0
1973	Newcastle United	A	League Division 1	1–1
1979	Wolverhampton Wanderers	H	League Division 1	1–2
1993	Leeds United	A	Premier League	1–1

MARCH 25

1911	Newcastle United		Birmingham	
			FA Cup semi-final	0–3
1916	West Ham United	H	London Combination League (Part Two)	4–0
1922	Manchester City	A	League Division 1	0–0
1931	Birmingham City	H	League Division 1	1–0

1931 First appearance of John Patterson Rankin, signed from Charlton Athletic, for whom he had played over 200 games, in May 1930. He managed only 66 starts in his time at the Bridge scoring 9 League goals in the process. He was transferred to Notts County in May 1934.

1932	Bolton Wanderers	H	League Division 1	3–0
1933	West Bromwich Albion	H	League Division 1	1–2
1939	Aston Villa	H	League Division 1	2–1
1940	Fulham	A	Football League South C	3–4
1944	West Ham United	A	Football League South Cup Group B	1–6
1950	Portsmouth	A	League Division 1	0–4
1958	Cdna Bulgaria	H	Friendly	1–1
1961	Newcastle United	A	League Division 1	6–1
1967	Newcastle United	H	League Division 1	2–1
1970	Sheffield Wednesday	H	League Division 1	3–1
1972	West Ham United	H	League Division 1	3–1
1975	Woking	A	Friendly	3–4
1978	West Ham United	A	League Division 1	1–3
1989	Bournemouth	H	League Division 2	2–0
1990	Middlesbrough	Wembley	ZDS Cup final	1–0

MARCH 26

1909	Bristol City	H	League Division 1	3–1
1910	Manchester United	H	League Division 1	1–1
1921	Bradford City	A	League Division 1	1–1
1927	Blackpool	A	League Division 2	1–3
1932	Everton	H	League Division 1	0–0
1937	Charlton Athletic	H	League Division 1	3–0
1938	Everton	H	League Division 1	2–0
1948	Manchester City	H	League Division 1	2–2
1949	Aston Villa	A	League Division 1	1–1
1951	Burnley	H	League Division 1	0–2
1966	Hull City	H	FA Cup 6th round	2–2
1977	Arsenal '	H	Friendly	3–0
1982	Newcastle United	A	League Division 2	0–1
1983	Barnsley	H	League Division 2	0–3

Keith Jones played his first senior game.

1988	Southampton	A	League Division 1	0–3
1994	West Ham United	H	Premier League	2–0

MARCH 27

1915	Everton	Villa Park		
			FA Cup semi-final	2–0
1920	Aston Villa	Bramall Lane		
			FA Cup semi-final	1–3
1926	Wolverhampton Wanderers	H	League Division 2	3–3
1937	Huddersfield Town	H	League Division 1	0–0
1943	Tottenham Hotspur	H	Football League Cup South Group 3	0–2
1946	Aston Villa	A	Football League South	3–0
1948	Preston North End	H	League Division 1	2–0
1954	Tottenham Hotspur	H	League Division 1	1–0
1959	Blackpool	A	League Division 1	0–5
1963	Derby County	H	League Division 2	3–1
1965	Liverpool	Villa Park		
			FA Cup semi-final	0–2
1967	Blackpool	A	League Division 1	2–0
1971	Leeds United	H	League Division 1	3–1
1973	Manchester City	A	League Division 1	1–0
1976	Bolton Wanderers	A	League Division 2	1–2
1978	Arsenal	H	League Division 1	0–0
1993	Ifk Gothenburg	A	Friendly	0–0
1995	Tottenham Hotspur	H	Friendly	5–1

MARCH 28

1901 John Ernest Townrow was born Stratford, East London. An England international who initially played for Clapton Orient, he signed for Chelsea in February 1927 at a cost of £5,000. He accumulated 140 starts and 3 goals in a spell that lasted until a transfer to Bristol Rovers in May 1932.

1910	Woolwich Arsenal	H	League Division 1	0–1
1914	Manchester City	H	League Division 1	1–0
1921	Aston Villa	A	League Division 1	0–3
1931	Leeds United	H	League Division 1	1–0
1936	Brentford	A	League Division 1	1–2
1942	Fulham	A	London War Cup Group 4	0–1
1953	Cardiff City	A	League Division 1	3–3
1959	Leeds United	A	League Division 1	0–4

Chelsea debut of Sylvan James Anderton.

1964	Birmingham City	A	League Division 1	4–3
1970	Everton	A	League Division 1	2–5
1979	Nottingham Forest	A	League Division 1	0–6
1981	Newcastle United	A	League Division 2	0–1
1989	Ipswich Town	A	League Division 2	1–0
1992	Manchester City	A	League Division 1	0–0

MARCH 29

1907	Hull City	H	League Division 2	3–0
1911	West Bromwich Albion	H	League Division 2	2–1
1913	Blackburn Rovers	H	League Division 1	1–6
1918	Queens Park Rangers	H	London Combination League	1–0
1919	Clapton Orient	A	London Combination League	0–0
1921	Aston Villa	H	League Division 1	5–1
1929	Grimsby Town	A	League Division 2	0–1
1930	Wolverhampton Wanderers	A	League Division 2	1–0
1933	Derby County	A	League Division 1	1–0
1937	Charlton Athletic	A	League Division 1	0–1
1941	Brentford	A	London Cup 'A' Competition	2–2
1947	Aston Villa	A	League Division 1	0–2
1948	Manchester City	A	League Division 1	0–1
1950	Middlesbrough	H	League Division 1	2–1
1955	Sunderland	H	League Division 1	2–1

Peter Brabrook made his League debut.

1958	Sunderland	H	League Division 1	0–0
1966	Tsv 1860 Munich	H	Fairs Cup 4th round	1–0
1969	Everton	A	League Division 1	2–1
1972	Sheffield United	H	League Division 1	2–0
1975	West Ham United	A	League Division 1	1–0
1977	Chelsea 1970 XI	H	Houseman Fund	3–0
1980	Charlton Athletic	A	League Division 2	2–1
1986	West Ham United	H	League Division 1	0–4
1988	Watford	A	League Division 1	3–0
1998	Middlesbrough	Wembley	League Cup final	2–0

New manager Gianluca Vialli took his first trophy barely two months after assuming the role for Chelsea. He decided against playing in the game himself and instead nominated Mark Hughes and Gianfranco Zola to start with Tore Andre Flo on the substitutes' bench. Although Chelsea dominated throughout, it took a period of extra time to seal the win with the goals coming from Frank Sinclair and Roberto Di Matteo, who had also notched a goal in the FA Cup final the previous year against the same opponents.

MARCH 30

1907	Barnsley	A	League Division 2	1–3
1918	Fulham	H	London Combination League	7–0
1923	Aston Villa	A	League Division 1	0–1

Debut of William Ferguson.

1929	Millwall	H	League Division 2	0–3
1934	Portsmouth	A	League Division 1	2–0
1935	Blackburn Rovers	H	League Division 1	4–2

1940	West Ham United	H	Football League South C	3–0
1946	Charlton Athletic	A	Football League South	0–0
1956	Luton Town	A	League Division 1	2–2
1957	Luton Town	A	League Division 1	4–0
1959	Blackpool	H	League Division 1	3–1
1960	Blackburn Rovers	A	League Division 1	0–1
1963	Walsall	H	League Division 2	0–1
1964	Nottingham Forest	H	League Division 1	1–0
1968	Birmingham City	A	FA Cup 6th round	0–1
1970	West Bromwich Albion	A	League Division 1	1–3
1974	Manchester United	H	League Division 1	1–3
1985	Sunderland	A	League Division 1	2–0
1991	Leeds United	H	League Division 1	1–2
1994	Sheffield Wednesday	A	Premier League	1–3

MARCH 31

1906	Leeds City	H	League Division 2	4–0
1909	Bury	A	League Division 1	1–2
1917	Arsenal	H	London Combination League	2–0
1923	Manchester City	A	League Division 1	0–3
1928	Nottingham Forest	A	League Division 2	2–2
1934	West Bromwich Albion	H	League Division 1	3–2
1945	Southampton	H	Football League South	3–4
1951	Manchester United	A	League Division 1	1–4
1956	Preston North End	H	League Division 1	0–1
1961	Tottenham Hotspur	A	League Division 1	2–4
1962	Bolton Wanderers	A	League Division 1	2–4
1964	Nottingham Forest	A	League Division 1	1–0
1965	Everton	A	League Division 1	1–1
1966	Hull City	A	FA Cup 6th round replay	3–1
1973	Crystal Palace	A	League Division 1	0–2
1975	Ipswich Town	H	League Division 1	0–0

Steve Wicks made his senior debut for the club.

1984	Cardiff City	A	League Division 2	3–3
1986	Queens Park Rangers	A	League Division 1	0–6
1990	Derby County	H	League Division 1	1–1
1996	Manchester United	Villa Park		
			FA Cup semi-final	1–2

APRIL 1

| 1908 | Everton | A | League Division 1 | 3–0 |

Thomas Law was born in Glasgow. One of the most celebrated names in Chelsea's history, Law played his entire professional career with the club commencing June 1925 and finishing in May 1939. In that time he made over 300 appearances and scored 19 goals, a respectable tally for a full-back. He also won two full Scottish international caps.

1911	Hull City	A	League Division 2	1–1
1916	Croydon Common	A	London Combination League (Part Two)	4–1
1918	Queens Park Rangers	A	London Combination League	2–1
1922	Everton	H	League Division 1	1–0
1925	Crystal Palace	A	League Division 2	0–1
1929	Grimsby Town	H	League Division 2	3–2
1933	Sheffield United	A	League Division 1	2–2
1939	Wolverhampton Wanderers	A	League Division 1	0–2
1944	Reading	White Hart Lane		
			Football League South Cup semi-final	3–2
1950	Huddersfield Town	H	League Division 1	3–1
1961	Cardiff City	H	League Division 1	6–1
1963	Luton Town	H	League Division 2	3–1
1967	Leeds United	A	League Division 1	0–1
1972	Ipswich Town	A	League Division 1	2–1
1978	Nottingham Forest	A	League Division 1	1–3
1989	Barnsley	H	League Division 2	5–3
1991	Coventry City	A	League Division 1	0–1
1995	Newcastle United	H	Premier League	1–1

APRIL 2

1910	Bradford City	A	League Division 1	1–4
1915	Bradford City	H	League Division 1	2–0

1915 At the same time that the Blues were beating Bradford City, Manchester United played Liverpool at Old Trafford. United were battling against relegation whilst Liverpool were safe in mid-table; this was a match United had to win and which they did 2-0. A couple of days later a letter appeared in the *Athletic News* asking the football authorities to look more closely into the game, which was said to have been the most sterile in football history. The crowd were booing the players, particularly those from Liverpool, for their lack of effort throughout, especially after Liverpool missed a penalty. The letter, most probably written by a disgruntled bookmaker (the bookies had taken a rush of bets on upsetting the form book and beating Liverpool 2-0) did indeed alert the authorities, who questioned just about everyone connected with this match and then, over a year later, announced the result to have been fixed. Life suspensions from the game were handed to a number of players who took part, although most were lifted immediately after the First World War in recognition of the service given by the players to the war effort. The one exception was Enoch West, who as well as losing a libel case against the *Athletic News* did not have his suspension lifted until 1945, when he was 62 – a suspension of over 30 years. The result of this game was allowed to stand and had several repercussions when football resumed after the war – the two points United collected were enough to lift them above Chelsea in the League and out of a relegation spot; when the League was extended immediately after the war. Chelsea were allowed to keep their place in the First Division because the United v Liverpool match had been fixed. Spurs, who would have finished bottom regardless, were voted out in preference to Arsenal, who finished fifth in the Second Division. One other participant in the United v Liverpool match was Billy Meredith, who had earlier been embroiled in a similar match-rigging claim whilst playing for Manchester City.

1920	Aston Villa	H	League Division 1	2–1
1921	Bradford City	H	League Division 1	3–1
1923	Aston Villa	H	League Division 1	1–1
1926	Southampton	H	League Division 2	0–0
1927	Reading	H	League Division 2	0–0
1932	Arsenal	A	League Division 1	1–1
1934	Portsmouth	H	League Division 1	4–0
1938	Manchester City	A	League Division 1	0–1
1945	West Ham United	H	Football League South	3–4
1949	Huddersfield Town	H	League Division 1	5–0
1955	Tottenham Hotspur	A	League Division 1	4–2
1956	Luton Town	H	League Division 1	0–0
1957	Esporte Clube Bahia	H	Friendly	3–1
1960	Manchester City	H	League Division 1	3–0

First appearance made by Peter 'The Cat' Bonetti.

1977	Blackburn Rovers	H	League Division 2	2–0
1980	Queens Park Rangers	H	League Division 2	0–2
1983	Fulham	A	League Division 2	1–1

1984 Death of Frank Rawlinson Mitchell.

1988	Arsenal	A	League Division 1	1–3
1994	Southampton	H	Premier League	2–0
1998	Vicenza	A	Cup-Winners' Cup semi-final	0–1

APRIL 3

1909	Woolwich Arsenal	A	League Division 1	0–0
1915	Sunderland	H	League Division 1	3–0
1920	Manchester City	H	League Division 1	1–0
1926	Swansea Town	A	League Division 2	0–0

George William Pearson, born in West Stanley 1907, made his debut for the club having signed from Bury two months earlier. In all he made 215 appearances and scored 35 goals before moving to Luton Town in June 1933. Finished his career with Walsall.

1937	Everton	A	League Division 1	0–0
1943	Millwall	A	Football League Cup South Group 3	2–1
1946	Charlton Athletic	H	Football League South	0–1
1948	Stoke City	A	League Division 1	0–2
1953	Arsenal	H	League Division 1	1–1

1954	Burnley	A	League Division 1	2–1
1961	Tottenham Hotspur	H	League Division 1	2–3
1965	Birmingham City	H	League Division 1	3–1
1971	Arsenal	A	League Division 1	0–2
1973	Tottenham Hotspur	H	League Division 1	0–1
1974	Tottenham Hotspur	A	League Division 1	2–1
1982	Oldham Athletic	H	League Division 2	2–2
1993	Middlesbrough	H	Premier League	4–0

APRIL 4

1908	Manchester City	A	League Division 1	3–0
1914	Bradford City	A	League Division 1	0–0
1925	Bradford City	A	League Division 2	0–2
1927	Southampton	A	League Division 2	1–1
1931	Arsenal	A	League Division 1	1–2
1936	Huddersfield Town	H	League Division 1	1–0
1942	Crystal Palace	A	London War Cup Group 4	3–0
1947	Blackburn Rovers	H	League Division 1	0–2
1949	Sidney Bishop died in Chelsea.			
1953	Newcastle United	H	League Division 1	1–2
1958	Nottingham Forest	H	League Division 1	0–0
1959	Manchester City	H	League Division 1	2–0
1966	Leeds United	A	League Division 1	0–2
1969	Newcastle United	H	League Division 1	1–1
1970	Tottenham Hotspur	H	League Division 1	1–0
1978	Middlesbrough	A	League Division 1	0–2
1979	Derby County	H	League Division 1	1–1
	Debut of Mickey Fillery.			
1981	Cardiff City	H	League Division 2	0–1
1983	Queens Park Rangers	H	League Division 2	0–2
1987	Everton	H	League Division 1	1–2
1989	Birmingham City	H	League Division 2	3–1
1992	West Ham United	H	League Division 1	2–1
1994	Newcastle United	A	Premier League	0–0

APRIL 5

1913	Derby County	A	League Division 1	1–3
1915	Burnley	A	League Division 1	0–2
1919	Arsenal	A	London Combination League	1–2
1924	Manchester City	A	League Division 1	0–1
1926	Southampton	A	League Division 2	1–0
1930	Bradford City	H	League Division 2	3–2
1941	Crystal Palace	H	London Cup 'A' Competition	1–3
1947	Derby County	H	League Division 1	3–0

1952	Arsenal		White Hart Lane	
			FA Cup semi-final	1–1
1958	Luton Town	A	League Division 1	2–0
1965	Leicester City	A	League Cup final	0–0

1967 Erland Johnsen was born in Fredrikstad, Norway. Bought from Bayern Munich in Germany, where Johnsen had been a member of a team that had won the Bundesliga and reached the semi-finals of the UEFA Cup, he cost just over £300,000 in December 1989. He played over 150 games for the Blues before his release in the summer of 1997.

1969	Burnley	H	League Division 1	2–3
1975	Stoke City	A	League Division 1	0–3
1980	Leicester City	A	League Division 2	0–1
1986	Ipswich Town	H	League Division 1	1–1
1997	Arsenal	A	Premier League	0–3
1998	Derby County	A	Premier League	1–0

APRIL 6

1907	Chesterfield	H	League Division 2	7–1
1912	Glossop North End	A	League Division 2	2–1
1917	Queens Park Rangers	A	London Combination League	2–2
1918	Clapton Orient	A	London Combination League	6–1
1920	Sheffield Wednesday	A	League Division 1	2–0
1921	Everton	A	League Division 1	1–5
1928	Oldham Athletic	H	League Division 2	2–1
1929	Port Vale	A	League Division 2	0–1
1931	Leicester City	H	League Division 1	1–0
1932	Liverpool	A	League Division 1	1–2
1935	Arsenal	A	League Division 1	2–2
1940	Charlton Athletic	H	Football League South C	1–4
1942	Fulham	H	London War Cup Group 4	2–2
1946	Fulham	A	Football League South	2–3
1953	Arsenal	A	League Division 1	0–2
1957	Aston Villa	H	League Division 1	1–1
1963	Norwich City	A	League Division 2	1–4
1964	Leicester City	H	League Division 1	1–0
1968	Sheffield Wednesday	A	League Division 1	2–2
1974	Southampton	A	League Division 1	0–0
1976	Fulham	H	League Division 2	0–0
1985	Queens Park Rangers	H	League Division 1	1–0
1991	Luton Town	H	League Division 1	3–3

Andy Myers, at 17 years old, made his League debut along with Frank Sinclair.

1993	Ipswich Town	A	Premier League	1–1
1995	Real Zaragoza	A	Cup-Winners' Cup semi-final	0–3
1996	Aston Villa	H	Premier League	1–2

APRIL 7

1906	Burton United	A	League Division 2	4–2
1917	Millwall	A	London Combination League	1–2
1923	Manchester City	H	League Division 1	1–1
1928	Port Vale	H	League Division 2	1–0
1931	Leicester City	A	League Division 1	1–2
1934	Birmingham City	A	League Division 1	3–0
1939	Charlton Athletic	A	League Division 1	0–2
1945	Millwall	Wembley	Football League South Cup final	2–0

Goals by McDonald and Wardle clinched the trophy for Chelsea.

1947	Blackburn Rovers	A	League Division 1	2–1
1950	Bolton Wanderers	H	League Division 1	1–1
1951	Aston Villa	H	League Division 1	1–1
1952	Arsenal	White Hart Lane		
			FA Cup semi-final replay	0–3
1956	Sheffield United	A	League Division 1	1–2
1958	Nottingham Forest	A	League Division 1	1–1
1962	Manchester City	H	League Division 1	1–1
1973	Stoke City	H	League Division 1	1–3
1979	Nottingham Forest	H	League Division 1	1–3
1980	Luton Town	H	League Division 2	1–1
1982	Cambridge United	H	League Division 2	4–1
1984	Fulham	H	League Division 2	4–0
1987	Charlton Athletic	A	League Division 1	0–0
1990	Luton Town	H	League Division 1	1–0

APRIL 8

1911	Fulham	H	League Division 2	2–0
1912	Derby County	A	League Division 2	0–2
1916	Fulham	H	London Combination League (Part Two)	6–3
1922	Everton	A	League Division 1	3–2
1933	Leeds United	H	League Division 1	6–0
1939	Everton	H	League Division 1	0–2
1944	Tottenham Hotspur	H	Football League South	1–1
1950	Aston Villa	A	League Division 1	0–4
1955	Sheffield United	H	League Division 1	1–1
1961	Manchester City	A	League Division 1	1–2
1967	Sheffield Wednesday	H	FA Cup 6th round	1–0
1969	Nottingham Forest	A	League Division 1	2–1
1972	Crystal Palace	H	League Division 1	2–1
1977	Fulham	A	League Division 2	1–3
1989	West Bromwich Albion	A	League Division 2	3–2

The last match in a run of 27 games in which Chelsea remained unbeaten in the Second Division either at home or away and thereby established a club record.

| 1996 | Bolton | A | Premier League | 1–2 |
| 1998 | Leeds United | A | Premier League | 1–3 |

APRIL 9

| 1909 | Middlesbrough | H | League Division 1 | 3–0 |

First game for Samuel Downing.

1910	Sheffield Wednesday	H	League Division 1	4–1
1917	Queens Park Rangers	H	London Combination League	3–1
1921	Huddersfield Town	A	League Division 1	0–2
1927	Swansea Town	A	League Division 2	1–2
1928	Oldham Athletic	A	League Division 2	1–2

William Russell made his debut. Joined the club in June 1927 from junior football and over the course of eight years with the Blues made 160 appearances (6 goals) before moving to Heart of Midlothian in December 1935.

| 1932 | Sheffield United | H | League Division 1 | 1–1 |
| 1938 | Leicester City | H | League Division 1 | 4–1 |

1946 David James Webb was born in Stratford, East London. One of the greatest characters in the history of Chelsea, Webby began his career at Leyton Orient and moved to Southampton from where the Blues secured his services for £40,000 and the contract of Joe Kirkup. In six years at the Bridge he made very nearly 300 appearances and scored 33 goals, the most important of which was clearly the winning goal against Leeds United in the 1970 FA Cup final replay. He was also a member of the side that won the European Cup-Winners' Cup in 1971 and, when the club was in the middle of a goalkeeping crisis, he made a faultless appearance between the posts in a 2–0 win over Ipswich Town (in December 1971). He was sold to Queens Park Rangers for £100,000 in May 1974 and later moved on to Leicester City, Derby County, AFC Bournemouth and Torquay United (as player-manager at his last two clubs). Went into football management on a full time basis and after experience gained with Southend United, took over for a short time at Chelsea but was not given an extended contract when the club preferred instead to appoint Glenn Hoddle from Swindon Town. Webb then took charge at Brentford, first as manager, later as a share-holder.

1949	Manchester United	A	League Division 1	1–1
1955	Wolverhampton Wanderers	H	League Division 1	1–0
1960	Arsenal	A	League Division 1	4–1
1966	West Ham United	H	League Division 1	6–2
1977	Luton Town	H	League Division 2	2–0
1983	Oldham Athletic	A	League Division 2	2–2
1986	Manchester United	A	League Division 1	2–1
1988	Derby County	A	League Division 1	0–2
1994	Luton Town	Wembley	FA Cup semi-final	2–0
1997	Coventry City	A	Premier League	1–3

APRIL 10

1909	Notts County	H	League Division 1	3–2
1915	Sheffield Wednesday	A	League Division 1	2–3
1920	Manchester City	A	League Division 1	0–1
1922	Huddersfield Town	H	League Division 1	1–0

1923 Sidney Tickeridge was born in Stepney. Sid was signed to the Tottenham Hotspur groundstaff in 1937 and sent to their Northfleet nursery. During the war he played for Spurs, Aldershot, Fulham and Millwall and at the end of the war signed professional forms with Spurs in April 1946. He was transferred to Chelsea in March 1951 for £10,000 and although he played only one full season in the first team, he nevertheless remained at the club over a period of four years during which time he made 73 appearances. Departed July 1955 on a free transfer to Brentford where an injury called a halt to his career. Later joined the Millwall training staff.

1926	Sheffield Wednesday	H	League Division 2	0–0
1936	Derby County	H	League Division 1	1–1
1937	Bolton Wanderers	H	League Division 1	0–1
1939	Charlton Athletic	H	League Division 1	1–3
1943	Reading	H	Football League Cup South Group 3	0–4
1944	Fulham	A	Football League South	3–2
1946	Coventry City	H	Football League South	2–1
1948	Sheffield United	H	League Division 1	1–0
1950	Bolton Wanderers	A	League Division 1	0–1
1954	Bolton Wanderers	H	League Division 1	2–0
1967	West Bromwich Albion	H	League Division 1	0–2
1971	Crystal Palace	H	League Division 1	1–1
1976	Bristol City	A	League Division 2	2–2
1979	Bristol City	A	League Division 1	1–3
1982	Queens Park Rangers	H	League Division 2	2–1
1985	Nottingham Forest	A	League Division 1	0–2
1993	Southampton	A	Premier League	0–1
1995	Wimbledon	A	Premier League	1–1

APRIL 11

1908	Preston North End	H	League Division 1	0–0
1914	Blackburn Rovers	H	League Division 1	2–0
1925	Port Vale	H	League Division 2	1–0
1931	Derby County	H	League Division 1	1–1
1936	Portsmouth	A	League Division 1	0–2
1942	Portsmouth	A	London War Cup Group 4	0–2
1953	West Bromwich Albion	A	League Division 1	1–0
1959	Arsenal	A	League Division 1	1–1
1962	Leicester City	A	League Division 1	0–2
1964	Bolton Wanderers	A	League Division 1	0–1
1966	Nottingham Forest	H	League Division 1	1–0

1970	Leeds United		Wembley FA Cup final	2–2

After the anticipation of reaching another FA Cup final, the result, if not the game itself, came as something of an anti-climax. A full house of 100,000 was treated to extra time but still the sides could not be separated. Chelsea's goals were supplied by Peter Houseman and Ian Hutchinson, ensuring a replay would take place 18 days later at Old Trafford.

1977	Charlton Athletic	A	League Division 2	0–4
1978	Wimbledon	A	Testimonial	0–3
1978	James Argue died in Lennoxtown.			
1981	Oldham Athletic	A	League Division 2	0–0
1992	Leeds United	A	League Division 1	0–3
1998	Tottenham Hotspur	H	Premier League	2–0

APRIL 12

1896 Frederick Barrett was born in Kent. He got his career underway with Belfast Celtic before joining Chelsea in June 1920 to serve the club for seven years mostly in a reserve capacity. He made a total of 70 appearances and scored 6 goals, all in the League.

1913	Tottenham Hotspur	H	League Division 1	1–0
1919	Crystal Palace	H	London Combination League	3–0
1924	Newcastle United	A	League Division 1	1–2
1930	Swansea Town	A	League Division 2	0–3
1941	Fulham	A	London Cup 'A' Competition	0–4
1947	Everton	A	League Division 1	0–2
1952	Preston North End	A	League Division 1	0–1
1958	Bolton Wanderers	H	League Division 1	2–2
1963	Bury	H	League Division 2	2–0
1965	West Ham United	A	League Division 1	2–3
1966	Nottingham Forest	A	League Division 1	2–1
1968	Manchester City	A	League Division 1	0–1
1969	West Ham United	A	League Division 1	0–0
1971	Liverpool	H	League Division 1	1–0
1972	Wolverhampton Wanderers	A	League Division 1	2–0
1975	Manchester City	H	League Division 1	0–1
1980	Preston North End	A	League Division 2	1–1
1982	Crystal Palace	A	League Division 2	1–0

Paul Canoville made history as the first black player to appear for Chelsea.

1986	Nottingham Forest	A	League Division 1	0–0
1993	Wimbledon	H	Premier League	4–2
1995	Southampton	H	Premier League	0–2

APRIL 13

1906	Manchester United	H	League Division 2	1–1

1907	Wolverhampton Wanderers	H	League Division 2	4–0
1912	Hull City	H	League Division 2	1–0
1914	Bolton Wanderers	H	League Division 1	2–1
1918	Tottenham Hotspur	H	National War Fund Competition	1–1
1925	Manchester United	H	League Division 2	0–0
1929	Hull City	H	League Division 2	0–0
1935	Portsmouth	H	League Division 1	1–1
1936	Derby County	A	League Division 1	1–1
1940	Southampton	A	Football League South C	0–3
1946	Fulham	H	Football League South	0–0
1957	Blackpool	A	League Division 1	0–1
1963	Grimsby Town	H	League Division 2	2–1
1968	Tottenham Hotspur	H	League Division 1	2–0
1970	Stoke City	A	League Division 1	2–1
1974	Arsenal	A	League Division 1	1–3
1985	West Ham United	A	League Division 1	1–1
1991	Everton	A	League Division 1	2–2
1994	Queens Park Rangers	A	Premier League	1–1
1996	Leeds United	H	Premier League	4–1
1997	Wimbledon	Highbury	FA Cup semi-final	3–0

A one-sided affair in which Chelsea dominated from first to last. Wimbledon showed none of their customary fight and slipped out of a second cup competition at the semi-final stage that season having already been beaten by Leicester City in the Coca-Cola Cup. The Blues meanwhile prepared to face relegation-threatened Middlesbrough for what would be the second of their three Cup final meetings in the Nineties (the Full Members' and the League Cup also being contested).

APRIL 14

1906	Grimsby Town	A	League Division 2	1–1
1911	Leeds City	H	League Division 2	4–1
1914	West Bromwich Albion	A	League Division 1	1–3
1915	Bolton Wanderers	A	League Division 1	1–3
1917	Brentford	H	London Combination League	3–2
1922	Aston Villa	H	League Division 1	1–0
1923	Bolton Wanderers	A	League Division 1	1–1
1928	South Shields	A	League Division 2	1–2
1932	Newcastle United	H	League Division 1	4–1
1933	Leicester City	H	League Division 1	4–1
1934	Everton	H	League Division 1	2–0
1941	Arsenal	H	Football League South	3–1
1945	Luton Town	A	Football League South	1–1
1948	Everton	A	League Division 1	3–2
1951	Derby County	A	League Division 1	0–1

1952	Aston Villa	H	League Division 1	2–2
1956	Everton	H	League Division 1	6–1
1962	West Bromwich Albion	A	League Division 1	0–4
1971	Manchester City	H	Cup-Winners' Cup semi-final	1–0

A single goal by Derek Smethurst gave the Blues the narrowest of advantages to take into the second leg at Maine Road.

1973	Norwich City	A	League Division 1	0–1
1975	Fulham	A	Friendly	1–0
1979	Southampton	H	League Division 1	1–2
1984	Crystal Palace	A	League Division 2	1–0
1987	Watford	A	League Division 1	1–3
1990	Aston Villa	A	League Division 1	0–1

APRIL 15

1911	Bradford Park Avenue	A	League Division 2	1–2
1916	Luton Town	A	London Combination League (Part Two)	1–1
1922	Sunderland	H	League Division 1	1–0

1923   William Dickson was born in Lurgan, County Armagh. Joined Chelsea in November 1947 from Notts County in an exchange deal that saw Tommy Lawton move in the opposite direction plus cash adjustment. Made 101 League and 18 FA Cup appearances scoring 4 goals before being transferred to Arsenal in October 1953 for £15,000. Later played for Mansfield Town and then Glenavon.

1933	Everton	A	League Division 1	2–3
1938	Preston North End	H	League Division 1	0–2
1939	Huddersfield Town	A	League Division 1	1–3

1940   Edward Graham McCreadie was born in Glasgow. He was virtually unknown when signed from East Stirlingshire in April 1962 for £6,000 but was an instant success in the Football League and flourished until his switch to a coaching role in November 1974. At the time he was Chelsea's most capped player with 23 appearances for Scotland whilst for the club he made over 400 appearances and scored 5 goals. Became manager in April 1975 when taking over from Ron Stuart and guided the club back to the First Division in May 1976 but left in a contractual dispute shortly after.

1944	Charlton Athletic	Wembley	Football League South Cup final	1–3
1949	Manchester City	A	League Division 1	0–1
1950	Wolverhampton Wanderers	H	League Division 1	0–0
1952	Aston Villa	A	League Division 1	1–7
1959	Nottingham Forest	A	League Division 1	3–1

Ken Shellito played his first senior game for the club.

1960	Tottenham Hotspur	H	League Division 1	1–3
1961	Arsenal	H	League Division 1	3–1
1970	Burnley	A	League Division 1	1–3
1972	Tottenham Hotspur	A	League Division 1	0–3

1974	Tottenham Hotspur	H	League Division 1	0–0
1978	Aston Villa	A	League Division 1	0–2
1985	Death of Samuel Weaver.			
1986	West Ham United	A	League Division 1	2–1
1989	Leicester City	A	League Division 2	0–2
1995	Aston Villa	H	Premier League	1–0

APRIL 16

| 1906 | Glossop North End | H | League Division 2 | 0–0 |

George Hunter Henderson played the first of his 64 games for the club. Signed from Middlesbrough in April 1905, he moved to Glossop after four years at the Bridge.

| 1910 | Bristol City | A | League Division 1 | 0–1 |

Robert Whittingham made his debut. He cost £1,300 when signed from Bradford City in January 1909 and repaid his fee with 80 goals in 129 games up to his transfer to Stoke in September 1919.

1921	Huddersfield Town	H	League Division 1	1–1
1927	Nottingham Forest	H	League Division 2	2–0
1932	Manchester City	A	League Division 1	1–1
1938	Huddersfield Town	A	League Division 1	2–1

1938 Anthony Wallace Nicholas was born in West Ham. Product of the Chelsea youth system who signed professional forms in May 1955 and made 63 appearances with 20 goals before moving on to Brighton and Hove Albion in November 1960 for a fee of £15,000.

1949	Derby County	H	League Division 1	0–3
1954	Manchester City	H	League Division 1	0–1
1955	Portsmouth	A	League Division 1	0–0
1960	Nottingham Forest	H	League Division 1	1–1
1963	Bury	A	League Division 2	0–2
1965	Liverpool	H	League Division 1	4–0
1966	Sunderland	A	League Division 1	0–2
1968	Manchester City	H	League Division 1	1–0
1976	Luton Town	A	League Division 2	2–2
1977	Nottingham Forest	H	League Division 2	2–1
1979	Arsenal	A	League Division 1	2–5
1983	Newcastle United	H	League Division 2	0–2
1985	Aston Villa	H	League Division 1	3–1
1990	Crystal Palace	H	League Division 1	3–0
1994	Arsenal	A	Premier League	0–1
1997	Newcastle United	A	Premier League	1–3
1998	Vicenza	H	Cup-Winners' Cup semi-final	3–1

APRIL 17

| 1909 | Newcastle United | A | League Division 1 | 3–1 |

1915	West Bromwich Albion	H	League Division 1	4–1
1920	Derby County	H	League Division 1	0–0
1922	Aston Villa	A	League Division 1	4–1
1926	Stoke City	A	League Division 2	3–1
1929	West Bromwich Albion	H	League Division 2	2–5
1937	Brentford	A	League Division 1	0–1
1940	Arsenal	H	Football League South C	2–2
1948	Manchester United	A	League Division 1	0–5
1954	Preston North End	A	League Division 1	0–1
1965	West Bromwich Albion	H	League Division 1	2–2
1967	Sheffield United	A	League Division 1	0–3
1971	Manchester City	A	League Division 1	1–1
1973	Everton	A	League Division 1	0–1
1976	Orient	H	League Division 2	0–2
1980	Notts County	H	League Division 2	1–0
1982	Grimsby Town	A	League Division 2	3–3
1991	Norwich City	A	League Division 1	3–1
1993	Manchester United	A	Premier League	0–3
1995	Manchester United	A	Premier League	0–0
1996	Sheffield Wednesday	A	Premier League	0–0

APRIL 18

1908	Bury	A	League Division 1	1–1
1911	Huddersfield Town	A	League Division 2	1–3
1914	Sunderland	A	League Division 1	0–2
1919	Queens Park Rangers	A	London Combination League	2–3
1924	Liverpool	H	League Division 1	2–1
1925	Middlesbrough	A	League Division 2	1–1
1927	Wolverhampton Wanderers	H	League Division 2	1–0
1930	Bristol City	H	League Division 2	2–1
1931	Sunderland	A	League Division 1	0–2
1933	Leicester City	A	League Division 1	1–1
1936	Preston North End	H	League Division 1	5–2
1938	Preston North End	A	League Division 1	0–0

1940 Michael Harrison was born in Ilford. Came straight from school and worked his way through the youth set-up, signing as a professional in April 1957. He made 64 appearances with 9 goals until he realised that his chances of establishing himself as a first team regular at the Bridge were limited and he moved to Blackburn Rovers in September 1962 for £18,000. Later played for Plymouth Argyle and Luton Town.

On the same day Ken Shellito was born a few miles away from Harrison in East Ham. His early career followed a remarkably similar pattern in that a professional contract was also awarded him in April 1957. Their fortunes differed though with the outstanding Shellito going on to make 123 appearances for the Blues and only prevented from making many more by a knee injury that forced him to retire prematurely in January 1969. He was appointed to Chelsea's coaching staff and progressed to the post of manager prior to the start of season 1977–78, a job he held for 15 months.

1942	Portsmouth	H	London War Cup Group 4	0–0
1949	Manchester City	H	League Division 1	1–1
1951	Huddersfield Town	A	League Division 1	1–2
1953	Middlesbrough	H	League Division 1	1–1

1958 Eamonn Bannon was born in Edinburgh. After starting with Heart of Midlothian he was purchased by Chelsea for £200,000 in January 1979 but never properly established himself in English football. He made just 27 appearances and scored a single goal before returning to Scotland to join Dundee United in a deal worth £170,000 in November 1979.

| 1959 | Everton | H | League Division 1 | 3–1 |
| 1960 | Tottenham Hotspur | A | League Division 1 | 1–0 |

1961 Kevin Wilson was born in Banbury. After an introduction to senior football at Derby County followed by a spell with Ipswich Town, Wilson was snapped up by the Blues for a fee of £335,000 in June 1987. A Northern Ireland international he won a Full Members' Cup medal in 1990 and played over 150 games for Chelsea, a large proportion of which saw him coming off the substitutes' bench, scoring more than 50 goals.

1964	Everton	H	League Division 1	1–0
1970	Liverpool	H	League Division 1	2–1
1972	Southampton	A	League Division 1	2–2
1981	Bristol City	A	League Division 2	0–0
1987	Queens Park Rangers	A	League Division 1	1–1

Goalkeeper Roger Freestone made his League debut for the Blues.

| 1992 | Queens Park Rangers | H | League Division 1 | 2–1 |

APRIL 19

1913	Middlesbrough	A	League Division 1	3–0
1915	Manchester United	H	League Division 1	1–3
1919	Crystal Palace	Highbury	London Victory Cup semi-final	4–0
1924	Newcastle United	H	League Division 1	1–0
1930	Cardiff City	H	League Division 2	1–0
1935	Wolverhampton Wanderers	H	League Division 1	4–2
1941	Fulham	H	London Cup 'A' Competition	4–3
1946	Plymouth Argyle	H	Football League South	2–0
1947	Huddersfield Town	H	League Division 1	1–0
1952	Burnley	H	League Division 1	4–1
1954	Manchester City	A	League Division 1	1–1
1957	Newcastle United	A	League Division 1	2–1

1958	Leeds United	A	League Division 1	0–0
1965	Liverpool	A	League Division 1	0–2
1967	Everton	A	League Division 1	1–3
1969	Queens Park Rangers	H	League Division 1	2–1
1975	Tottenham Hotspur	A	League Division 1	0–2
1976	Charlton Athletic	A	League Division 2	1–1
1977	Oldham Athletic	A	League Division 2	0–0

Clive Walker made his first appearance.

1986	Newcastle United	H	League Division 1	1–1
1997	Leicester City	H	Premier League	2–1
1998	Sheffield Wednesday	A	Premier League	4–1

APRIL 20

1900 Albert Edward Thain was born in Southall. Played junior football for Metropolitan Railway and Southall before joining Chelsea in April 1922 where he went on to make just over 150 appearances and score 50 goals in a nine-year career. He was transferred to Bournemouth and Boscombe in June 1931 where an injury put paid to his endeavours.

1907	Clapton Orient	A	League Division 2	1–0
1908	Liverpool	H	League Division 1	0–2
1909	Bradford City	A	League Division 1	0–3
1918	Tottenham Hotspur	A	National War Fund Competition	1–0
1925	South Shields	H	League Division 2	1–1
1929	Tottenham Hotspur	A	League Division 2	1–4
1935	Liverpool	A	League Division 1	0–6
1940	West Ham United	A	Football League War Cup 1st round	2–3
1946	Portsmouth	A	Football League South	0–3
1957	Everton	H	League Division 1	5–1
1962	Wolverhampton Wanderers	H	League Division 1	4–5
1963	Plymouth Argyle	A	League Division 2	1–2
1968	Everton	A	League Division 1	1–2
1974	Leicester City	A	League Division 1	0–3
1981	Luton Town	H	League Division 2	0–2
1982	Luton Town	A	League Division 2	2–2
1985	West Bromwich Albion	A	League Division 1	1–0
1987	Southampton	H	League Division 1	1–1
1991	Nottingham Forest	A	League Division 1	0–7

Not for the first time the Blues leaked seven goals to equal their worst margin of defeat.

| 1992 | Aston Villa | A | League Division 1 | 1–3 |
| 1995 | Real Zaragoza | H | Cup-Winners' Cup semi-final | 3–1 |

APRIL 21

1906	Gainsborough Trinity	H	League Division 2	1–3
1916	Arsenal	H	London Combination League (Part Two)	9–0
1917	Fulham	A	London Combination League	4–0
1918	Brentford	A	London Combination League	0–0
1919	Queens Park Rangers	H	London Combination League	3–0
1923	Bolton Wanderers	H	League Division 1	3–0
1928	Leeds United	H	League Division 2	2–3
1930	Bristol City	A	League Division 2	1–2
1934	Manchester City	A	League Division 1	2–4
1945	Brighton & Hove Albion	H	Football League South	0–2
1947	Heart of Midlothian	A	Friendly	4–1

This was the first meeting of the sides commencing a series of annual challenge matches that later were played for The Stamford Bridge Trophy (from 1951) as provided by the then Chairman of Chelsea, Joe Mears.

1951	Liverpool	H	League Division 1	1–0

Goalkeeper Bill Robertson made his debut, kept a clean sheet and inspired Chelsea to a first win in fifteen games. Three more consecutive victories helped the Blues escape relegation (on goal average) from the First Division.

1952	Manchester United	A	League Division 1	0–3
1956	Newcastle United	A	League Division 1	1–1
1962	Ipswich Town	H	League Division 1	2–2
1964	Celtic	A	Friendly (abandoned)	1–1
1969	Charlton Athletic	H	Friendly	5–1
1973	Southampton	H	League Division 1	2–1
1979	Middlesbrough	H	League Division 1	2–1

First appearance of Gary Chivers.

1980	Chelsea Past XI	H	Testimonial	0–1
1984	Shrewsbury Town	H	League Division 2	3–0
1990	Liverpool	A	League Division 1	1–4

APRIL 22

1911	Burnley	H	League Division 2	3–0
1912	Blackpool	H	League Division 2	4–1
1916	Croydon Common	H	London Combination League (Part Two)	3–1
1922	Sunderland	A	League Division 1	2–1
1933	Arsenal	H	League Division 1	1–3
1935	Wolverhampton Wanderers	A	League Division 1	1–6
1936	Portsmouth	H	League Division 1	1–0
1939	Portsmouth	H	League Division 1	1–0
1944	Watford	H	Football League South	2–1
1946	Plymouth Argyle	A	Football League South	4–1

1950	Blackpool	A	League Division 1	0–0
1957	Newcastle United	H	League Division 1	6–2
1958	Canto Do Rio Brazil	H	Friendly	3–2
1959	West Bromwich Albion	H	League Division 1	0–2
1961	West Bromwich Albion	A	League Division 1	0–3
1967	Stoke City	H	League Division 1	1–0
1968	Burnley	H	League Division 1	2–1
1972	Newcastle United	H	League Division 1	3–3
1978	Wolverhampton Wanderers	H	League Division 1	1–1
1989	Leeds United	H	League Division 2	1–0
1997	Wimbledon	A	Premier League	1–0

APRIL 23

1910	Bury	H	League Division 1	2–0
1921	Middlesbrough	A	League Division 1	0–0
1927	Barnsley	A	League Division 2	0–3
1932	West Bromwich Albion	H	League Division 1	0–2
1934	Leicester City	H	League Division 1	2–0
1938	Derby County	H	League Division 1	3–0
1949	Arsenal	A	League Division 1	2–1
1952	Heart of Midlothian	H	Friendly	3–2
1955	Sheffield Wednesday	H	League Division 1	3–0
1960	Bolton Wanderers	A	League Division 1	0–2
1962	Wolverhampton Wanderers	A	League Division 1	1–1
1966	Sheffield Wednesday	Villa Park	FA Cup semi-final	0–2

A crowd of 61,321 saw the Blues crash out of the competition but the experience gathered enabled Chelsea to go a step further the following year.

1973	Coventry City	H	League Division 1	2–0
1975	Sheffield United	H	League Division 1	1–1
1977	Burnley	A	League Division 2	0–1
1983	Burnley	A	League Division 2	0–3
1985	March Town	A	Friendly	11–0
1988	Wimbledon	H	League Division 1	1–1
1993	Le Havre	A	Cross Channel Tournament	1–1
1994	Leeds United	H	Premier League	1–1

APRIL 24

| 1915 | Sheffield United | Old Trafford | FA Cup final | 0–3 |

With the Crystal Palace ground having already been requisitioned owing to the First World War, Old Trafford was chosen to stage the FA Cup between Sheffield

United and Chelsea. In what later became known as the 'Khaki Cup final' owing to the abundance of soldiers in the crowd of 49,557, the Blues were unable to lift the first major trophy in their history.

1916	Arsenal	A	London Combination League (Part Two)	3–1
1920	Derby County	A	League Division 1	0–5
1926	Middlesbrough	H	League Division 2	0–1
1937	Arsenal	H	League Division 1	2–0
1940	Millwall	H	Football League South C	2–1
1948	Burnley	H	League Division 1	0–2

1949 Christopher Stephen Garland was born in Bristol. Spent five years at local club Bristol City before signing for Chelsea in a £100,000 move in September 1971. He made 115 appearances and scored 31 goals in his time with the club but was tempted into a £95,000 transfer to Leicester City (February 1975) from where he went full circle back to Bristol City.

1964	Heart of Midlothian	A	Friendly	0–2
1965	Burnley	A	League Division 1	2–6
1969	Arsenal	H	League Division 1	2–1
1971	Coventry City	H	League Division 1	2–1
1972	Stoke City	H	League Division 1	2–0
1976	York City	A	League Division 2	2–2
1982	Derby County	H	League Division 2	0–2
1984	Portsmouth	A	League Division 2	2–2
1996	Leicester City	A	Friendly	3–0

APRIL 25

1908	Aston Villa	H	League Division 1	1–3
1912	Barnsley	A	League Division 2	2–0
1914	Everton	H	League Division 1	2–0

League debut of goalkeeper Colin Michael Kenneth Hampton who spent the majority of his time (11 years) at the Bridge playing in the reserves. He was signed from Motherwell in April 1914 having earlier gained experience at Brechin City to whom he returned when released by Chelsea. He made 82 appearances in total for the Blues.

1923	West Bromwich Albion	H	League Division 1	2–2
1925	Barnsley	H	League Division 2	0–1
1931	Portsmouth	H	League Division 1	2–0
1936	Wolverhampton Wanderers	A	League Division 1	3–3
1942	Fulham	A	Friendly	1–4
1951	Wolverhampton Wanderers	H	League Division 1	2–1
1953	Liverpool	A	League Division 1	0–2
1959	Birmingham City	A	League Division 1	1–4
1966	West Bromwich Albion	H	League Division 1	2–3
1969	Charlton Athletic	A	Friendly	0–1

1977	Oxford United	A	Houseman Fund	3–1
1981	Swansea City	A	League Division 2	0–3
1986	Gareth Hall signed professional terms.			
1987	Newcastle United	A	League Division 1	0–1
1992	Arsenal	H	League Division 1	1–1
1998	Liverpool	H	Premier League	4–1

APRIL 26

1911	Bolton Wanderers	A	League Division 2	0–2
1913	Notts County	H	League Division 1	5–2
1915	Everton	A	League Division 1	2–2
1917	Luton Town	H	London Combination League	4–0
1919	Fulham	Highbury	London Victory Cup final	3–0
1920	West Bromwich Albion	H	League Division 1	2–0
1924	Sunderland	H	League Division 1	4–1
1926	Derby County	H	League Division 2	2–1
1930	Preston North End	A	League Division 2	2–1
1939	Birmingham City	A	League Division 1	1–1
1941	Reading	A	Football League South	3–2
1947	Wolverhampton Wanderers	A	League Division 1	4–6
1948	Heart of Midlothian	A	Friendly	4–1
1950	Heart of Midlothian	H	Friendly	3–2
1952	Charlton Athletic	A	League Division 1	1–1
1958	Manchester United	H	League Division 1	2–1
1961	Sheffield Wednesday	H	League Division 1	0–2
1965	Blackpool	A	League Division 1	2–3
1971	Burnley	H	League Division 1	0–1
1975	Everton	H	League Division 1	1–1
1978	Leicester City	A	League Division 1	2–0
1980	Swansea City	A	League Division 2	1–1
1986	Aston Villa	A	League Division 1	1–3

APRIL 27

1907	Gainsborough Trinity	H	League Division 2	4–1
1912	Bradford Park Avenue	H	League Division 2	1–0
1918	West Ham United	A	National War Fund Competition	3–3
1925	Stoke City	H	League Division 2	2–1
1929	Reading	H	League Division 2	2–1
1935	Manchester City	H	League Division 1	4–2
1936	Arsenal	A	League Division 1	1–1
1938	Charlton Athletic	H	League Division 1	1–1
1940	West Ham United	H	Football League War Cup 1st round	0–2
1946	Portsmouth	H	Football League South	3–0

1955	Hayes	A	Friendly	8–0
1957	Preston North End	A	League Division 1	0–1
1963	Preston North End	H	League Division 2	2–0
1966	CF Barcelona	A	Fairs Cup semi-final	0–2

Chelsea suffered a defeat they would reverse at Stamford Bridge to force a play-off on a neutral ground.

1968	Sunderland	H	League Division 1	1–0
1972	West Bromwich Albion	A	League Division 1	0–4
1974	Stoke City	H	League Division 1	0–1
1985	Tottenham Hotspur	H	League Division 1	1–1
1994	Swindon Town	H	Premier League	2–0
1996	Tottenham Hotspur	A	Premier League	1–1

APRIL 28

1906	Bristol City	A	League Division 2	1–2

'Pom-Pom' Whiting was given his debut.

1907 Alexander George Cheyne was born in Glasgow. He was purchased from Aberdeen in June 1930 for £6,000 where he had won five Scottish international caps (he did not add to his tally at Chelsea), and after being sold to Nimes in France in 1932, returned for a second spell at the Bridge in March 1934. In his time with Chelsea he amassed 69 appearances and scored 13 goals. He left for his last club, Colchester United, in 1936.

1915	Notts County	A	League Division 1	0–2
1917	Watford	A	London Combination League	6–3
1918	West Ham United	H	London Combination League	3–1
1923	Blackburn Rovers	A	League Division 1	0–0
1927	Clapton Orient	A	League Division 2	0–3
1928	Wolverhampton Wanderers	A	League Division 2	2–1
1934	Arsenal	H	League Division 1	2–2
1945	Arsenal	A	Football League South	0–3
1951	Fulham	A	League Division 1	2–1
1956	Blackpool	H	League Division 1	2–1

Debuts given to John Mortimore and Richard Whittaker.

1958	Reading	A	Friendly	0–0
1962	Burnley	A	League Division 1	1–1
1971	Manchester City	A	Cup-Winners' Cup semi-final	1–0
1973	Manchester United	H	League Division 1	1–0

Bobby Charlton bowed out of the game he had graced for so long at Stamford Bridge, making the last of his 606 League appearances for United. Both teams had formed a guard of honour as he strode out onto the pitch for the last time and Chelsea made a presentation to him in recognition of his feat. There was to be no fairy-tale ending, however, as Chelsea won 1–0. Meanwhile, down at Southampton, brother Jack was playing his last League game for Leeds United as they lost 3–1.

1979	Aston Villa	A	League Division 1	1–2
1984	Leeds United	H	League Division 2	5–0
1990	Everton	H	League Division 1	2–1

APRIL 29

1908	Notts County	H	League Division 1	1–2
1909	Leicester Fosse	H	League Division 1	1–0
1911	Gainsborough Trinity	A	League Division 2	1–3
1916	Queens Park Rangers	H	London Combination League (Part Two)	3–0
1934	Sheffield Wednesday	H	League Division 1	1–2
1939	Preston North End	A	League Division 1	1–1
1940	West Ham United	A	Football League South C	2–4

1941 Barry Bridges was born in Horsford, Norfolk. Chelsea was his first club and he was an important member of the first team squad for eight years as he clocked up over 200 appearances and scored 93 goals. He won a Football League Cup winners' medal with the Blues in 1965 and also four England international caps, before being sold to Birmingham City for £55,000 in May 1966. Later played for QPR, Millwall, Brighton and Hove Albion and then Highland Park in South Africa.

1944	Reading	H	Football League South	3–1
1950	Newcastle United	H	League Division 1	1–3
1951	KB Copenhagen	A	Friendly	2–1
1953	Manchester City	H	League Division 1	3–1
1959	Ville De Belgrade	H	Fairs Cup 2nd round	1–0
1961	Nottingham Forest	H	League Division 1	4–3
1964	Southampton	A	Friendly	2–3
1965	Charlton Athletic	A	Friendly	3–2
1967	Leeds United	Villa Park		
			FA Cup semi-final	1–0
1968	Wolverhampton Wanderers	H	League Division 1	1–0
1970	Leeds United	Old Trafford		
			FA Cup final replay	2–1

For the first time in the history of Chelsea Football Club the FA Cup was brought back to Stamford Bridge, the third major prize to be won by the club. As with the original game extra time was required but this time a result was produced in favour of the Blues. Leeds had gone ahead in the first period with a neatly taken goal by Mick Jones having been set up by strike partner Alan 'Sniffer' Clarke. However, the longer the game went on the stronger Chelsea grew and it therefore came as no surprise when Peter Osgood brought the scores level after a superb ball played to him by the mercurial Charlie Cooke. The goal that won the final for Chelsea arrived in the 14th minute of the additional period. A throw-in by the left-hand corner flag was launched by Ian Hutchinson. David Webb was first to the ball with a header that gave Leeds goalkeeper Harvey no chance. Although Leeds mounted a last gasp rally the Blues' defence held firm and the Cup went to London!

1978	Everton	A	League Division 1	0–6
1986	Arsenal	A	League Division 1	0–2
1989	Shrewsbury Town	A	League Division 2	1–1
1995	Queens Park Rangers	H	Premier League	1–0
1998	Blackburn Rovers	H	Premier League	0–1

APRIL 30

1910	Tottenham Hotspur	A	League Division 1	1–2

In the final match of the season Chelsea faced Tottenham Hotspur at White Hart Lane. Before the kick-off Spurs held 30 points to Chelsea's 29, defeat for either club would send them down into the Second Division with Bolton Wanderers. A crowd of 35,000 saw Spurs scrape home to escape an immediate return to the division they had crawled out of the previous year and condemn Chelsea to relegation.

1921	Middlesbrough	H	League Division 1	1–1
1924	Manchester City	H	League Division 1	3–1
1927	Manchester City	H	League Division 2	0–0
1932	Birmingham City	A	League Division 1	0–4
1938	Wolverhampton Wanderers	A	League Division 1	1–1
1949	Sunderland	H	League Division 1	0–1

Billy Gray made his Chelsea debut.

1952	Tottenham Hotspur	H	League Division 1	0–2
1955	Manchester United	A	League Division 1	1–1
1956	Southend United	A	Friendly	3–4
1960	Wolverhampton Wanderers	H	League Division 1	1–5
1963	Leeds United	H	League Division 2	2–2
1966	Liverpool	A	League Division 1	1–2
1973	Liverpool	A	Testimonial	2–4
1977	Sheffield United	H	League Division 2	4–0
1983	Rotherham United	H	League Division 2	1–1
1988	Liverpool	A	League Division 1	1–2
1994	Manchester City	A	Premier League	2–2

MAY 1

1920	West Bromwich Albion	A	League Division 1	0–4
1926	Portsmouth	A	League Division 2	0–4
1937	Liverpool	A	League Division 1	1–1
1948	Portsmouth	A	League Division 1	1–2
1961	Hapoel, Israel	A	Friendly	1–0
1970	Cambridge United	A	Friendly	3–4
1971	Ipswich Town	A	League Division 1	0–0
1972	Leeds United	A	League Division 1	0–2

1974	Manchester United	H	Testimonial	1–2
1982	Sheffield Wednesday	A	League Division 2	0–0
1989	Stoke City	H	League Division 2	2–1

Dutchman Ken Monkou made his debut.

| 1993 | Coventry City | H | Premier League | 2–1 |

MAY 2

1883 George Henry Dale was born in Nottingham. Before the First World War he played for Notts County, joining Chelsea after the end of hostilities. Made 52 appearances with just a single goal.

1921	Blackburn Rovers	A	League Division 1	0–0
1931	Newcastle United	H	League Division 1	1–1
1936	Blackburn Rovers	H	League Division 1	5–1
1942	Reading	A	London War League	2–3
1955	Shamrock Rovers	A	Friendly	2–3
1957	Leicester City	H	Friendly	2–1
1966	Sheffield Wednesday	A	League Division 1	1–1

1967 David Carlyle Rocastle was born in Lewisham. A star at Arsenal, he failed to reproduce his form with Leeds United or Manchester City from whom he was purchased in August 1994 for £1.25 million. He made just 40 appearances over the period of his four-year contract and was released on a free transfer when it came to an end.

1978	Queens Park Rangers	H	League Division 1	3–1
1981	Notts County	H	League Division 2	0–2
1983	Sheffield Wednesday	H	League Division 2	1–1
1987	Leicester City	H	League Division 1	3–1
1988	West Ham United	H	League Division 1	1–1
1992	Everton	A	League Division 1	1–2
1998	Newcastle United	A	Premier League	1–3

MAY 3

1930	Bury	A	League Division 2	0–1
1933	Manchester City	A	League Division 1	4–1
1941	Queens Park Rangers	H	London Cup 'A' Competition	2–3
1947	Sheffield United	H	League Division 1	1–4
1952	Derby County	A	League Division 1	1–1
1956	Walthamstow Avenue	A	Friendly	3–1

1959 Edward Niedzwiecki was born in Bangor. The Welsh international goalkeeper commenced his career at Wrexham and was transferred to Chelsea at a cost of £45,000 in May 1983. He had made 175 appearances for the club when forced to retire with a serious knee injury in May 1988. He was appointed to the Chelsea coaching staff and later moved in a similar capacity to Reading.

| 1980 | Oldham Athletic | H | League Division 2 | 3–0 |
| 1986 | Liverpool | H | League Division 1 | 0–1 |

| 1995 | Everton | A | Premier League | 3–3 |
| 1997 | Leeds United | H | Premier League | 0–0 |

MAY 4

1918	West Ham United	H	National War Fund Competition	4–1
1927	Portsmouth	H	League Division 2	0–0
1935	Middlesbrough	A	League Division 1	2–2
1940	Portsmouth	A	Football League South C	1–3
1946	Derby County	A	Football League South	1–1
1949	Bolton Wanderers	A	League Division 1	1–1
1953	Fulham	A	Coronation Match	1–1
1961	Israel XI	A	Friendly	2–0
1966	Blackburn Rovers	H	League Division 1	1–0
1968	Wolverhampton Wanderers	A	League Division 1	0–3
1984	Manchester City	A	League Division 2	2–0
1985	Liverpool	A	League Division 1	3–4
1991	Liverpool	H	League Division 1	4–2
1994	Coventry City	H	Premier League	1–2

MAY 5

1923	Blackburn Rovers	H	League Division 1	1–1
1928	Barnsley	H	League Division 2	1–2
1934	Leeds United	A	League Division 1	1–3
1945	Watford	H	Football League South	3–4
1951	Bolton Wanderers	H	League Division 1	4–0
1971	Standard Liege	H	Testimonial	1–2
1972	Brighton & Hove Albion	A	Testimonial	3–2
1978	Manchester City	H	League Division 1	0–0
1979	Ipswich Town	H	League Division 1	2–3
1980	Crystal Palace	A	Testimonial	1–3
1982	Orient	H	League Division 2	2–2
1986	Watford	H	League Division 1	1–5

Gordon Durie made his debut for Chelsea.

| 1987 | Wimbledon | A | League Division 1 | 1–2 |

First game for Gareth Hall.

| 1990 | Millwall | A | League Division 1 | 3–1 |
| 1996 | Blackburn Rovers | H | Premier League | 2–3 |

MAY 6

1922	Huddersfield Town	A	League Division 1	0–2
1933	Sunderland	H	League Division 1	1–1
1939	Bolton Wanderers	H	League Division 1	1–1

1944	Millwall	A	Football League South	2–4
1950	Sunderland	A	League Division 1	1–4
1961	Israel-Maccabi	A	Friendly	5–2
1967	Leeds United	H	League Division 1	2–2
1968	Queens Park Rangers	H	Testimonial	6–3
1980	Telford United	A	Friendly	2–1
1985	Sheffield Wednesday	H	League Division 1	2–1
1989	Bradford City	H	League Division 2	3–1
1995	Leicester City	A	Premier League	1–1
1998	Nottingham Forest	H	Friendly	3–3

MAY 7

1921	Blackburn Rovers	H	League Division 1	1–2
1927	Darlington	A	League Division 2	2–2
1932	West Ham United	H	League Division 1	3–2
1938	Grimsby Town	A	League Division 1	0–2
1949	Wolverhampton Wanderers	A	League Division 1	1–1

1951 Michael Droy was born in Highbury. Signed from Slough in October 1970 and became the rock at the centre of the Chelsea defence for the best part of a 15-year stay at the Bridge. A giant of a man who often displayed playing skills that many thought were beyond his capabilities. He made in excess of 300 appearances with 19 goals before accepting a free transfer to Crystal Palace in March 1985, joining Brentford a year later to see out what remained of his professional career.

1955	Lens, France	A	Friendly	1–1
1966	Sheffield United	H	League Division 1	2–0
1976	Crystal Palace	H	Testimonial	2–2
1977	Wolverhampton Wanderers	A	League Division 2	1–1
1979	Fulham	A	Friendly	0–0
1983	Bolton Wanderers	A	League Division 2	1–0
1984	Barnsley	H	League Division 2	3–1

Keith Dublin's debut.

1988	Charlton Athletic	A	League Division 1	2–2
1994	Sheffield United	H	Premier League	3–2
1996	Hitchin	A	Friendly	5–2

MAY 8

1951	Floriana Malta	H	Friendly	5–1

This match was played as part of the Festival of Britain celebrations.

1953	Bohemians Dublin	A	Friendly	1–1

1964 James Peter O'Dowd died.

1965	New South Wales	A	Tour	5–0
1982	Luton Town	H	League Division 2	1–2

| 1985 | Luton Town | H | League Division 1 | 2–0 |
| 1993 | Sheffield United | A | Premier League | 2–4 |

MAY 9

1942	Brentford	A	Friendly	0–2
1954	Fortuna Dusseldorf	New York		
			Friendly	3–2
1967	Leicester City	A	League Division 1	2–3
1978	Brentford	A	Friendly	8–2

Death of Leonard Hector Allum in Reading.

| 1987 | Liverpool | H | League Division 1 | 3–3 |

MAY 10

1941	Cardiff City	A	Football League South	2–1
1947	Middlesbrough	H	League Division 1	2–0
1977	Leicester City	A	Testimonial	0–3
1998	Bolton Wanderers	H	Premier League	2–0

MAY 11

1940	Brentford	H	Football League South C	0–2
1955	Dutch National XI	A	Friendly	2–2
1963	Stoke City	H	League Division 2	0–1
1966	CF Barcelona	H	Fairs Cup semi-final	2–0

Charlie Cooke played his first game for Chelsea.

1968	Sheffield United	A	League Division 1	2–1
1985	Stoke City	A	League Division 1	1–0
1991	Aston Villa	A	League Division 1	2–2
1997	Everton	A	Premier League	2–1

MAY 12

1905 Alexander Skinner Jackson was born in Renton. Although he was still only 25 years old when he joined Chelsea, Jackson already had a string of clubs, a wealth of experience and a fine reputation behind him. His first professional club was Dumbarton, followed by spells with Aberdeen, Bethlehem Star (USA), Aberdeen and Huddersfield Town. He signed for Chelsea in September 1930 and notched up 77 games and 30 goals before being transferred to non-League side Ashton Nationals in August 1932. Followed this move with a brief stint at Margate before playing for French sides Le Touquet, Nice and Olympique.

1951	Heart of Midlothian	A	Friendly	2–0
1965	Combined XI, Australia	A	Tour	7–0
1984	Grimsby Town	A	League Division 2	1–0
1993	Chesham	A	Friendly	1–4

MAY 13

1959	Ville De Belgrade	A	Fairs Cup 2nd round	1–4
1968	Queens Park Rangers	A	Testimonial	2–1
1978	Jerv, Norway	A	Tour	2–0
1989	Portsmouth	A	League Division 2	3–2

Graham Le Saux made his debut.

| 1998 | VFB Stuttgart | Stockholm | | |
| | | | Cup-Winners' Cup final | 1–0 |

Diminutive striker Gianfranco Zola weaved his magic for Chelsea scoring 23 seconds after coming on as substitute to hand the Blues a 1–0 victory over Vfb Stuttgart in the European Cup-Winners' Cup final. Zola, who had been kept on the bench for fear of aggravating a groin injury, replaced Tore Andre Flo in the 71st minute. He was immediately found by a glorious pass from captain Dennis Wise and the Italian moved on and struck an unstoppable half-volley into the back of the net. Chelsea had to survive the closing minutes with ten men after the sending off of Dan Petrescu but in truth always looked worthy of their 'favourites' tag. The Chelsea team on the night was: De Goey, Petrescu, Leboeuf, Clarke, Poyet (sub Newton 81), Duberry, Wise, Granville, Di Matteo, Vialli and Flo (sub Zola 71).

MAY 14

1889 Robert Lawrence Abrams was born in Banks. A wing half who spent his early career with Southport Central, Colne, Stockport County and Heart of Midlothian before joining Chelsea in June 1914, his misfortune was to arrive just prior to the outbreak of the First World War. He nevertheless managed a total of 49 senior games in which he scored 7 goals before moving on to Cardiff City in 1920. He subsequently played for Southport before retiring in 1923.

1955	Rouen, France	A	Friendly	4–2
1977	Hull City	H	League Division 2	4–0
1979	Arsenal	H	League Division 1	1–1
1983	Middlesbrough	H	League Division 2	0–0
1984	Brentford	A	Friendly	6–3
1985	Norwich City	H	League Division 1	1–2
1994	Manchester United	Wembley	FA Cup final	0–4

After early double successes by Preston and Aston Villa, the football world had to wait over sixty years for the feat to be done again, with Spurs finally achieving what had been beyond the Arsenal side of the 1930s and both Manchester United and Wolves in the 1950s. Ten years later Arsenal won the double, followed a further fifteen years later by Liverpool. Having safely secured the title in 1994, Manchester United's attention could now turn to the other half of the domestic dream, the FA Cup. Lady Luck seemed to be on their side as they survived a scare in the semi-final before finally overcoming Oldham after a replay. Even so they were facing a resurgent Chelsea team who had proven to be something of a bogey side for United in recent years. Indeed, United's first two defeats during the season had both been inflicted by Chelsea! On Wembley's lush and spacious turf, both teams began hesitantly, not wishing to give too much away to their opponents. If anything Chelsea, whose search for a major trophy had stretched over twenty years, had the better of the opening half, fashioning a number of lively attacks. Slowly but surely, however, Manchester United got the better of Chelsea and finally took the lead on the hour thanks to a penalty scored by Eric Cantona. He added another penalty seven minutes later, and the fight seemed to visibly drain from Chelsea. The final score of 4-0 (Hughes and McClair added later goals) may well have flattered United who completed the double, but for the Blues the positive aspect taken away from this game was that the team had gained invaluable experience from the occasion. It would serve them well the next time they went to Wembley for a Cup final!

| 1995 | Arsenal | H | Premier League | 2–1 |

MAY 15

| 1951 | KB Copenhagen | H | Friendly | 1–0 |

This match was played as a part of the Festival of Britain celebrations.

| 1957 | Feyenoord | A | Friendly | 4–1 |

1960 Gary Chivers was born in Stockwell. Joined as a schoolboy and rose through the ranks making his debut nine months after signing professional terms. Played 148 games and scored 4 goals before departing for Swansea City, later with Queens Park Rangers, Watford and Brighton and Hove Albion.

1965	Northern New South Wales	A	Tour	6–2
1982	Blackburn Rovers	A	League Division 2	1–1
1988	Blackburn Rovers	A	Play-off semi-final	2–0
1998	Auxerre	Martinique Friendly		0–3

MAY 16

1942	West Ham United	A	Friendly	2–5
1954	Glasgow Rangers	Montreal Friendly		0–1
1957	Fortuna Geleen,Holland	A	Friendly	2–2
1965	Victoria, Australia	A	Tour	1–0
1966	Aston Villa	H	League Division 1	0–2
1978	Voss, Norway	A	Tour	6–1
1979	Manchester United	A	League Division 1	1–1
1984	Oxford United	A	Friendly	1–2
1985	Glasgow Rangers	H	Friendly	3–2

MAY 17

1924 Roy Thomas Frank Bentley was born in Bristol. One of the greatest names in Chelsea's history, Bentley started with local club Bristol Rovers in 1937 but spent only a year on their books before joining rivals Bristol City and then, after the Second World War, Newcastle United. In 1948 Chelsea paid £11,000 for his services and as leading goalscorer for eight consecutive seasons he must be rated as one of the club's best ever buys.

Roy Bentley captained the 1955 Football League Championship winning team and made 366 League and Cup appearances in which he scored 149 goals. He also netted in the 1955 FA Charity Shield.

He departed Stamford Bridge for Fulham in August 1956 with the Blues receiving £8,500 as his transfer fee. He later played for Queens Park Rangers and managed Reading and Swansea Town.

1941	Northampton Town	A	Football League South	1–4
1977	Stromsgodset, Norway	A	Friendly	2–1
1978	Hauger, Norway	A	Tour	4–1
1982	Wigan Athletic	A	Friendly	0–0
1990	Frank Sinclair signed professional forms.			
1997	Middlesbrough	Wembley	FA Cup final	2–0

After the disappointment of 1994, this was the game that Chelsea (as firm favourites) had to win to step out of the shadows of the past. The expensively assembled side needed to establish their own reputations to leave behind the constant references to the last great cup-winning side of the early 1970s. This time the whole team came good with the best of all possible starts given them by a Roberto Di Matteo goal in a record-breaking 43 seconds. This was followed by a second goal added by Eddie Newton to erase the painful memories of the 1994 final when a penalty was awarded against him. Roberto Di Matteo was voted 'Man of the Match' and Ruud Gullit became the first ever foreign manager to win the FA Cup final.

1998	Martinique XI	A	Friendly	3–1

MAY 18

1963	Sunderland	A	League Division 2	1–0
1972	Barbados XI	A	Tour	5–0
1973	Persepolis, Iran	A	Tour	1–1
1988	Blackburn Rovers	H	Play-off semi-final	4–1

MAY 19

1945	West Ham United	A	Football League South	1–2
1951	Algiers Combination	A	Friendly	2–1
1954	Ian Britton was born in Dundee.			

Ian Britton was born in Dundee. A regular member of the first-team squad for more than ten years, he joined Chelsea from junior club Hillside Rangers, and went on to play nearly 300 games for the club scoring 34 times. Left for Dundee United in August 1982 and later played for Blackpool and Burnley.

1965	Western Australia	A	Tour	6–1
1971	Real Madrid, Spain	Athens	Cup-Winners' Cup final	1–1

Disappointment for Chelsea as Peter Osgood's goal in the second half of the game was wiped out with the last kick of normal time. Extra time failed to separate the sides and a replay was required at the same venue two days later.

1977	Orn Horten, Norway	A	Friendly	3–1

MAY 20

1902 Harold Sydney Miller was born in St Albans. He won an international cap for England prior to joining from Charlton Athletic in June 1923 to embark on a stay of almost 17 years. In that time he made over 350 appearances for the club and scored 44 goals before leaving on a free transfer to Northampton Town (May 1939).

1951	FC Vienna	A	Friendly	4–0
1967	Tottenham Hotspur	Wembley	FA Cup final	1–2

The first all-London FA Cup final clash pitted the experienced Spurs, winners of the FA Cup on a previous four occasions, with a young Chelsea side that had yet to win the FA Cup and were making their first appearance at Wembley. The two managers could not have been more different either; Bill Nicholson, the taciturn coach who was not renowned for his verbal skills, and Tommy Docherty, seldom lost for words but yet to prove himself as a tactician. The talking before the game turned out to be rather more interesting than the match itself, for Chelsea's inexperience showed and they allowed Spurs to take the game to them almost throughout. This proved their undoing, for after Jimmy Robertson (hitting the rebound after an Alan Mullery shot had been blocked) and Frank Saul (turning well to meet a cross and firing home) had fired Spurs 2-0 ahead there was little likelihood that Chelsea were going to force their way back. Bobby Tambling's goal, four minutes from the end, was no more than a consolation effort.

1972	New South Wales	Barbados	Tour	4–1
1997	South China	A	Friendly	2–3

MAY 21

1954	Baltimore Rockets	Westport	Friendly	7–1
1963	Portsmouth	H	League Division 2	7–0
1964	Barbados	A	Tour	7–0
1971	Real Madrid, Spain	Athens	Cup-Winners' Cup final replay	2–1

One of the greatest nights in the history of Chelsea Football Club when the Blues won a European trophy for the first time. An injury to John Hollins facilitated a change of tactics from the first game with replacement Tommy Baldwin playing a more attacking role. Chelsea took the lead from a John Dempsey volley from about 15 to 20 yards out and when a second goal was added minutes later by Peter Osgood, the tie looked to be settled in the Blues' favour. However a late goal from the Spanish side gave them the impetus to be more positive in search of an equaliser and Chelsea fans had to endure some heart-stopping moments before the final whistle. The Blues gallantly held on to secure a famous victory.

1973	Taj, Iran	A	Tour	1–0

MAY 22

1945	Southampton	A	Friendly	6–4
1965	Southern Australia	A	Tour	2–1
1974	Northern Territories	A	Tour	6–1
1994	Hong Kong XI	A	Friendly	1–2

MAY 23

1884 James McLachlan Turnbull was born in East Plain in Bannockburn. Signed by Manchester United from Leyton FC in May 1907 he helped the club win the League Championship at the end of his first season at Old Trafford. The following season he added an FA Cup winners' medal but he and United were unable to agree terms in the close season of 1910 and United signed Enoch West as replacement, allowing Jimmy to sign for Bradford in September 1910. After a spell at Chelsea in which he played 22 games and scored 8 goals Jimmy returned to United in September 1914 for a one-month trial and did well enough for them to consider signing him full time. However, Chelsea's insistence on a £300 fee at a time when football was likely to be halted owing to the First World War was considered 'too much in the present crisis.'

1954	Borrussia Dortmund	New York		
			Friendly	1–6
1965	Australian Select XI	A	Tour	2–2
1972	Barbados XI	A	Tour	10–0

MAY 24

1927 William Patrick Gray was born in Dinnington, County Durham. Joined Chelsea in March 1949 from Leyton Orient and played 172 games (13 goals) on the wing where he was a regular for four seasons before being transferred to Burnley for £16,000 in August 1953. Later played for Nottingham Forest and Millwall where he embarked on a management career.

| 1941 | West Ham United | A | Football League South | 3–3 |

1956 Douglas Rougvie was born in Ballingry, Fife. Granite-hard Scot who had played for 12 seasons in the Granite City, Aberdeen, before signing for Chelsea in July 1984 for £150,000. He made exactly 100 appearances for the Blues, won a Full Members Cup medal in 1986 and then transferred to Brighton and Hove Albion in June 1987. Later played for Shrewsbury Town and Fulham.

| 1971 | Slough Town | A | Friendly | 2–2 |
| 1997 | Brunei | A | Friendly | 6–0 |

MAY 25

| 1940 | Tottenham Hotspur | A | Football League South C | 2–3 |
| 1966 | CF Barcelona | A | Fairs Cup semi-final play-off | 0–5 |

The defeat inflicted by Barcelona ranks as Chelsea's heaviest ever reverse in European competition.

1967	Dundee	A	Friendly	2–4
1973	Tehran Combined, Iran	A	Tour	0–1
1977	Seattle Sounders, USA	A	Friendly	0–2
1988	Middlesbrough	A	Play-off final	0–2

MAY 26

1915 Thomas Walker, OBE, was born in Livingston Station. He joined Chelsea in September 1946 in a £6,000 deal from Heart of Midlothian at the age of 31 at a time when his career was naturally winding down. A Scottish international who won a total 20 caps, he began with Hearts in 1932 and returned there as a player and assistant-manager after leaving Stamford Bridge in December 1948 and was later appointed as manager, serving them in this capacity from 1951 until 1966. His Chelsea career comprised 104 games with 24 goals.

1945	Millwall	A	Football League South	2–1
1947	Portsmouth	H	League Division 1	0–3
1951	Oran Combination	A	Friendly	0–0
1954	Eastern Seaboard Allstars		Fall River	
			Friendly	6–0
1965	Tasmania	A	Tour	12–0
1974	Western Australia	A	Tour	1–0
1994	Paul Furlong was purchased for £2,300,000 from Watford.			

MAY 27

1951	Valladolid Spain	A	Friendly	2–1
1967	British Columbia All Stars	A	Tour	5–2
1977	Vancouver Island, Canada	A	Friendly	3–0
1997	Thailand	A	Friendly	1–0

MAY 28

1967	North West Allstars	A	Tour	5–0
1988	Middlesbrough	H	Play-off final	1–0

MAY 29

1964   Stephen Francis was born in Billericay. Signed professional terms in May 1982 after having made his Senior debut in October 1981. Played 88 games in goal before joining Reading in February 1987 for £15,000 where he appeared on over 250 occasions before moving to Huddersfield Town for £150,000 in August 1993.

1970   Roberto Di Matteo was born in Switzerland of Italian parents. Began his career with Swiss sides Schaffhausen, FC Zurich and FC Aarrac (where he was voted Swiss Player of the Year for his part in the club's first post-war championship) before moving on to Lazio in Rome. Whilst playing in Serie A, he became an automatic choice for the Italian national team and has played regularly since his move to London, although was edged out of the starting line-up in the World Cup in France 1998. He became one of Ruud Gullit's most inspired signings for the club in July 1996 when he joined Chelsea in a £4.9 million from Lazio and has played a major part in the club's advance and recent successes. He scored a memorable record-breaking 43-second goal in the 1997 FA Cup final against Middlesbrough and a critical second goal in the Coca-Cola League Cup semi-final second leg against Arsenal at Stamford Bridge in 1998. He is thus the owner of three Cup-winners' medals.

1974	South Australia	A	Tour	4–0

MAY 30

1954	American Allstars	Harrison	Friendly	2–0
1965	Australian World Cup XI	A	Tour	1–1
1967	O'Keefe's Club	A	Tour	3–2
1971	Southampton	San Salvador	Tour	8–3

1977 Mark Nicholls was born in Hillingdon.

MAY 31

1998 The incoming transfer of Pierluigi Casiraghi, an Italian international from Lazio in Rome was confirmed at the same time that the club emphasised that neither Roberto Di Matteo or Gianfranco Zola would be heading back to their native country. Di Matteo, himself a £4.9 million acquisition from Lazio two years previously, was thought to interest his old club as well as a host of others in Italy's Serie A. It was, in any case, irrelevant as the midfielder was tied to a contract signed with Chelsea in December 1997 that reportedly runs until 2002. Zola had been linked with the Sardinian club Cagliari who wanted to take the player back to his native island to finish his career there. Manager Gianluca Vialli rebutted the approach and insisted that he wanted to retain Zola's services despite the arrival of new strikers Pierluigi Casiraghi and Brian Laudrup.

JUNE 1

1950 Dennis Rofe was born in Fulham. Enjoyed a brief two-year spell at the Bridge after signing from Leicester City in April 1972 in a deal worth £80,000. He had begun his career in London with Leyton Orient where he spent four years as a professional before moving to the Foxes. Made 63 appearances for Chelsea then transferred to Southampton.

1071	El Salvador	A	Tour	1–0
1977	San Jose Earthquake, USA	A	Friendly	2–1

JUNE 2

1945	Bolton Wanderers	H	Friendly	1–2

1960 Joseph McLaughlin was born in Greenock. Started with Morton and made Chelsea his second club in May 1983 when he was the subject of a £95,000 transfer. He made over 250 League and Cup appearances with 7 goals then moved to Charlton Athletic in August 1989 for £600,000. Later played for Watford.

1965	South Coast XI, Australia	A	Tour	1–0
1974	Queensland, Australia	A	Tour (abandoned)	1–0

JUNE 3

1879 Vivian J. Woodward born in Kennington, South London. One of the finest players of his or any other age, Vivian Woodward would have shone in any team. An amateur for his entire career, he began playing with local sides in Clacton and then signed with Chelmsford City. He signed with Spurs in March 1901 but did not become a regular in the side until 1902-03 as he had business commitments and also because he had no wish to let down Chelmsford. He was a regular feature of the Spurs side until 1909 and to him fell the honour of scoring first goal as a Football League side, in the match against Wolves at White Hart Lane in September 1908. His amateur status saw him make 67 appearances for the England amateur team and he was good enough to also represent the full side on 23 occasions, scoring 28 goals. He was also captain of the United Kingdom teams that won consecutive Olympic titles in 1908 and 1912. He was appointed a director of Spurs in 1908 but the following year announced his retirement from the top level of the game in order to return playing for Chelmsford. Less than three months later he signed with Chelsea and remained on the playing staff until midway through the First World War, in this time he made 116 appearances and scored 34 goals. This of course included Chelsea's first appearance in the FA Cup final, and Woodward was given leave by the Army to play in the match against Sheffield United. However, Woodward's principles were such that if he had played, Bob Thomson (who had scored most of the goals that got Chelsea to the final) would have missed out and so Woodward declined Chelsea's offer. He did however become a director of the club in 1922 and served them in this capacity until 1930. Having previously been an architect for most of his professional life he became a gentleman farmer and died in Ealing in January 1954.

1924   Kenneth Armstrong was born in Bradford. He joined Chelsea in December 1946 after a start with Bradford Rovers and a spell in the Army to become one of the club's most consistent performers who, until overtaken by Peter Bonetti, held the League appearance record with 362 games in which he scored 25 goals. Ken also clocked up 39 games in the FA Cup and scored 5 goals in that competition but rather surprisingly was asked only once to represent his country, playing for England against Scotland at Wembley in 1955. After Chelsea he emigrated to New Zealand where he became coach to the national team before passing away there in 1984.

1957   John Sparrow was born in Bethnal Green. He made his debut for the senior team at the tender age of 16 in March 1974 and did not sign professional forms until three months later. However, he did not fulfil his early potential, and after a loan spell with Millwall settled on a full transfer in January 1981 to Exeter City who paid £5,000 to secure his services. His Chelsea record ended; Played 74 Goals 2.

1977   Los Angeles Aztecs,   A   Friendly   3–1
         USA

JUNE 4

1967	Dundee		Hertford, Conn	
			Tour	2–2
1971	Trinidad	A	Tour	3–2

1993   Glenn Hoddle, fresh from taking Swindon Town into the Premier League, was appointed Chelsea player-manager. He later brought Peter Shreeve to the club to assist him in his duties and, perhaps more significantly, introduced Graham Rix to coach the youth team set-up.

JUNE 5

1954	Glasgow Rangers	Toronto	Friendly	4–1

JUNE 6

1954	Glasgow Rangers	New York Friendly	0–0
1965	Queensland, Australia	A	Tour	4–0
1971	Southampton	Trinidad	Tour	6–2

1991 Tony Dorigo left Chelsea to join Leeds United in a then record outgoing deal of £1,300,000.

JUNE 7

1964	Haiti	A	Tour (abandoned)	1–2
1967	Devonshire Club	A	Tour	8–0
1974	Illawarra District, Australia	A	Tour	4–1

JUNE 8

1933 Ronald Michael Collins was born in Redcar. A goalkeeper who signed for Chelsea in November 1951 from his local side Redcar Albion, he spent over five years at the Bridge and made only one senior appearance in a League match in March 1954. His misfortune was to be at the club at the same time as Harry Medhurst, Bill Robertson and Charlie Thomson all of whom were a good deal more experienced than Collins. Disillusioned, he moved on to Watford in July 1957 where he held the first team position for a couple of seasons before drifting into non-League football.

1937 Clifford Huxford was born in Stroud. A talented junior who joined from the youth ranks in February 1955 and broke into the first team in September 1958. However, after just seven games, it was realised that he would not make the grade at Chelsea and he was therefore used in part-exchange in the deal that brought Charlie Livesey to the Bridge from Southampton in May 1959. He played some 300 games for the Saints before ending up at Exeter City.

JUNE 9

1964 Darren Terrence Wood was born in Scarborough. Signed from Middlesborough in September 1984 for £50,000 and remained until January 1989 when he transferred to Sheffield Wednesday for £350,000. By the time of his departure he had made 178 appearances and contributed 3 goals. He picked up a Full Members' Cup winners' medal in 1986.

1967	PHC Bermuda	A	Tour	2–0
1974	New South Wales	A	Tour	1–2

JUNE 10

1945 Tommy Baldwin was born in Gateshead. He was signed from Arsenal in a deal that saw George Graham move in the opposite direction and made 239 appearances in total for the club scoring 92 goals in a career that saw him win an FA Cup winners' medal in 1970. He moved to Millwall in November 1974.

1967 Bermuda Olympic XI   A   Tour   4–2

1998 Norway, with Tore Andre Flo, drew 2–2 with Morocco on the opening day of the Group stages of the World Cup finals. This game was played in Montpellier.

JUNE 11

1946 Keith Weller was born in Islington. Chelsea was his third London club after previous spells at Tottenham Hotspur and Millwall from whom the Blues signed him for £100,000 in May 1970. An English international (4 caps), he had appeared 53 times in Chelsea's colours when Leicester City purchased him for £100,000 in September 1971. He won a European Cup-Winners' Cup medal for Chelsea in 1971. The latter part of his career was played in the North American Soccer League with two clubs, New England Tea Men and Fort Lauderdale Strikers.

1957 The legendary Hughie Gallacher took his own life when he stepped in front of an express train near his home in Gateshead.

1967 Eintracht Braunschweig Boston   Tour   1–3

1998 Roberto Di Matteo started for Italy in their Group B match against Chile which ended all square at 2–2 in the World Cup finals in France.

JUNE 12

1956 Colin Lee was born in Torquay. He began his career in modest surroundings with Bristol City moved to Hereford United, Torquay United and then Tottenham Hotspur before finally arriving in the big time when he joined the Blues in January 1980 for £200,000. In a career in which he was transformed from forward to full-back, he made over 200 appearances and scored 41 goals during his time at the Bridge. He won a Second Division Championship medal in 1984 and a Full Members Cup winners' medal in 1986.

1965 John Jackson died in Nova Scotia, Canada.

1998 Brian Laudrup played for Denmark in their 1–0 defeat of Saudi Arabia in Group C of the World Cup finals in France. On the same day Marcel Desailly was in the French team that beat South Africa 3–0 in the same group.

JUNE 13

1967 Rochester USA.   A   Tour   6–1

1989 Damian Matthew signed full professional forms.

1998 In France at Nantes, Chelsea's new signing Albert Ferrer started for Spain in their 3–2 defeat at the hands of Nigeria who included Celastine Babayaro in their ranks for the Group D clash in the World Cup finals.

JUNE 14

1918 David Thomas Winter was born in Tonypandy. He played for Bolton Wanderers before the Second World War and joined Chelsea, after making 57 guest appearances during the hostilities, in December 1945. He then proceeded to make over 150 regular appearances until the end of season 1950–51 when he transferred to non-League Worcester City.

JUNE 15

1924 Phillip McKnight was born in Camlachie. After a start with Alloa Athletic he was transferred to Chelsea in January 1947 and remained with the club until July 1954 when he joined Leyton Orient. Despite the length of time at the Bridge most of his duties were with the Reserves but he performed as a capable deputy when called upon which happened 33 times in League games. He was happier with the O's and made nearly 200 appearances for the East London club.

1989 Graham Stuart was upgraded to full professional.

1998 Graham Le Saux was in the starting line-up for England as they kicked off their World Cup finals campaign with a 2–0 win against Tunisia in Marseille. Meanwhile in Lyon in the same Group G, Dan Petrescu played for Romania as they beat Colombia by 1–0.

JUNE 16

1981 William Marshall Hughes died in Birmingham.

1998 Norway, with Tore Andre Flo, drew 1–1 with Scotland (whose goal was scored by former Chelsea player Craig Burley) in the opening Group matches of the World Cup finals.

JUNE 17

1998 Roberto Di Matteo was introduced as a 62nd minute substitute for Italy as the *Azzuri* beat Cameroon by 3–0 in Group B of the World Cup finals in France.

JUNE 18

1998 In Group C of the World Cup finals in France, Denmark with Brian Laudrup drew 1–1 with South Africa in Toulouse whilst France including Marcel Desailly beat Saudi Arabia 4–0 in Paris.

JUNE 19

1964 John McNaught was born in Glasgow. Chelsea invested £75,000 for the services of McNaught when buying his contract from Hamilton Academical in May 1986. Unfortunately what had seemed a highly promising talent in Scotland failed to nurture and develop in London and only 13 first class games were achieved before he was released on a free transfer to return north to Partick Thistle.

1998 Celestine Babayaro played for his native Nigeria against Bulgaria as they won 1–0 in Group D of the World Cup finals in Paris.

JUNE 20

1948   Colin Viljoen was born in Johannesburg, South Africa. Ipswich Town were the first club in England to recognise Viljoen's talents and he signed for them in August 1967 after playing for South Transvaal. Subsequently went to Manchester City before joining Chelsea for £45,000 in August 1978 at the age of 31. He had played for the Blues just 23 times when his contract was cancelled in May 1982. After adopting British nationality, Viljoen had won 2 England international caps prior to his arrival at Stamford Bridge.

1983   Nigel Spackman joined the club (for the first time) from Bournemouth for £40,000.

JUNE 21

1951   Alan Anthony Hudson was born in Chelsea. He joined as an apprentice and signed professional forms in June 1968 making his debut In February 1969 but was one of the band of players that, having established their reputations at the Bridge, left in their prime for greener pastures only to return as their careers were winding down. Hudson first left Chelsea for Stoke City in January 1974 for a fee of £240,000 and rejoined in August 1983, after periods with Arsenal and Seattle Sounders, at a cost of £23,500. His second spell lasted only a matter of months before he again departed for Stoke City. For all his undoubted talent, Hudson won only two caps for England and his only other honour was the European Cup-Winners' Cup medal he won with Chelsea in 1971. He appeared 188 times and scored 14 goals for the club.

JUNE 22

1894   Robert Hamilton Turnbull was born in Dumbarton. Had previous form with Royal Engineers, Arsenal and Charlton Athletic prior to joining the Blues in February 1925 to boost the goalscoring potential of the club as it tried to come to terms with life in the Second Division. Made 87 starts in Chelsea's colours, in which he netted an impressive tally of 58 goals, fulfilling the purpose for which he was acquired. After losing his place in the first team, he was transferred to Clapton Orient in March 1928 and later played for Southend United, Chatham and Crystal Palace.

1998   Graham Le Saux and Dan Petrescu were on opposing sides as England met Romania in their Group G clash in the World Cup finals staged at Toulouse. The club rivalry ended in disastrous circumstances when Petrescu out-fought Le Saux for a ball that he should have cleared and squeezed the ball under England's goalkeeper David Seaman to ensure a 2–1 victory for Romania.

JUNE 23

1995   Mark Hughes signed for Chelsea in a deal worth £1.5 million from Manchester United. Although Mark was over 31 years of age at the time of his transfer, there were many that felt he still had much to offer. Certainly his record at Chelsea seemed to prove the point as he helped them win the FA Cup, Coca-Cola Cup and European Cup-Winners' Cup whilst at Stamford Bridge. Left in July 1998 for Southampton.

CLOCKWISE FROM TOP LEFT:
cigarette cards of Thomas Law,
Ben Warren, Ben Howard Baker
and Jack Harrow

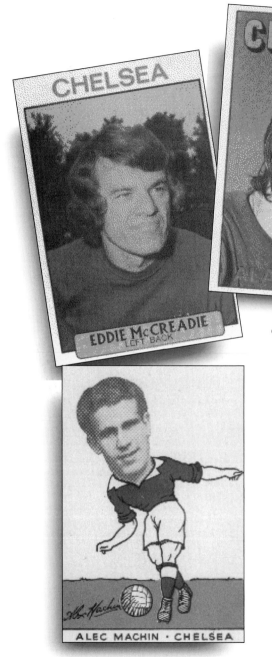

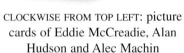

CLOCKWISE FROM TOP LEFT: picture cards of Eddie McCreadie, Alan Hudson and Alec Machin

ABOVE: picture card of Peter
Osgood
RIGHT: cigarette card of
Roy Bentley

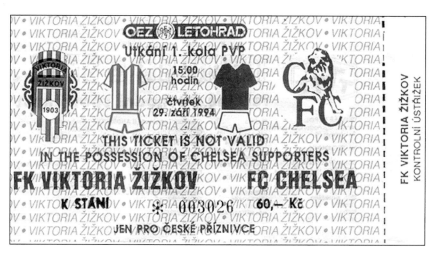

Ticket stub for Viktoria Zizkov against Chelsea in 1994

Ticket stub from the 1950
FA Cup semi-final between
London rivals Chelsea and
Arsenal

Ticket stub from the 1952 FA
Cup semi-final between
Chelsea and Arsenal

Ticket stub from the 1970
FA Cup final between
Chelsea and Leeds United

Ticket stub from the 1994 FA
Cup final between Manchester
United and Chelsea which was
won 4–0 by United

Programme for the 1967 FA Cup
final between Spurs and Chelsea

Programme for the 1970 FA Cup
final between Chelsea and Leeds
at Wembley, which ended all
square at 2–2

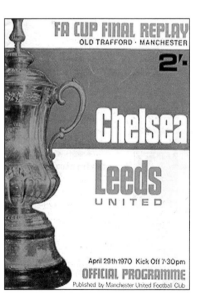

Programme from the 1970 FA Cup
final replay at Old Trafford

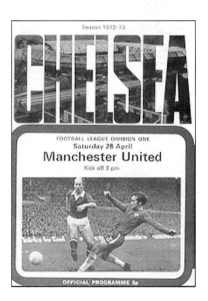

Programme for Chelsea against
Manchester United in 1973

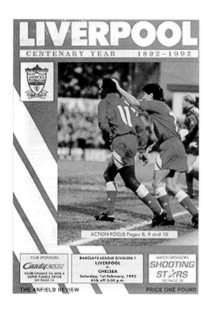

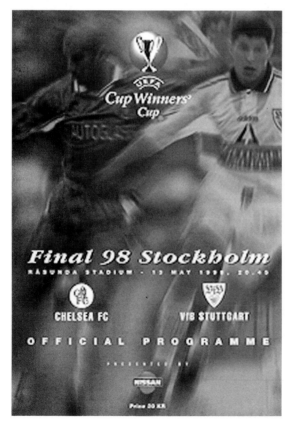

TOP LEFT: Programme for Liverpool against Chelsea on 1 February 1992

TOP RIGHT: Programme for the 1972 League Cup final between Stoke City and Chelsea, which Stoke won 2–1

LEFT: Programme for the 1997 European Cup-Winners' Cup final

TOP: Ticket stub from the 1994 European Cup-Winners' Cup match against FK Austria Memphis

MIDDLE: Ticket stub from the 1995 European Cup-Winners' Cup semi-final against Real Zaragoza

BOTTOM: Ticket stub from Tromso against Chelsea in the European Cup-Winners' Cup of 1997–98

TOP LEFT: Player-manager
Gianluca Vialli

TOP RIGHT: Ruud Gullit

LEFT: Gianfranco Zola

1998   Norway, including Tore Andre Flo, pulled off a last-gasp surprise defeat of defending champions Brazil by 2–1 in the Group stages of the World Cup finals in France. Flo contributed an 83rd-minute equaliser to Norway's cause.

JUNE 24

1884   William Cartwright was born in Burton upon Trent. Commenced his career at Gainsborough Trinity where he spent two years before linking up with Chelsea in May 1908 making his first team debut a few months later and progressing to a total 46 outings before accepting a transfer to Tottenham Hotspur. Later with Swansea Town.

1998   The clash between France and Denmark in Group C of the World Cup finals in Lyon placed new team-mates Marcel Desailly, Frank Leboeuf and Brian Laudrup on opposing sides. France emerged as 2–1 winners.

JUNE 25

1998   The free transfer of Brian Laudrup to Chelsea was rumoured to have hit a snag as Glasgow Rangers were reportedly looking for compensation to release the player. However, with Laudrup at the end of his contract and the European Ruling following the 'Bosman case', it was not sufficient to halt the move from going through.

JUNE 26

1927   James Leonard Lewis was born in Hackney. An amateur with Walthamstow Avenue and Leyton Orient he continued in the same manner with Chelsea from September 1952 to summer 1958 when he rejoined Walthamstow Avenue. In his six seasons at the Bridge he played 95 games and scored 40 goals in all as an amateur.

1957   Clive Walker was born in Oxford. Began his long and varied career at Chelsea when signing professional forms in April 1975 and progressing to over 200 first team appearances with 65 goals. He had a short spell with Fort Lauderdale Strikers in 1979 but finally left the Bridge in July 1984 for Sunderland in a £75,000 deal. Thereafter returned south to play for Queens Park Rangers, Fulham and Brighton and Hove Albion before establishing himself as one of the most consistent players at the top of the non-League pyramid.

1998   In the closing round of Group G matches at the World Cup finals in France, Dan Petrescu played for Romania in Paris as they ensured pole position in the group with a 1–1 draw against Tunisia. Meanwhile in Lens, Graham Le Saux was in the England side that partly redeemed itself from the previous performance by winning 2–0 against Colombia.

JUNE 27

1894   Harry Thomas Wilding was born in Wolverhampton. Signed for Chelsea in April 1914 just prior to the outbreak of the First World War and had to wait until hostilities had ceased before making his debut for the club. Nevertheless he managed to make 265 appearances in the time available to him and clock up 25 goals in the process.

When his career at the Bridge came to a halt in November 1928, he moved to a lower level playing first for Tottenham Hotspur and later for Bristol Rovers.

1998   Norway, with Tore Andre Flo as striker, lost 1–0 to Italy at the second round stage of the World Cup.

JUNE 28

1922   Robert Inglis Campbell was born in Glasgow. Signed for Chelsea in May 1947 from Falkirk and became a regular first team player for six consecutive seasons making over 200 appearances and scoring 40 goals before being granted a free transfer to Reading in August 1954. He won five Scottish caps.

1955   Graham Wilkins was born in Hillingdon. Elder brother of Ray 'Butch' Wilkins and son of former professional footballer, George who played for Brentford. He signed professional forms in July 1972 and was a Chelsea player for 10 years during which time he was one appearance short of 150 games. He was released on a free transfer to join Brentford and later served Southend United on loan.

1998   France, including Marcel Desailly, overcame Paraguay by a single (golden) goal in the second round of the World Cup finals. On the same night Denmark shocked the world by the ease with which they disposed of Nigeria by 4–1 at the same stage of the competition. Chelsea's Brian Laudrup scored the second goal for the Danes whilst Celastine Babayaro had to catch the plane home.

JUNE 29

1998   Dan Petrescu had a date at the barbers. Together with all the other members of the Romanian World Cup squad, Dan had his hair dyed a fetching colour of 'bottle blonde' keeping a pledge the team had made between each other after the defeat of England, that they would enter the knock-out stages in shocking fashion. The only problem was that the anticipated time for the hair to grow out and thereby remove the colour would be approximately four months!

JUNE 30

1917   John Harris was born in Glasgow. Joined Chelsea after the Second World War having made over 100 appearances as a guest player during the hostilities. His formative career had been spent with Swindon Town, Swansea Town, Tottenham Hotspur and Wolverhampton Wanderers. His Chelsea period lasted until 1956 when he joined Chester as player-manager during which time he clocked up over 350 games and scored 14 goals.

1998   Romania, with Dan Petrescu, fell by a single goal to Croatia in the second round of the World Cup finals in France. On the same night England, complete with Graham Le Saux in the side, were condemned, by the sending-off of David Beckham of Manchester United, to defeat at the hands of Argentina. They fell 4–3 on penalties after a gutsy ten-man performance had held on to a 2–2 draw through extra time.

JULY 1

1988   David Lee was promoted from trainee to full professional.

1995 Ruud Gullit was signed on a free transfer from Sampdoria by manager Glenn Hoddle. On the same day Mark Nicholls signed as a full professional for the club.

JULY 2

1987 Tony Dorigo, an Australian by birth but qualified to play for England, agreed terms to join Chelsea in a £475,000 switch from Aston Villa.

JULY 3

1959 Graham Roberts born in Southampton. A classic case of a late developer as a player, Graham had been on the books of Bournemouth and Portsmouth as an apprentice but broke an ankle just before Portsmouth were to offer professional terms. After he recovered he joined Dorchester Town and then Weymouth. His performances at Weymouth received rave reviews and he was recommended to Bill Nicholson, of Spurs, by someone he met on a railway station! He went to see Roberts in action for himself and, suitably impressed, persuaded Keith Burkinshaw to invest £35,000 for his signature despite opposition from West Bromwich Albion. Graham made his Tottenham Hotspur debut in October 1980 and earned a regular place in the defence from December onwards. By the end of the season the former fitter's mate turned defender had picked up a winners' medal in the FA Cup final (having previously only visited Wembley as a ballboy!). Although he was surprisingly omitted from the side that lost the League Cup final against Liverpool in 1982, he did collect a second FA Cup winners' medal. In 1983 he collected the first of six full caps for England and the following year was captain on the evening Spurs lifted the UEFA Cup scoring the late goal which forced extra time and setting the example in the penalty shoot-out. In 1986 manager David Pleat sold him to Rangers where he helped them win the Scottish Premier title and in 1988 the Skol Cup. He fell out with manager Graeme Souness and was transferred to Chelsea in August 1988 for £475,000. He was immediately made captain, his inspirational leadership took the Blues to the Second Division title in 1989. He assumed the role of coach on Ian Porterfield's departure but a public row with chairman Ken Bates followed and he was transfer-listed and subsequently sold to West Bromwich Albion in November 1990. He made 83 appearances for Chelsea and scored 22 goals. He then drifted back into the non-League game, taking over as player-manager of Enfield in August 1992.

1998 In the World Cup quarter-finals, France (including Marcel Desailly) drew 0–0 at the end of normal time with Italy and then won through to the semi-final with a 4–3 penalty shoot-out victory. At the same stage of the competition Denmark were eased out 3–2 by defending champions Brazil despite another goal by Chelsea's Brian Laudrup.

JULY 4

1998 Speculation mounted that Michael Duberry would be the victim of Chelsea's success at attracting world-class talent to the Bridge and that such might result in his departure. The arrival of France's Marcel Desailly, seemingly to partner Frank

Leboeuf at the heart of the defence, meant that Duberry was increasingly looking like the odd man out. However, any immediate departure was rejected as the player emphasised his desire to remain a Chelsea player.

JULY 5

1957   Christopher Hutchings was born in Winchester. Whilst in non-League football with Harrow Borough he earned his keep as a bricklayer. He joined Chelsea in July 1980 for £5,000 and having been converted from playing in midfield to full-back clocked up just under 100 appearances for the club with 3 goals scored. He was sold to Brighton and Hove Albion for £50,000 in November 1983 and later played for Huddersfield Town and Walsall.

1966   Gianfranco Zola was born in Sardinia. An Italian international who would have won more caps for his country had he not been in competition with Roberto Baggio, he joined Chelsea from Parma in a deal worth £4,500,000 in November 1996. He was immediately a revelation in the Premiership whether playing as an out and out striker or in the 'hole' behind a front two. He has been an invaluable weapon in Chelsea's assault on the major prizes and has been rewarded with winners' medals for the FA Cup in 1997 , the Coca-Cola Cup and European Cup-Winners' Cup in 1998.

1990   Andy Townsend joined from Norwich City for £1,200,000 whilst Dennis Wise became the club's record incoming transfer at the cost of £1,600,000 from Wimbledon.

JULY 6

1920   Alexander Harold Machin was born in Shepherd's Bush. He was spotted by Chelsea whilst in the Army and was signed when demobilised in 1944. However, he found life as a full time professional, and League football at the highest level, somewhat difficult to adjust to and consequently played only 61 games (scored 9 goals) before moving to Plymouth Argyle where he finished his career.

JULY 7

1951   John Thomas Phillips was born in Shrewsbury. A goalkeeper who began with local club Shrewsbury Town and moved to Aston Villa from where he joined Chelsea in August 1970 for £25,000. A Welsh international, he struggled to hold down a first team place at club level due to competition from Peter Bonetti, but did manage to amass almost 150 appearances. Departed for Brighton and Hove Albion in March 1980 with later spells at Charlton Athletic and Crystal Palace.

1954   Michael Reginald Thomas was born in Mochdre near Colwyn Bay. Mickey began his professional career with Wrexham in April 1972 and was already a Welsh international by the time of his transfer to Manchester United in November 1978 for £300,000. He appeared in the 1979 FA Cup final against Arsenal, although following the arrival of Ron Atkinson in 1981 he was sold to Everton in an exchange deal with John Gidman worth £450,000. He then played for Brighton and Stoke City before joining Chelsea in January 1994 for £75,000 where he played 54 games and scored 11 goals. He was transferred to West Bromwich Albion in September 1985 for £100,000, later played for Derby, Shrewsbury, Leeds, Wrexham and had two further spells with Stoke!

1974   George Barber died in Ilford, Essex.

JULY 8

1991   The signing of Paul Elliott from Celtic for £1,400,000 was completed. It was to be Elliott's last move after a career that had encompassed Charlton Athletic, Luton Town and Bari in Italy before his spell in Scotland. It all came to an abrupt halt at the Bridge. He received a horrendous injury whilst playing for Chelsea in a clash with the much-travelled Dean Saunders that meant he had to retire on medical advice. Elliott sought compensation from Saunders in a claim that was rejected after an acrimonious dispute in the High Court. He now concentrates on media work.

1998   In the semi-final of the World Cup in Paris, France (including Chelsea's new signing Marcel Desailly) overcame Croatia, who were competing as a nation for the first time in the World Cup, by two goals to one. Thus France booked a place at the same venue in the final four days later. A late decision by the referee, influenced by some outrageous theatrics from Croatia's and Everton's Slaven Bilic, resulted in a red card for Laurent Blanc and meant that France would line up in the final with Chelsea's new partnership of Leboeuf and Desailly at the heart of their defence. In preparation for this event, Leboeuf had been introduced on 75 minutes as substitute.

JULY 9

1964   Gianluca Vialli was born in Italy. Began a celebrated career with Cremonese followed by a lengthy period spent at Sampdoria where he partnered Roberto Mancini in attack as the previously unfashionable Italian side made an impact both on Serie A and Europe. He was transferred to Juventus where he was prominent in the side that captured the European Champions' League before making his move to London as a free agent to play for Chelsea. In his first season at the Bridge he was not always selected by manager Ruud Gullit who often chose a pairing of Mark Hughes and Gianfranco Zola up front, nevertheless he battled on to make a late appearance as substitute in Chelsea's FA Cup final win against Middlesbrough. Season 1997–98 held some unexpected surprises for him and not least the ascendency to the managerial chair, which he filled comfortably, guiding the club to two Cup final victories. With the close season signings of Brian Laudrup, Marcel Desailly, Alberto Ferrer and Pierluigi Casiraghi, the manager's stated ambition is to bring the Championship trophy to Stamford Bridge for the first time since 1955.

1998   Mark Hughes' departure to Southampton was sealed in a £650,000 move to the south coast club. Although he had decided to leave the Bridge in the belief that his future chances in the Chelsea first team would be limited, Southampton manager David Jones warned that he would have to fight for a place in the Saints' starting line-up

JULY 10

1998   Mark Stein was released on a free transfer under the Bosman ruling.

JULY 11

1928   Stanley Maurice Wicks was born in Reading. He joined Chelsea from his local club at the cost of £10,500 in January 1954 and managed 80 games before an injury to his knee forced an early retirement at the age of 28 in 1956. He picked up a League Championship medal for the part he played in the successful 1954–55 campaign.

JULY 12

1954   Gary Locke was born in Kingsbury. Graduated through the Chelsea youth ranks to the first team, signing in July 1971 and making his debut in September 1972. He was a regular in the defence for most of the eleven years spent at the Bridge and amassed over 300 appearances before being transferred to Crystal Palace.

1996   Frank Leboeuf signed for Chelsea in a move from Strasbourg that cost £2,500,000.

1997   Kingstonian   A   Friendly   3–0

1998   Chelsea players Frank Leboeuf and Marcel Desailly (who received two yellow cards and was thus dismissed from the match in the second half) helped earn host nation France their first World Cup final victory in a 3–0 triumph over the previous world champions, Brazil. Leboeuf had been given the task of marking the man currently hailed as the greatest player in the world, Ronaldo, and although it was later claimed that the striker had been unfit to play the match, Frank had no problem at all in his task.

JULY 13

1950   Paul McMillan was born in Lennox Castle. A promising graduate of the youth programme, McMillan signed professional forms in August 1967 and made his one and only appearance in the first team less than one month after joining the seniors. He was forced to retire on medical advice just eight months after signing whilst still in his teens. He did later attempt a short-lived comeback with Clydebank.

1988   A tribunal set the fee for Pat Nevin to complete his move to Chelsea from Everton at £925,000.

JULY 14

1977   Dave Sexton was announced as the new manager of Manchester United following the sacking of Tommy Docherty. Sexton had seemingly been heading to Arsenal but chose instead to take over at Old Trafford. This was the second time in his career Sexton had replaced Docherty, for in 1967 he had succeeded him at Chelsea. Sexton had previously been a player with West Ham, Brighton and Crystal Palace before turning to coaching, and had been at the helm at QPR.

1983   Pat Nevin was signed from Clyde for £95,000.

JULY 15

1978   George Robert Mills died in Torquay.

JULY 16

1912   Len Goulden was born in Plaistow. Chelsea was the last club that Goulden played for prior to retirement in 1950, having signed from West Ham United in August 1945. An international player with 14 English caps to his name, he made 111 appearances for the Blues and scored 19 goals.

1946 John Hollins was born in Guilford. Joined the club straight from school and rapidly established a reputation as one of the best players ever to have worn the blue shirt. Enjoyed two distinct periods at the Bridge, the first extending from July 1963 (when he first signed professional forms) to June 1975 as he moved to Queens Park Rangers for £80,000 following Chelsea's relegation to Division 2. He then had a spell with Arsenal before returning in June 1983 as player-coach when his influence was a major factor in Chelsea winning the Second Division championship. Capped once by England he won an FA Cup winners' medal in 1970, a Football League Cup winners' medal in 1966 and a European Cup-Winners' Cup medal in 1971. He amassed just under 600 appearances and scored 64 goals in his Chelsea career.

1993 Kingstonian   A   Friendly   2–0

JULY 17

1996 Roberto Di Matteo joined the Chelsea ranks in a £4.9 million move from Lazio. On the same day Chelsea recouped £1.5 million from Birmingham City for Paul Furlong.

1998 Steve Clarke, at the age of 34 and with 421 appearances to his credit, was appointed player-coach under Gianluca Vialli, a position he was to hold for only a couple of months before joining Ruud Gullit at Newcastle.

JULY 18

1908 Richard Spence was born in Platt's Common near Barnsley. Chelsea paid £5,000 to secure his talents from Barnsley in October 1934 and he rewarded the club with 40 years of service. As a player, he made very nearly 250 appearances scoring 65 goals between his debut in October 1934 and his retirement in 1950 (although his final senior game was some three years previously when, at 40 years of age, he entered the record books as Chelsea's oldest ever player). After completing his playing career he joined the Stamford Bridge training staff.

JULY 19

1958 Jack Harrow, one of Chelsea's most famous players, died.
1992 Sligo Rovers   A   Friendly   2–2
1996 Kingstonian   A   Friendly   7–0
1997 Reading   A   Friendly   2–1

JULY 20

1936 John Charles Sillett was born in Southampton. Younger brother of Peter Sillett who enjoyed a more illustrious playing career, they both joined Chelsea in May 1953 from home town club, Southampton. John made just over 100 appearances for the Blues before moving on to Coventry City for £3,000 in April 1962. He completed his playing career at Plymouth Argyle before turning to management where the

highlight of his achievements was the 1987 FA Cup final in which his Coventry
City team destroyed Tottenham Hotspur.

| 1993 | Reading | A | Friendly | 1–2 |
| 1994 | Swindon Town | A | Friendly | 0–0 |

JULY 21

| 1992 | Derry City | A | Friendly | 1–1 |
| 1993 | Southend United | A | Friendly | 1–0 |

JULY 22

1980	Wimbledon	A	Friendly	2–2
1995	Kingstonian	A	Friendly	5–0
1996	Exeter City	A	Friendly	1–2
1997	West Bromwich Albion	A	Friendly	2–0

JULY 23

1963 Andrew David Townsend was born in London. From non-League Weymouth he
moved to Southampton followed by Norwich City from where Chelsea secured his
services in exchange for £1,200,000. A commanding midfield leader he assumed
the captaincy from the more limited Peter Nicholas and went on to make 131
appearances and score 19 goals before a £2,100,000 transfer in July 1993 took him
to Aston Villa. Later signed for Bryan (Man of the Match, not) Robson's
Middlesbrough outfit.

1979	Reading	A	Friendly	4–0
1992	Portadown	A	Friendly	3–0
1993	Ikast FS	A	Friendly	2–0
1994	Kingstonian	A	Friendly	10–0

JULY 24

1961 Kerry Michael Dixon was born in Luton. Bounced back from rejection by
Tottenham Hotspur when an apprentice at that club and, following a short spell in
non-League football, re-entered the League with a reputation-building period at
Reading. Signed by Chelsea in August 1983 for £175,000, he was leading goalscorer as Chelsea surged to promotion from Division 2. He played over 400 games
for the Blues and notched nearly 200 goals whilst establishing himself at
international level with England for whom he made eight full appearances.
Departed to Southampton in July 1992 for a transfer fee of £575,000 and
subsequently played for Luton Town, Millwall, Watford and Doncaster Rovers
where he had a brief and unsuccessful period in management.

| 1996 | Plymouth Argyle | A | Friendly | 3–0 |
| 1998 | Northampton Town | A | Friendly | 2–0 |

JULY 25

| 1992 | Cork City | A | Friendly | 2–1 |

1993	Viborg FF	A	Friendly	2–2
1994	Southend United	A	Friendly	2–1
1995	Gillingham	A	Friendly	3–1

JULY 26

1969	Bristol City	A	Friendly	1–1
1970	Ajax	A	Friendly	1–1
1972	St Etienne, France	A	Friendly	0–3
1980	Heart of Midlothian	A	Friendly	1–0
1993	Andy Townsend left to join Aston Villa.			
1997	Newcastle United	Goodison Park		
			Umbro Tournament	1–1

JULY 27

1885	James Anderson Croal was born in Glasgow. Began his career at Glasgow Rangers and arrived at the Bridge via Ayr Parkhouse, Alloa Athletic, Dunfermline Athletic and Falkirk. Cost Chelsea £2,000 in April 1914 and gave eight years of service before moving on to Fulham in March 1922, which proved to be his last club. Made 130 appearances and scored 26 goals with 3 caps for Scotland.			
1964	Peter Joseph McKenna died in London.			
1965	VFB Stuttgart, Germany	A	Friendly	1–1
1975	John Crawford died in Epsom.			
1976	Halmstad, Sweden	A	Friendly	1–2
1978	Gillingham	A	Friendly	1–3
1982	IFK Ostersund, Sweden	A	Friendly	0–1
1994	Watford	A	Friendly	1–0
1997	Everton	A	Umbro Tournament	3–1

JULY 28

1969	Crystal Palace	A	Friendly	2–0
1971	Stockholm XI	A	Friendly	1–1
1979	Wimbledon	A	Friendly	1–2
1980	Raith Rovers	A	Friendly	2–3
1993	Cambridge United	A	Friendly	1–0
1996	Swindon Town	A	Friendly	2–0

JULY 29

1970	Breda, Holland	A	Friendly	2–3
1976	Orgryte, Sweden	A	Friendly	3–1
1982	Multraa, Sweden	A	Friendly	2–1
1992	Bournemouth	A	Friendly	1–0

JULY 30

| 1964 | IFK Gothenburg | A | Friendly | 1–2 |

1965	SV Hamburg, Germany	A	Friendly	2–0
1980	Dundee United	A	Friendly	0–0
1994	Charlton Athletic	A	Friendly	3–1
1995	FC Porto	H	Friendly	1–1

JULY 31

1968	Crystal Palace	A	Friendly	1–1
1979	Luton Town	A	Friendly	0–1
1993	Ajax		White Hart Lane	
			Makita Tournament	1–1
1996	Wolverhampton Wanderers	A	Friendly	1–0
1997	Portsmouth	A	Friendly	4–1

AUGUST 1

1878 William Frederick Brawn was born in Wellingborough. He came to Chelsea in 1907 after a nomadic career that had seen him play for Wellingborough Town, Northampton Town, Sheffield United, Aston Villa, and Middlesbrough. In three seasons with the Blues he notched up 99 appearances and 11 goals before moving on again to join Brentford where, two years later, he finally hung up his boots.

1908 George Frederick Barber was born in West Ham. Signed on a free transfer from his first senior club, Luton Town, he gave the Blues over a decade of service in which he made 294 appearances and scored just a single goal in the FA Cup before going into retirement.

1965	Gothenburg Alliance	A	Friendly	2–4
1970	PSV Eindhoven	A	Friendly	0–2
1971	Vaxjo Osters, Sweden	A	Friendly	1–1
1973	Bochum, Germany	A	Friendly	2–0
1976	Gais, Gothenburg	A	Friendly	3–0
1978	Malawi National XI	A	Friendly	6–1
1982	IFK Stroemsund	A	Friendly	8–0
1992	Wokingham Town	A	Friendly	6–0
1993	Tottenham Hotspur	A	Makita Tournament	4–0
1995	Torquay United	A	Friendly	5–0

AUGUST 2

1964	Elfsborg Baras Sweden	A	Friendly	2–1
1967	Aberdeen	A	Friendly	1–2
1969	Alemannia Aachen, Germany	A	Friendly	1–3
1972	Den Bosch, Holland	A	Friendly	3–0
1975	Bristol City	H	Anglo Scottish Cup	1–0
1980	Millwall	A	Friendly	1–1

1994	FC Copenhagen	A	Tour	1–0
1994	FC Koln	Copenhagen	Tour	0–2

AUGUST 3

1963	St Mirren	A	Friendly	5–2
1965	Orebro SK, Sweden	A	Friendly	8–0
1966	Lugano, Switzerland	A	Friendly	3–2
1968	Kaiserslautern, Germany	A	Friendly	0–1
1973	Werder Bremen, Germany	A	Friendly	2–1
1974	Feyenoord, Holland	A	Friendly	1–3
1979	Ipswich Town	A	Friendly	2–3
1982	Mariehamn, Sweden	A	Friendly	6–1
1984	Aberystwyth	A	Friendly	4–1
1995	Plymouth Argyle	A	Friendly	2–0
1996	Nottingham Forest	A	Umbro Tournament	0–0
1997	Manchester United	Wembley	FA Charity Shield	1–1

AUGUST 4

1948 Ian Hutchinson was born in Codnor, Derbyshire. Chelsea acquired his services from Cambridge United for £5,000 in July 1968 and have rarely achieved such value for money. Despite being dogged by injuries he still managed to notch up just short of 150 appearances and score 57 goals, the most crucial of which was surely the second equaliser in the 1970 FA Cup final against Leeds United at Wembley.

1967	Clydebank	A	Friendly	2–2
1971	RFC Bruges, Belgium	A	Friendly	1–1
1980	Portsmouth	A	Friendly	0–0
1981	Woking	A	Friendly	2–2

1983 Kerry Dixon joined from Reading in a £175,000 deal.

1984	Wrexham	A	Friendly	1–0
1992	Burnley	A	Friendly	0–1
1993	Colchester United	A	Friendly	2–0
1996	Ajax	Nottingham	Umbro Tournament	2–0

AUGUST 5

1965	IFK Norrkoping, Sweden	A	Friendly	0–1
1972	Go Ahead Deventer, Holland	A	Friendly	2–2
1978	Portsmouth	A	Friendly	1–1

1981 Death of Albert Eric Oakton.

| 1983 | Aberystwyth | A | Friendly | 3–0 |

1983 Alexander Cheyne died in Arbroath.

AUGUST 6

1925 Eddie Baily born in Clapton, East London. Although he signed amateur forms with Tottenham Hotspur during the war, he was later reported missing in action and Spurs therefore allowed his registration to lapse. Upon arriving back in England he was persuaded by Chelsea to sign amateur forms with them, and it was only when he popped into White Hart Lane to collect his boots that the situation became clear. To their credit, Chelsea agreed to tear up their contract and Baily re-signed with Spurs in February 1946, being upgraded to professional status in October the following year.

| 1966 | VFB Stuttgart, Germany | A | Friendly | 0–2 |

1971 Scott Christopher Minto was born in Heswall. He followed his understudy, Anthony Barness, from Charlton Athletic to the Bridge in May 1994 at a cost of £775,000 and played 70-plus games before moving on a free transfer to play for Benfica in Lisbon when out of contract in the summer of 1997. Prone to injury he at least had an FA Cup winners' medal to take with him won against Middlesbrough in 1997.

1974	Borussia Moenchengladbach	A	Friendly	1–0
1977	Fulham	A	Anglo Scottish Cup	0–1
1980	Brentford	A	Friendly	0–3
1983	Newport County	A	Friendly	2–0
1992	Kingstonian	A	Friendly	3–1
1994	AS Napoli	Highbury	Makita Tournament	0–2
1995	Bristol City	A	Friendly	1–1

AUGUST 7

1971	Bolton Wanderers	A	Friendly	0–2
1973	Ado Den Haag, Holland	A	Friendly	2–0
1976	Fulham	H	Anglo Scottish Cup	0–0
1979	Charlton Athletic	A	Friendly	1–1
1984	Bristol City	A	Friendly	0–1
1993	West Bromwich Albion	A	Friendly	3–0
1994	Athletico Madrid	Highbury	Makita Tournament	1–0

AUGUST 8

1964	Fredrikshaven, Denmark	A	Friendly	3–1
1965	Aarhus, Denmark	A	Friendly	0–0
1966	Dundee	A	Friendly	2–1
1970	Everton	H	FA Charity Shield	1–2

1980	Norwich City	A	Friendly	1–1
1992	Bristol City	A	Friendly	1–2
1996	Sampdoria	A	Friendly	2–1

AUGUST 9

1924 James Duncan Bowie was born in Aberdeen. He signed for the club in 1944 during the Second World War in which he served as a Naval rating. He eventually made his debut in 1947 but still amassed over 80 appearances and 22 League and Cup goals before departing for Fulham in 1951 for £20,000. Later played for Brentford and Watford, before drifting into non-League football.

1969	Liverpool	A	League Division 1	1–4
1974	Wuppertal, Germany	A	Friendly	3–1
1975	Norwich City	H	Anglo Scottish Cup	1–1
1975	Fulham	A	Anglo Scottish Cup	0–1
1977	Orient	H	Anglo Scottish Cup	2–0
1978	Seville, Spain	A	Friendly	2–3
1995	Birmingham City	A	Friendly	4–0
1997	Coventry City	A	Premier League	2–3

AUGUST 10

1885 George Richard Hilsdon was born in Bow, London. Acquired on a free transfer from West Ham United in May 1906 he played 150 League games and 14 FA Cup matches scoring over 100 goals before rejoining West Ham again on a free transfer in the summer of 1912. In his first season at Stamford Bridge he scored 27 goals which made a huge contribution to Chelsea's promotion campaign to the First Division.

| 1958 | CDNA, Bulgaria | A | Friendly | 1–2 |

1961 Colin George Pates was born in Carshalton. Signed as a professional in July 1979 after an apprenticeship in the juniors and made his full debut five months later. He quickly established himself as a regular member of the first team graduating to the captaincy in the final few months of the promotion season in 1984. He left the Bridge in October 1988 in a £430,000 transfer to Charlton Athletic having played very nearly 350 games in which he had scored 10 goals. He later played for Arsenal and Brighton and Hove Albion.

1968	Waterford	A	Friendly	5–2
1980	Panathinaikos, Greece	A	Friendly	0–2
1994	Wycombe Wanderers	A	Friendly	2–1

AUGUST 11

1962	Brighton & Hove Albion	A	Friendly	1–1
1964	TSV 1860 Munich	A	Friendly	0–2
1965	Glasgow Select	A	Glasgow Charity Cup	3–0

1965 Robert William Fleck was born in Glasgow. Began his professional career at Glasgow Rangers where he enjoyed a favourable goals-to-games ratio, probably the major factor that convinced Norwich City to pay £580,000 for his services in December 1987. It was with the Canaries that he shot to fame until joining the Blues for £2,100,000 in August 1992. He was not the same player in London and rarely looked to have settled to the demands and expectations placed upon him in the capital. He mustered just 46 games and scored only 5 goals when, after loan spells at Bolton Wanderers and Bristol City, his unhappy period was brought to a conclusion with a £650,000 return transfer to Norwich City.

1967	Independiente, Argentina	A	Friendly	2–1
1969	West Ham United	A	League Division 1	0–2
1976	Norwich City	H	Anglo Scottish Cup	1–1
1978	Porto, Portugal	A	Friendly	1–2
1979	Crystal Palace	A	Friendly	0–5
1980	Aek Athens	A	Friendly	2–2
1981	Vasteras IFK, Sweden	A	Friendly	0–1
1996	Psv Eindhoven	H	Friendly	2–3

AUGUST 12

1961	Bournemouth & Boscombe	A	Friendly	3–4
1964	Chaux De Fonds, Switzerland	A	Friendly	1–0
1966	SV Hamburg, Germany	A	Friendly	1–3
1967	Real Sociedad, Spain	A	Friendly	1–2
1972	Leeds United	H	League Division 1	4–0
1981	Flens IF, Sweden	A	Friendly	2–0
1995	Feyenoord	A	Friendly	1–0

AUGUST 13

1977	Norwich City	H	Anglo Scottish Cup	2–2
1979	China	H	Friendly	3–1
1982	Aberystwyth	A	Friendly	4–0
1982	Robert Fleck signed for the club in a £2,100,000 deal from Norwich City.			
1994	Valencia	A	Friendly	1–1

AUGUST 14

1905 John William Horton was born in Castleford. He spent seven years at his first senior club, Charlton Athletic, before transferring to Chelsea in March 1933. He played 66 times and scored 15 goals in a stay that lasted until June 1937 when he departed for his final club, Crystal Palace.

1963	MTK Hungary	A	Friendly	3–1
1964	Rapid Vienna, Austria	A	Friendly	2–1
1966	Eintracht Frankfurt, Germany	A	Friendly	0–1

| 1968 | Nottingham Forest | H | League Division 1 | 1–1 |
| 1971 | Arsenal | A | League Division 1 | 0–3 |

John Hollins commenced a run of 167 consecutive appearances that would extend through to 25 September 1974 (inclusive).

| 1976 | Orient | A | Anglo Scottish Cup | 1–2 |

1979 Ray Wilkins left the club to join Manchester United in a deal worth £850,00. The move reunited Wilkins with the manager who had signed him as a 15-year-old for the Blues, Dave Sexton.

1981	BK Forward, Sweden	A	Friendly	0–1
1982	Cardiff City	A	Friendly	3–1
1993	Blackburn Rovers	H	Premier League	1–2

AUGUST 15

1970	Derby County	H	League Division 1	2–1
1977	Celtic	A	Friendly	2–2
1984	Brentford	A	Friendly	3–0
1987	Sheffield Wednesday	A	League Division 1	0–3

Tony Dorigo and Clive Wilson made their first appearances for the club.

| 1992 | Oldham Athletic | H | Premier League | 1–1 |

AUGUST 16

| 1959 | Ajax | A | Friendly | 3–2 |

1968 Dmitri Kharine was born in Moscow, Russia. A long-established first-choice Russian international goalkeeper, he joined the club in a bargain £200,000 transfer from CSKA Moscow in December 1992. He suffered more than his fair share of injuries and that fact alone was probably what prompted Chelsea to sign a rival goalkeeper, Ed de Goey, to fight for the first team duties. Kharine has played around 150 games for the Blues.

1969	Ipswich Town	H	League Division 1	1–0
1972	Leicester City	A	League Division 1	1–1
1975	Sunderland	A	League Division 2	1–2

Gary Stanley made his senior debut.

| 1980 | Wrexham | H | League Division 2 | 2–2 |
| 1983 | Wimbledon | A | Friendly | 1–2 |

AUGUST 17

1888 Thomas Logan was born in Burnhead. A Scot who won a single international cap for his country, he began his career north of the border with Arthurlie, and Falkirk before joining Chelsea in May 1913 for £2,500. Stayed with the Blues until retiring in 1921 during which time he played 117 League and Cup games and scored 8 goals.

1958	Levski, Sofia	A	Friendly	2–0
1965	Germany XI	A	Friendly	2–3
1968	West Bromwich Albion	H	League Division 1	3–1
1974	Carlisle United	H	League Division 1	0–2

David Hay played his first game for the club.

1981	Hofers Aif, Sweden	A	Friendly	1–2
1982	Hillingdon Borough	A	Friendly	4–1
1985	Sheffield Wednesday	A	League Division 1	1–1
1991	Wimbledon	H	League Division 1	2–2
1993	Wimbledon	A	Premier League	1–1

AUGUST 18

1924 Thomas Meehan died in St George's Hospital after a bout of sleeping sickness. Such was his popularity that some 2,000 mourners turned out for his funeral in Wandsworth and a fund established to help his widow and four children raised £1,580.

1951	Blackpool	A	League Division 1	2–1
1956	Burnley	A	League Division 1	0–2
1957	Ajax	A	Friendly	4–2
1962	Rotherham United	A	League Division 2	1–0

Eddie McCreadie played his first game for the club.

1971	Manchester United	H	League Division 1	2–3
1973	Orense, Spain	A	Friendly	1–1
1979	Sunderland	H	League Division 2	0–0
1987	Portsmouth	H	League Division 1	0–0
1996	Southampton	A	Premier League	0–0

AUGUST 19

1900 John Priestley was born in Johnstone, Renfrew. Signed from his local club in May 1920, he had made over 200 starts for the Blues and scored 19 goals when he was transferred to Grimsby Town in May 1928. He subsequently returned to St Johnstone before finishing his career with Cowdenbeath.

| 1950 | Sheffield Wednesday | H | League Division 1 | 4–0 |
| 1953 | Manchester United | A | League Division 1 | 1–1 |

Peter Sillett played in Chelsea colours for the first time.

| 1961 | Nottingham Forest | H | League Division 1 | 2–2 |

First game for Frank Upton.

| 1963 | Charlton Athletic | A | Friendly | 4–2 |
| 1967 | West Bromwich Albion | A | League Division 1 | 1–0 |

1968 Roger Freestone was born in Caerleon, Newport. Made his League debut with local club Newport County and signed for Chelsea in March 1987 for £75,000. He appeared a total of 53 times in goal for Chelsea before returning to his native Wales to join Swansea City first on loan and then on a permanent basis for a £45,000 transfer fee in September 1991. Made over 300 appearances for the Swans. Whilst at Chelsea he also went for a short loan spell with Hereford United.

1970	Manchester United	A	League Division 1	0–0
1972	Derby County	A	League Division 1	2–1
1973	Celta, Spain	A	Friendly	3–3
1978	Everton	H	League Division 1	0–1

1989	Wimbledon	A	League Division 1	1–0
1992	Norwich City	A	Premier League	1–2
1995	Everton	H	Premier League	0–0

AUGUST 20

1904 Harry Burgess was born in Alderley Edge, Cheshire. After experience with Stockport County and Sheffield Wednesday, he joined Chelsea in March 1935 and made over 150 appearances (scoring 37 goals) before the outbreak of the Second World War put paid to his career. He retired in 1945.

| 1919 | Everton | A | League Division 1 | 3–2 |

George Henry Dale made his Chelsea debut, as did Harry Thomas Wilding.

1925 John McNichol was born in Kilmarnock. He became manager Ted Drake's first signing in August 1952 when he joined from Brighton and Hove Albion in a £12,000 deal, and was an important part of the side Drake assembled that won the League Championship in 1955. McNichol made 200 plus appearances and scored 66 goals whilst at the Bridge. He had previously been with Newcastle United and went on to play for Crystal Palace whom he joined in March 1958 for £2,000.

| 1949 | Birmingham City | A | League Division 1 | 3–0 |

1949 Stewart Houston was born in Dunoon in Argyle. After unsuccessful spells with Chelsea (where he made just 14 appearances) and Brentford, Houston was signed by Manchester United for £55,000 in 1973. He was sold to Sheffield United in 1980 and later had spells coaching with Colchester and Plymouth before joining Arsenal's backroom staff as assistant manager. More recently he was manager at QPR and a coach at Ipswich Town.

1955	Bolton Wanderers	H	League Division 1	0–2
1960	Aston Villa	A	League Division 1	2–3
1966	West Ham United	A	League Division 1	2–1
1969	West Ham United	H	League Division 1	0–0
1975	West Bromwich Albion	A	League Division 2	0–0
1977	West Bromwich Albion	A	League Division 1	0–3
1979	West Ham United	A	League Division 2	1–0
1980	Derby County	A	League Division 2	2–3
1982	Arsenal	H	Friendly	1–3
1983	Queens Park Rangers	H	Friendly	2–1
1985	Coventry City	H	League Division 1	1–0
1994	Norwich City	H	Premier League	2–0

AUGUST 21

1948	Middlesbrough	H	League Division 1	1–0
1954	Leicester City	A	League Division 1	1–1
1965	Burnley	H	League Division 1	1–1
1968	Newcastle United	A	League Division 1	2–3
1971	Manchester City	H	League Division 1	2–2
1974	Burnley	H	League Division 1	3–3

| 1976 | Orient | A | League Division 2 | 1–0 |

Chelsea won the first home game of the season and kicked off an unbeaten sequence of matches at Stamford Bridge which lasted until the end of the 1976–77 campaign.

1981	Exeter City	A	Friendly	1–0
1984	Doncaster Rovers	A	Friendly	1–1
1991	Oldham Athletic	A	League Division 1	0–3
1992	Ken Monkou was transferred to Southampton for £750,000.			
1993	Ipswich Town	A	Premier League	0–1
1996	Middlesbrough	H	Premier League	1–0

AUGUST 22

1887 Charles Redfern Freeman was born in Overseal, Derbyshire. Joined Chelsea in 1907 from Fulham to commence a playing career that would endure at the Bridge until 1921 (when he departed for Gillingham). However, in this time he was most commonly a reserve and managed only a total of 105 games (22 goals) but obviously impressed with his attitude and, after retirement, returned as a member of the backroom staff to continue in Chelsea's employ until 1953.

1900 William Brown was born in Fence Houses, Co Durham. Signed from West Ham United in February 1924 and made only 57 appearances in a five-year stay. His career tailed off at Fulham, Stockport County and Hartlepool United.

1945 Alan John Birchenhall was born in East Ham. Manager Dave Sexton's first signing for the club from Sheffield United in November 1967 at a cost of £100,000, he made just short of 100 senior appearances and scored 28 goals for the Blues before being sold to Crystal Palace in June 1970. Chelsea recouped the outlay they had made on Birchenhall who ended with a string of clubs to his name.

1951	Arsenal	H	League Division 1	1–3
1953	Blackpool	A	League Division 1	1–2
1954	Burnley	H	League Division 1	1–0
1956	Sheffield Wednesday	A	League Division 1	0–4

Anthony Wallace Nicholas made his first appearance for the club.

1959	Preston North End	H	League Division 1	4–4
1962	Scunthorpe United	H	League Division 2	3–0
1964	Wolverhampton Wanderers	A	League Division 1	3–0
1970	West Ham United	A	League Division 1	2–2
1978	Wolverhampton Wanderers	A	League Division 1	1–0
1987	Tottenham Hotspur	H	League Division 1	0–0
1989	Queens Park Rangers	H	League Division 1	1–1
1992	Sheffield Wednesday	A	Premier League	3–3

AUGUST 23

1924 Stanley Willemse was born in Brighton. He was acquired from Brighton and Hove

Albion for £6,500 in July 1949 and made 220 appearances in a seven-year stay at the Bridge in which the highlight was the winning of a League Championship medal in 1955. He departed for Leyton Orient in June 1956 with the O's paying £4,500 to secure his services.

1947	Blackpool	A	League Division 1	0–3

Ken Armstrong's debut.

1952	Manchester United	A	League Division 1	0–2

John McNichol played his first game for the club.

1958	Manchester United	A	League Division 1	2–5
1961	Manchester United	A	League Division 1	2–3
1967	Newcastle United	H	League Division 1	1–1
1969	Southampton	A	League Division 1	2–2
1972	Liverpool	H	League Division 1	1–2
1975	Carlisle United	H	League Division 2	3–1
1980	Shrewsbury Town	A	League Division 2	2–2
1986	Norwich City	H	League Division 1	0–0
1995	Nottingham Forest	A	Premier League	0–0

AUGUST 24

1928   Tommy Docherty was born in Glasgow. He began his playing career with Celtic before moving to England and signing for Preston North End in November 1949. He picked up a runners-up medal in the FA Cup in 1954 and 22 full Scottish caps and then moved to Arsenal in 1958, with whom he won a further three caps. He then moved to Chelsea but after only four games moved onto the coaching side, eventually taking over from Ted Drake as manager in 1962. He guided them to the League Cup in 1965 and the FA Cup final in 1967, where they lost to Spurs. After leaving Chelsea he began a tour of the managerial hot-seats around the country; Aston Villa, two spells at Queen's Park Rangers, Rotherham United, Manchester United (with whom he won the FA Cup), Wolverhampton Wanderers, Derby County and spells managing overseas. His most successful appointment, at Manchester United, was ended when it was revealed he was involved in a relationship with the wife of a member of his staff. Although he later married her he was sacked from his post and later lost a highly publicised libel case.

1949	Arsenal	H	League Division 1	1–2
1955	Huddersfield Town	A	League Division 1	3–1
1957	Tottenham Hotspur	A	League Division 1	1–1

Debut of Jimmy Greaves.

1960	Leicester City	H	League Division 1	1–3
1963	West Ham United	H	League Division 1	0–0
1966	Nottingham Forest	H	League Division 1	2–1
1968	Manchester United	A	League Division 1	4–0
1974	Coventry City	A	League Division 1	3–1
1977	Birmingham City	H	League Division 1	2–0
1985	Birmingham City	H	League Division 1	2–0
1991	Tottenham Hotspur	A	League Division 1	3–1

| 1996 | Coventry City | H | Premier League | 2–0 |
| 1997 | Barnsley | A | Premier League | 6–0 |

Chelsea's biggest win in the Premier League was secured with four goals by Gianluca Vialli.

AUGUST 25

| 1878 | Edward Lawson Birnie was born in Sunderland. Joined Chelsea in August 1906 after spells at Newcastle United and Crystal Palace and immediately became an integral member of the first promotion side of 1906–07. Made 108 senior appearances, scoring three goals, before transferring to Tottenham Hotspur. | | | |
| 1923 | Blackburn Rovers | A | League Division 1 | 0–3 |

The debut of Harold Sydney Miller.

| 1928 | Swansea Town | H | League Division 2 | 4–0 |

Debut for Sidney Bishop.

1934	Derby County	A	League Division 1	0–3
1945	Nottingham Forest	H	Football League South	0–4
1948	Newcastle United	A	League Division 1	2–2
1950	Arsenal	A	League Division 1	0–0
1951	Liverpool	H	League Division 1	1–3
1953	Portsmouth	H	League Division 1	4–3
1956	Preston North End	H	League Division 1	1–0
1962	Charlton Athletic	H	League Division 2	5–0
1965	Stoke City	A	League Division 1	2–2
1971	Everton	A	League Division 1	0–2
1973	Derby County	A	League Division 1	0–1
1976	Notts County	H	League Division 2	1–1
1979	Wrexham	H	League Division 2	3–1
1984	Arsenal	A	League Division 1	1–1

Doug Rougvie made his first start for the club.

| 1986 | Oxford United | A | League Division 1 | 1–1 |
| 1990 | Derby County | H | League Division 1 | 2–1 |

Andy Townsend and Dennis Wise played for the Blues for the first time.

| 1993 | Queens Park Rangers | H | Premier League | 2–0 |

AUGUST 26

1944	Fulham	A	Football League South	4–7
1950	Middlesbrough	A	League Division 1	0–3
1959	Manchester United	A	League Division 1	1–0
1961	Aston Villa	A	League Division 1	1–3
1964	Aston Villa	H	League Division 1	2–1
1967	Fulham	H	League Division 1	1–1
1970	Everton	H	League Division 1	2–2
1972	Manchester City	H	League Division 1	2–1
1978	Tottenham Hotspur	A	League Division 1	2–2

1989	Sheffield Wednesday	H	League Division 1	4–0
1992	Blackburn Rovers	H	Premier League	0–0
1995	Middlesbrough	A	Premier League	0–2

AUGUST 27

| 1921 | Blackburn Rovers | A | League Division 1 | 1–1 |

George Smith played his initial game for the club. He went on to make a total of 370 League and Cup appearances until a serious injury curtailed his career at the Bridge in 1932 when he moved on to East Fife.

1923	Tottenham Hotspur	H	League Division 1	0–1
1927	Reading	A	League Division 2	2–1
1928	Bradford Park Avenue	A	League Division 2	2–1
1932	Blackburn Rovers	A	League Division 1	2–2

Albert Eric Oakton made his first Chelsea appearance.

1938	Liverpool	A	League Division 1	1–2
1939	Bolton Wanderers	H	League Division 1 (Expunged)	3–2
1947	Blackburn Rovers	H	League Division 1	1–0
1949	Derby County	H	League Division 1	1–2
1952	Derby County	H	League Division 1	1–1
1955	Arsenal	A	League Division 1	1–1
1958	Tottenham Hotspur	H	League Division 1	4–2
1960	Wolverhampton Wanderers	H	League Division 1	3–3
1963	Burnley	A	League Division 1	0–0
1966	Sheffield Wednesday	H	League Division 1	0–0
1969	Tottenham Hotspur	A	League Division 1	1–1
1974	Burnley	A	League Division 1	2–1
1975	Oxford United	H	League Division 2	3–1
1977	Coventry City	H	League Division 1	1–2
1980	Cardiff City	A	League Cup 2nd round	0–1
1983	Derby County	H	League Division 2	5–0

Chelsea debuts for Kerry Dixon, Joe McLaughlin, Eddie Niedzwiecki and Nigel Spackman.

1984	Sunderland	H	League Division 1	1–0
1988	Blackburn Rovers	H	League Division 2	1–2
1994	Leeds United	A	Premier League	3–2
1997	Wimbledon	A	Premier League	2–0

AUGUST 28

1894 Samuel Johnstone Irving was born in Belfast. Joined Chelsea late in his career from Cardiff City in February 1928 but nevertheless played an important part in helping the club climb out of the Second Division in 1930. He made just under 100 appearances before moving on to Bristol Rovers in May 1932.

1904 Robert Macaulay was born in Wishaw. Played for Glasgow Rangers twice, with a spell at Fall River USA sandwiched in between, from where he joined Chelsea in May 1932. He had played 74 games and scored just one goal when transferred to Cardiff City then finished with spells at Workington and Raith Rovers.

1920	Derby County	A	League Division 1	0–0

Debut of David Cameron.

1922	Birmingham City	H	League Division 1	1–1
1922	Stoke City	A	League Division 1	2–1
1926	Middlesbrough	H	League Division 2	3–0
1933	Stoke City	A	League Division 1	0–1
1937	Liverpool	H	League Division 1	6–1
1943	Queens Park Rangers	H	Football League South	1–3
1948	Birmingham City	A	League Division 1	0–1
1954	Bolton Wanderers	H	League Division 1	3–2
1957	Manchester City	H	League Division 1	2–3
1962	Scunthorpe United	A	League Division 2	0–3
1965	Fulham	A	League Division 1	3–0
1968	Sheffield Wednesday	H	League Division 1	1–0
1971	Huddersfield Town	A	League Division 1	2–1
1973	Burnley	A	League Division 1	0–1
1976	Carlisle United	H	League Division 2	2–1
1979	Plymouth Argyle	A	League Cup 2nd round	2–2
1982	Cambridge United	A	League Division 2	1–0
1985	Leicester City	A	League Division 1	0–0
1990	Crystal Palace	A	League Division 1	1–2
1991	Notts County	H	League Division 1	2–2
1993	Sheffield Wednesday	H	Premier League	1–1

AUGUST 29

1921	Birmingham City	H	League Division 1	1–2
1925	Bradford City	H	League Division 2	2–0

The start of a new campaign got Chelsea off to winning ways. It established a platform from which the team went on to establish a record (opening) unbeaten run of 14 games.

1931	Middlesbrough	A	League Division 1	2–0

Goalkeeper Vic Woodley played his first game in senior football. He did so well he remained Chelsea's number one for the greater part of fifteen years and England's regular pre-war goalie.

1936	Leeds United	A	League Division 1	3–2

Samuel Weaver played his first game for the Blues.

1942	Queens Park Rangers	H	Football League South	1–1
1951	Arsenal	A	League Division 1	1–2
1953	Charlton Athletic	H	League Division 1	3–1
1955	Huddersfield Town	H	League Division 1	0–0
1959	Leicester City	A	League Division 1	1–3

1963   Steve Clarke was born in Saltcoats. Joined Chelsea in January 1987 from St Mirren for £422,000. A Scottish international who, with more than a decade and a completed testimonial season at the Bridge, has written his name large in Chelsea's history. He was elevated to club captain in season 1996–97 and has been an integral part of the recent successful cup teams, picking up medals for the FA Cup, Coca-Cola (League Cup) and European Cup-Winners' Cup. At the end of season 1997–98 he had made over 420 appearances for the club and was appointed to a player-coach role. At the start of the following season he left to join Ruud Gullit at Newcastle.

1964	Sunderland	H	League Division 1	3–1

George Graham's debut.

1970	Arsenal	H	League Division 1	2–1
1978	Bolton Wanderers	A	League Cup 2nd round	1–2
1981	Bolton Wanderers	H	League Division 2	2–0
1987	Luton Town	A	League Division 1	0–3
1989	Charlton Athletic	A	League Division 1	0–3
1992	Queens Park Rangers	H	Premier League	1–0

AUGUST 30

1924	Coventry City	H	League Division 2	1–0
1926	Wolverhampton Wanderers	A	League Division 2	3–0
1930	Grimsby Town	A	League Division 1	1–0

First game for Alexander Cheyne and Hugh Gallacher.

1941	Charlton Athletic	A	London War League	1–2
1947	Derby County	H	League Division 1	1–0
1950	Arsenal	H	League Division 1	0–1
1952	Portsmouth	H	League Division 1	2–0
1958	Wolverhampton Wanderers	H	League Division 1	6–2
1961	Manchester United	H	League Division 1	2–0
1966	Nottingham Forest	A	League Division 1	0–0
1967	Newcastle United	A	League Division 1	1–5
1969	Crystal Palace	H	League Division 1	1–1
1972	Manchester United	A	League Division 1	0–0
1975	Luton Town	A	League Division 2	0–3
1977	Liverpool	A	League Cup 2nd round	0–2
1980	Queens Park Rangers	H	League Division 2	1–1
1983	Gillingham	A	League Cup 1st round	2–1
1986	Sheffield Wednesday	A	League Division 1	0–2
1988	Crystal Palace	A	League Division 2	1–1
1991	Hard-man Vinnie Jones joined from Sheffield United for £575,000.			
1995	Coventry	H	Premier League	2–2
1997	Southampton	H	Premier League	4–2

AUGUST 31

1925	Nottingham Forest	A	League Division 2	5–1
1929	Nottingham Forest	H	League Division 2	2–0
1931	West Ham United	A	League Division 1	1–3
1932	Portsmouth	A	League Division 1	0–2
1935	Liverpool	H	League Division 1	2–2
1938	Preston North End	H	League Division 1	3–1
1939	Manchester United	H	League Division 1 (Expunged)	1–1
1940	Crystal Palace	A	Football League South	3–6
1946	Bolton Wanderers	H	League Division 1	4–3
1949	Arsenal	A	League Division 1	3–2

Stanley Wilelmse played his first game for Chelsea.

1954	Burnley	A	League Division 1	1–1
1957	Birmingham City	H	League Division 1	5–1
1960	Leicester City	A	League Division 1	3–1

1960 Death of William Ferguson.

1963	Sheffield United	A	League Division 1	1–1
1964	Aston Villa	A	League Division 1	2–2
1968	Tottenham Hotspur	H	League Division 1	2–2
1974	Liverpool	H	League Division 1	0–3
1982	Wolverhampton Wanderers	H	League Division 2	0–0
1984	Everton	H	League Division 1	0–1
1985	West Bromwich Albion	H	League Division 1	3–0
1987	Manchester United	H	League Division 1	1–2
1991	Luton Town	H	League Division 1	4–1
1994	Manchester City	H	Premier League	3–0

SEPTEMBER 1

1906 Glossop North End   H   League Division 2   9–2

This game, which ranks as Chelsea's biggest win in Division Two, marked the debut of George Hilsdon who established a club record by scoring five goals on his first appearance. It was also the first time in action for Joseph Walton who joined the club the previous month from New Brompton and spent nearly five years at the Bridge before being released in May 1911. However, despite the length of service, Walton was unable to command a regular first team spot and ended with only 53 appearances to his credit.

1908 Preston North End   H   League Division 1   0–0

First games for Scot, Angus Douglas, and English international, Benjamin Warren. The latter was capped 22 times for his country and, after joining the Blues from Derby County in August 1908 for £1,250, made in excess of 100 appearances in Chelsea's colours (5 goals). He retired in 1912 and was later classified insane, spending time in a lunatic asylum before his death in 1917. A benefit game was played between the North and South at Stamford Bridge for his dependants in April 1914.

1909	Notts County	H	League Division 1	2–2
1917	Millwall	H	London Combination League	3–4
1919	Sunderland	H	League Division 1	2–0
1920	Bolton Wanderers	H	League Division 1	1–0
1923	Blackburn Rovers	H	League Division 1	2–0
1924	Leicester City	A	League Division 2	0–4
1928	Blackpool	A	League Division 2	1–0
1934	Leicester City	H	League Division 1	3–1
1937	Leeds United	A	League Division 1	0–2
1945	Nottingham Forest	A	Football League South	1–0
1948	Newcastle United	H	League Division 1	2–3
1951	Portsmouth	A	League Division 1	0–1
1956	Leeds United	A	League Division 1	0–0

Debut of Les Allen.

| 1962 | Stoke City | A | League Division 2 | 0–0 |

1962 Ruud Gullit was born in Surinam. His playing career at international (he won 64 caps for Holland) and club level marked him out as one of the greatest ever talents of any generation. He established his credentials with Haarlem, PSV Eindhoven, AC Milan and Sampdoria from where he joined Chelsea on a free transfer in July 1995. A European Cup-winner with Milan, he was at the end of his glittering career when, in the close season of 1996, he was asked to assume the managerial duties from Glenn Hoddle who in turn had progressed to the England national team coaching role. Ruud's astute dealings saw him introduce Gianluca Vialli, Frank Leboeuf, Roberto Di Matteo and then Gianfranco Zola in his first season in charge and it was fitting that, following the untimely death of Matthew Harding, the club should win the FA Cup by beating Middlesbrough at Wembley in May 1997. The shock departure of Gullit from Stamford Bridge came at a time when the club was riding high in three of the four competitions entered for in season 1997–98 but conversely also when Gullit's playing abilities were being called into question. His performance in the first leg of the Coca-Cola Cup semi-final at Highbury against Arsenal was one of his worst in a Chelsea shirt and it appeared obvious that his days on the field were numbered. Nevertheless, it was still a huge surprise that his total departure from the Bridge came so soon and before he got the chance to challenge for 'the cup with the big ears'.

1965	Stoke City	H	League Division 1	1–2
1970	Burnley	A	League Division 1	0–0
1971	West Bromwich Albion	H	League Division 1	1–0
1973	Sheffield United	H	League Division 1	1–2
1976	Sheffield United	H	League Cup 2nd round	3–1
1979	Newcastle United	A	League Division 2	1–2
1990	Queens Park Rangers	A	League Division 1	0–1

Jason Cundy made his League debut.

| 1993 | Tottenham Hotspur | A | Premier League | 1–1 |

1905 Stockport County   A   League Division 2   0–1

This was Chelsea's first League game! Therefore the entire team made their club League debuts, but those listed below carved careers of some note with the Blues; George Key played his first game, out of a total 56 games, having joined from Heart of Midlothian the previous month. He retired at the end of season 1908–09. John Kirwan also made his debut having signed from Tottenham Hotspur in May 1905. An Irish international, he played 76 games and scored 18 goals before being transferred to Clyde in May 1908.

It was also the first outing for the superbly named Robert McRoberts who hailed from Coatbridge and was Chelsea's first signing, coming to the club from Small Heath in April 1905 for £100. He made over 100 appearances and scored 10 goals before turning to management with his old club (which had renamed itself Birmingham).

Another significant debut was made by Thomas Miller. He was born in, and played for, Falkirk before joining the Blues in May 1905. He went on to complete 120 games for the club before returning to play for his hometown club. His story bore a remarkable similarity with that of Kevin McAllister some 80 years later.

Martin Moran, the muscular midget, played at right-wing at the start of a three-year stay that saw him make 67 appearances with 8 goals. His career began at Glasgow Celtic and was followed by spells at Sheffield United, Millwall and Heart of Midlothian before Chelsea and a return to Celtic in 1908.

Finally, James 'The Wizard' Windridge who appeared for the first time stayed at Chelsea longer than any other of his counterparts amassing 152 League and Cup games and 58 goals before departing to Middlesbrough in November 1911 for £1,000.

1911	Stockport County	H	League Division 2	0–0
1912	Aston Villa	A	League Division 1	0–1
1916	Tottenham Hotspur	A	London Combination League	2–0
1922	Birmingham City	A	League Division 1	1–0
1933	Wolverhampton Wanderers	H	League Division 1	5–2
1936	Grimsby Town	H	League Division 1	3–2
1939	Liverpool	A	League Division 1 (Expunged)	0–1
1944	Aldershot	H	Football League South	1–1
1950	Huddersfield Town	H	League Division 1	1–2
1953	Portsmouth	A	League Division 1	2–3
1959	Manchester United	H	League Division 1	3–6
1961	Fulham	H	League Division 1	0–0
1967	Southampton	H	League Division 1	2–6
1969	Coventry City	A	League Cup 2nd round	1–0
1972	Arsenal	A	League Division 1	1–1
1978	Leeds United	H	League Division 1	0–3
1986	Coventry City	H	League Division 1	0–0
1992	Aston Villa	A	Premier League	3–1

SEPTEMBER 3

| 1910 | Derby County | A | League Division 2 | 4–1 |

James Molyneux, born in Port Sunlight in 1887, made his first start for the Blues. He had been signed during the previous month from Stockport County at a cost of £550, stayed at the Bridge for nearly 13 years before returning to his original club and made close to 250 appearances in the interim.

1921	Blackburn Rovers	H	League Division 1	1–0
1923	Tottenham Hotspur	A	League Division 1	1–0
1927	Blackpool	H	League Division 2	3–0
1930	Newcastle United	A	League Division 1	0–1
1932	Huddersfield Town	A	League Division 1	0–2

Robert Macauly played his first game for the club.

| 1934 | Sheffield Wednesday | A | League Division 1 | 1–3 |

1935 Stanley Crowther was born in in Bilston. Played for Bilston Town, Aston Villa and Manchester United before joining Chelsea for £10,000 in December 1958. Made 58 appearances over three seasons before a transfer to Brighton and Hove Albion in March 1961.

1938	Leicester City	H	League Division 1	3–0
1949	West Bromwich Albion	A	League Division 1	1–1
1952	Derby County	A	League Division 1	2–3
1955	Portsmouth	H	League Division 1	1–5
1958	Tottenham Hotspur	A	League Division 1	0–4
1960	Bolton Wanderers	A	League Division 1	1–4
1966	Southampton	A	League Division 1	3–0

Goalkeeper Alex Stepney played his one and only game for the club, sandwiched between a £50,000 move from Millwall and a £50,000 move to Manchester United.

1968	Birmingham City	A	League Cup 2nd round	1–0
1977	Ipswich Town	A	League Division 1	0–1
1978	Napoli, Italy	A	Friendly	1–0
1980	Cardiff City	H	League Cup 2nd round	1–1
1983	Brighton & Hove Albion	A	League Division 2	2–1
1988	Bournemouth	A	League Division 2	0–1
1991	Sheffield United	A	League Division 1	1–0

SEPTEMBER 4

| 1905 | Liverpool | H | Friendly | 4–0 |
| 1909 | Liverpool | H | League Division 1 | 2–1 |

Alec Ormiston played his first game for the club.

1915	Clapton Orient	H	London Combination League (Part One)	3–1
1920	Derby County	H	League Division 1	1–1
1922	Stoke City	H	League Division 1	3–2
1926	Port Vale	A	League Division 2	0–0
1933	Huddersfield Town	A	League Division 1	1–6

1935	Stoke City	H	League Division 1	3–5
1937	West Bromwich Albion	A	League Division 1	0–4

1937 Leslie William Allen was born in Dagenham, Essex. After impressing for Briggs Sports (who reached the FA Amateur Cup semi-final in 1954) Les was signed by Chelsea in September 1954 and scored 11 goals in 44 League appearances for the club. These appearances took five years to amass as Les was more often than not stuck in the reserves. According to Bill Nicholson, Chelsea manager Ted Drake approached Spurs with a view to signing the popular Johnny Brooks in an attempt to stave off relegation. Nicholson took a look at Chelsea's reserve team and selected Les Allen, with the pair swapping clubs in a £20,000 deal. It has to be said that Spurs did far better out of this particular deal. An ever-present when Spurs won the 'double' in 1960-61. Allen's Spurs career was effectively ended with the arrival of Alan Gilzean and in 1965 he joined Third Division Queen's Park Rangers for £21,000. There his experience was allied to the up-and-coming talents of Rodney Marsh et al and QPR won the Third Division championship and the League Cup in 1966-67. When Tommy Docherty left the club in 1968 Les took over as player-manager, holding the reigns until 1971 when he left to take over at Woodford Town. He returned to League management with Swindon and then had a spell in Greece before returning to England and working in the car industry. Of course, Les is one part of the exceptional Allen clan, which has seen Les, his son Clive and nephew Paul all play for Spurs and his two other sons Martin and Bradley turned out for QPR, West Ham and and QPR respectively. His brother Dennis played for Charlton, Reading and Bournemouth.

1943	Brighton & Hove Albion	A	Football League South	3–1
1946	Manchester United	H	League Division 1	0–3
1948	Bolton Wanderers	H	League Division 1	2–2
1950	Bolton Wanderers	A	League Division 1	0–1

Bobby Smith, at seventeen years of age, made his League debut.

1954	Cardiff City	H	League Division 1	1–1
1957	Manchester City	A	League Division 1	2–5
1962	Wealdstone	A	Friendly	3–1
1963	Burnley	H	League Division 1	2–0
1965	Arsenal	A	League Division 1	3–1
1971	Coventry City	H	League Division 1	3–3

Chris Garland played his first game for the club.

1976	Millwall	A	League Division 2	0–3
1979	Plymouth Argyle	H	League Cup 2nd round	1–2
1982	Leicester City	H	League Division 2	1–1
1985	Tottenham Hotspur	A	League Division 1	1–4
1996	Arsenal	A	Premier League	3–3

SEPTEMBER 5

1908	Liverpool	A	League Division 1	1–2

1914 Tottenham Hotspur   A   League Division 1   1–1
Debut of Robert Lawrence Abrams and James Croal.
Also the initial appearance of Robert McNeil, born in Glasgow and signed from Hamilton Academical, he went on to play over 300 games for Chelsea and score 32 goals in a career that was disrupted by the First World War. He retired in May 1929 with only a runners-up medal from the 1915 FA Cup final to show for his 15 years in London.

Year	Opponent	H/A	Competition	Score
1921	Birmingham City	A	League Division 1	1–5
1925	Port Vale	A	League Division 2	6–0
1928	Bradford Park Avenue	H	League Division 2	3–1
1931	Huddersfield Town	H	League Division 1	0–1
1936	Birmingham City	H	League Division 1	1–3
1938	Bolton Wanderers	A	League Division 1	2–0
1942	Brighton & Hove Albion	A	Football League South	2–1
1951	Derby County	H	League Division 1	0–1
1953	Sheffield United	H	League Division 1	1–2

Derek Saunders made his debut.

Year	Opponent	H/A	Competition	Score
1955	Blackpool	A	League Division 1	1–2
1956	Manchester United	H	League Division 1	1–2
1959	Burnley	H	League Division 1	4–1
1964	Leicester City	A	League Division 1	1–1
1970	Leeds United	A	League Division 1	0–1
1973	Birmingham City	H	League Division 1	3–1
1981	Cardiff City	A	League Division 2	2–1
1984	Manchester United	A	League Division 1	1–1
1987	Nottingham Forest	A	League Division 1	2–3
1992	Liverpool	A	Premier League	1–2

SEPTEMBER 6

1913 Tottenham Hotspur   H   League Division 1   1–3
Debut of Harold James Halse who had signed for the Blues in May 1913 in a transfer from Aston Villa with whom he had won a League Championship medal. His previous clubs included Clapton Orient, Southend United and Manchester United. He had played 111 games for Chelsea and scored 25 goals when he was transferred to Charlton Athletic (in July 1921) where he finished his playing days. Also the first game played by Thomas Logan.

Year	Opponent	H/A	Competition	Score
1919	Everton	H	League Division 1	0–1
1920	Bolton Wanderers	A	League Division 1	1–3
1924	Oldham Athletic	A	League Division 2	5–0
1926	Notts County	H	League Division 2	2–0
1930	Manchester United	H	League Division 1	6–2
1941	West Ham United	H	London War League	4–8
1947	Huddersfield Town	A	League Division 1	1–3

1952	Bolton Wanderers	A	League Division 1	1–1
1954	Preston North End	H	League Division 1	0–1
1958	Portsmouth	A	League Division 1	2–2
1961	Cardiff City	A	League Division 1	2–5

1963 Patrick Kevin Francis Michael Nevin was born in Glasgow. A Scottish international, Pat joined from Clyde in May 1983 for £95,000 and remained at the Bridge for five years before moving to Everton in July 1988 for £925,000. Instrumental in the promotion campaign of 1984, he played approaching 250 games and scored 45 goals in his Chelsea career. Also won a Full Members Cup winners' medal in 1986. After Everton, he played for Tranmere Rovers before returning to Scottish football.

1967	Sheffield United	H	League Division 1	4–2
1969	Manchester City	A	League Division 1	0–0
1972	Southend United	A	League Cup 2nd round	1–0
1975	Nottingham Forest	H	League Division 2	0–0
1980	West Ham United	H	League Division 2	0–1
1986	Luton Town	H	League Division 1	1–3

SEPTEMBER 7

1907	Sheffield United	H	League Division 1	2–4
1908	Preston North End	A	League Division 1	0–6
1912	Bolton Wanderers	A	League Division 1	0–1

Henry Thomas Ford made his debut for Chelsea having joined from junior club Tunbridge Wells Rangers in April 1912. Stayed at the Bridge all his career until retirement in 1924 and, had it not been for the First World War, would probably have established a club appearance record. As it was he managed to achieve just short of 250 games in which he scored 46 times.

1918	Millwall	A	London Combination League	6–1
1925	Nottingham Forest	H	League Division 2	0–0
1927	Notts County	H	League Division 2	5–0
1929	Oldham Athletic	A	League Division 2	2–4
1932	Portsmouth	H	League Division 1	4–4
1935	Grimsby Town	A	League Division 1	3–1
1940	Brentford	H	Football League South	2–1
1946	Liverpool	A	League Division 1	4–7
1949	Sunderland	H	League Division 1	3–1

1956 Raymond Lewington was born in Lambeth. Joined Chelsea as a schoolboy and progressed to the first team making his debut in February 1976. He eventually totalled 92 matches and 4 goals before manager Danny Blanchflower sold him to Vancouver Whitecaps for £40,000 in February 1979. Later returned to the UK to play for Wimbledon, Fulham and Sheffield United and then went into management and coaching.

1957	Everton	A	League Division 1	0–3
1960	Blackburn Rovers	H	League Division 1	5–2
1963	Liverpool	H	League Division 1	1–3

1966	Leicester City	H	League Division 1	2–2
1968	Everton	H	League Division 1	1–1
1974	Middlesbrough	A	League Division 1	1–1
1983	Blackburn Rovers	A	League Division 2	0–0
1985	Luton Town	A	League Division 1	1–1
1991	West Ham United	A	League Division 1	1–1
1996	Sheffield Wednesday	A	Premier League	2–0

SEPTEMBER 8

| 1906 | Blackpool | A | League Division 2 | 0–0 |

Ted Birnie made his debut.

1913	West Bromwich Albion	H	League Division 1	1–1
1917	Tottenham Hotspur	A	London Combination League	4–0
1923	Aston Villa	H	League Division 1	0–0
1924	Leicester City	H	League Division 2	4–0
1928	Middlesbrough	H	League Division 2	2–0
1930	Sheffield Wednesday	A	League Division 1	1–1
1934	Sunderland	A	League Division 1	0–4
1936	Grimsby Town	A	League Division 1	0–3
1937	Leeds United	H	League Division 1	4–1
1945	Newport County	A	Football League South	3–1
1948	Charlton Athletic	A	League Division 1	1–1
1951	Fulham	H	League Division 1	2–1
1953	Arsenal	A	League Division 1	2–1
1956	Cardiff City	A	League Division 1	1–1
1962	Sunderland	H	League Division 2	1–0
1962	Hounslow Town	A	Friendly	4–1
1971	Plymouth Argyle	H	League Cup 2nd round	2–0
1973	Liverpool	A	League Division 1	0–1
1979	Birmingham City	H	League Division 2	1–2
1982	Derby County	A	League Division 2	0–1
1984	Aston Villa	A	League Division 1	2–4
1990	Sunderland	H	League Division 1	3–2

SEPTEMBER 9

1905	Blackpool	A	League Division 2	1–0
1911	Leeds City	A	League Division 2	0–0
1912	Liverpool	H	League Division 1	1–2
1914	Bradford City	A	League Division 1	2–2
1916	Crystal Palace	H	London Combination League	4–1
1922	Middlesbrough	H	League Division 1	1–1
1931	Sheffield Wednesday	H	League Division 1	2–3
1933	Sheffield United	A	League Division 1	1–4
1935	Stoke City	A	League Division 1	0–3

1944	Brentford	A	Football League South	5–0
1946	Sheffield United	A	League Division 1	2–2

Tommy Walker made his first competitive start for the Blues having earlier appeared in Chelsea colours as a wartime guest.

1950	Newcastle United	A	League Division 1	1–3
1959	Birmingham City	A	League Division 1	1–1
1961	Sheffield United	H	League Division 1	6–1

The day Chelsea 'called for the Doc', Tommy Docherty made his debut as a player for the club.

1964	Sheffield Wednesday	H	League Division 1	1–1
1967	Liverpool	A	League Division 1	1–3
1970	Sheffield Wednesday	A	League Cup 2nd round	1–1
1972	West Ham United	H	League Division 1	1–3

Bill Garner made his first appearance for Chelsea.

1978	Coventry City	A	League Division 1	2–3
1989	Nottingham Forest	H	League Division 1	2–2

SEPTEMBER 10

1910	Barnsley	H	League Division 2	3–1
1919	Sunderland	A	League Division 1	2–3
1921	Manchester United	H	League Division 1	0–0
1927	Fulham	A	League Division 2	1–1
1932	Sheffield United	H	League Division 1	3–0
1938	Middlesbrough	A	League Division 1	1–1
1947	Sunderland	H	League Division 1	1–1
1949	Manchester United	H	League Division 1	1–1
1952	Blackpool	H	League Division 1	4–0

Roy Bentley scored to kick off a run of eight consecutive matches in which he found the back of the net for the Blues.

1955	Sunderland	A	League Division 1	3–4
1958	Newcastle United	H	League Division 1	6–5
1960	West Ham United	H	League Division 1	3–2
1962	Southampton	H	League Division 2	2–0
1966	Sunderland	H	League Division 1	1–1
1968	Coventry City	A	League Division 1	1–0
1975	Crewe Alexandra	A	League Cup 2nd round	0–1
1977	Derby County	H	League Division 1	1–1
1983	Cambridge United	H	League Division 2	2–1
1987	Benjamin Howard Baker died in Warminster.			
1988	Oxford United	H	League Division 2	1–1
1992	Vinnie Jones returned to Wimbledon in a £700,000 move.			
1994	Newcastle United	A	Premier League	2–4

SEPTEMBER 11

1905	Hull City	H	League Division 2	5–1
1909	Aston Villa	A	League Division 1	1–4
1911	Derby County	H	League Division 2	1–0
1915	West Ham United	A	London Combination League (Part One)	0–0
1920	Manchester United	A	League Division 1	1–3
1926	Southampton	H	League Division 2	2–3
1929	Barnsley	H	League Division 2	2–0
1937	Birmingham City	H	League Division 1	2–0
1943	Portsmouth	H	Football League South	6–2
1948	Everton	H	League Division 1	6–0
1954	Manchester City	A	League Division 1	1–1
1957	West Bromwich Albion	H	League Division 1	2–2
1963	Blackburn Rovers	H	League Division 1	1–0
1965	Everton	H	League Division 1	3–1

1970   Little John Spencer was born in Glasgow. Played a handful of games for Glasgow Rangers before moving south to Chelsea for £450,000 in August 1992. An early success, he struggled to find a way into the team when Mark Hughes and Gianluca Vialli became the preferred choice. Thus after approaching 150 games he left to join Queens Park Rangers in the First Division with Chelsea receiving £2,500,000 for his services in November 1996.

1971	West Ham United	A	League Division 1	1–2
1973	Birmingham City	A	League Division 1	4–2
1974	Newport County	H	League Cup 2nd round	4–2
1976	Plymouth Argyle	A	League Division 2	3–2
1982	Newcastle United	A	League Division 2	1–1
1993	Manchester United	H	Premier League	1–0
1995	West Ham United	A	Premier League	3–1

SEPTEMBER 12

1902   David Cameron was born in Borthwick, Middleton. Joined Chelsea from Scottish club Queen's Park in June 1920 but was plagued by injury problems and consequently played only 81 games (2 goals) before returning north of the border to Heart of Midlothian in 1925. Later played for Dunfermline Athletic and Nottingham Forest.

1908	Bury	H	League Division 1	4–1
1914	Newcastle United	H	League Division 1	0–3
1925	Barnsley	H	League Division 2	3–2
1931	Newcastle United	A	League Division 1	1–4
1936	Middlesbrough	A	League Division 1	0–2
1942	Portsmouth	H	Football League South	2–1
1945	Southampton	H	Football League South	1–0
1953	Huddersfield Town	A	League Division 1	1–3
1959	Leeds United	A	League Division 1	1–2
1964	Fulham	H	League Division 1	1–0

1970	Wolverhampton Wanderers	H	League Division 1	2–2
1972	Fortuna Dusseldorf, Germany	A	Friendly	0–0
1981	Watford	H	League Division 2	1–3
1987	Queens Park Rangers	H	League Division 1	1–1
1992	Norwich City	H	Premier League	2–3

SEPTEMBER 13

1913	Oldham Athletic	A	League Division 1	2–3
1919	Newcastle United	H	League Division 1	0–0
1924	Sheffield Wednesday	H	League Division 2	0–0
1926	Notts County	A	League Division 2	0–5
1930	West Ham United	A	League Division 1	1–4
1933	Huddersfield Town	H	League Division 1	2–3

Robert Gregg's first game for the club.

1941	Watford	A	London War League	3–1
1947	Bolton Wanderers	H	League Division 1	1–1

Richard Spence, at the age of 40 years and 57 days, played his final senior game for the club (he continued for another three years at the Bridge before retiring) to set the record as the oldest man ever to appear in a first class match for Chelsea.

1952	Aston Villa	H	League Division 1	4–0
1957				

Mal Donaghy was born in Belfast. Mal signed for Luton in 1978 and enjoyed a ten-year career at Kenilworth Road before a surprising switch to Manchester United for £650,000 in 1988, a big fee for a player over 30 years of age. He spent a brief spell on loan to Luton before signing for Chelsea in 1992 for £100,000.

1958	Aston Villa	H	League Division 1	2–1
1967	Middlesbrough	A	League Cup 2nd round	1–2
1969	Wolverhampton Wanderers	H	League Division 1	2–2
1975	Oldham Athletic	A	League Division 2	1–2
1980	Cambridge United	A	League Division 2	1–0
1983	Gillingham	H	League Cup 1st round	4–0

Pat Nevin made his first appearance for Chelsea.

1986	Tottenham Hotspur	A	League Division 1	3–1
1997	Crystal Palace	A	Premier League	3–0

SEPTEMBER 14

1907	Newcastle United	A	League Division 1	0–1

Debut of Norrie Fairgray.

1912	Sheffield United	H	League Division 1	4–2
1918	Fulham	H	London Combination League	4–2
1929	Millwall	H	League Division 2	3–0
1935	Leeds United	H	League Division 1	1–0

1940	Tottenham Hotspur	A	Football League South	2–3
1946	Leeds United	H	League Division 1	3–0
1955	Newcastle United	H	FA Charity Shield	3–0

The Blues emerged victorious from this prestigious season opener with goals from Bentley, Blunstone and an own goal by McMichael. The most disappointing aspect was that the crowd numbered only 12,802 for a game played at Stamford Bridge.

1956 Ray Wilkins born in Hillingdon in Middlesex. Known by his nickname of 'Butch', Ray was signed by Chelsea straight from school and was their youngest ever captain when appointed at the age of 18. Whilst at Stamford Bridge he made 199 appearances for the Blues and scored 34 goals. In 1979 former Chelsea manager Dave Sexton, by this time occupying the hot seat at Old Trafford, paid £825,000 to take him to Manchester United. The highlight of his United career was the 1983 FA Cup final in which he won a winners' medal, and his performances in midfield alongside Bryan Robson were repeated with England. In July 1984 he was sold to AC Milan for £1.5 million, where he remained for three years before spending a brief spell with Paris St Germain. He returned to Britain with Glasgow Rangers and then came south of the border to play for QPR in 1989. After five years at Loftus Road he joined Crystal Palace but returned six months later as player-manager. He resigned this position in September 1996 and after brief spells playing for Wycombe Wanderers, Hibernian, Millwall and Leyton Orient was appointed manager at Fulham but was relieved from his post toward the end of season 1997–98.

1957	Newcastle United	A	League Division 1	1–1
1963	Aston Villa	A	League Division 1	0–2
1966	Charlton Athletic	H	League Cup 2nd round	5–2
1968	Queens Park Rangers	A	League Division 1	4–0
1974	Arsenal	H	League Division 1	0–0
1985	Southampton	H	League Division 1	2–0

Kevin McAllister made his first appearance.

| 1991 | Leeds United | H | League Division 1 | 0–1 |

SEPTEMBER 15

1906	Bradford City	H	League Division 2	5–1
1917	Crystal Palace	A	London Combination League	3–0
1923	Aston Villa	A	League Division 1	0–0
1928	Barnsley	H	League Division 2	1–0
1930	Sheffield Wednesday	H	League Division 1	0–0

The Chelsea debut of Alexander Skinner Jackson, dubbed the 'Gay Cavalier', and such was his reputation that 51,000 people turned up to watch this match.

1934	Tottenham Hotspur	H	League Division 1	1–3
1937	Grimsby Town	H	League Division 1	1–0
1945	Newport County	H	Football League South	2–0
1951	Huddersfield Town	H	League Division 1	2–1
1952	Blackpool	A	League Division 1	1–3

1953	Arsenal	H	League Division 1	0–2
1954	Preston North End	A	League Division 1	2–1
1956	Birmingham City	H	League Division 1	1–0
1962	Leeds United	A	League Division 2	0–2
1965	Sheffield Wednesday	H	League Division 1	1–1
1971	Jeunesse Hautcharage	A	Cup-Winners' Cup 1st round	8–0

The victory established a record for a Chelsea away win in any competition. It also set up the record aggregate score of 21–0 that resulted after the second leg of the tie. Peter Osgood took advantage of the poor standard of defending to net a hat-trick.

1973	Coventry City	H	League Division 1	1–0
1979	Shrewsbury Town	A	League Division 2	0–3
1984	West Ham United	H	League Division 1	3–0
1990	Arsenal	A	League Division 1	1–4
1994	Viktoria Zizkov	H	Cup-Winners' Cup 1st round	4–2
1996	Aston Villa	H	Premier League	1–1

SEPTEMBER 16

1905	Bradford City	A	League Division 2	1–1
1911	Wolverhampton Wanderers	H	League Division 2	4–0
1916	Brentford	A	London Combination League	3–0
1922	Middlesbrough	A	League Division 1	1–2
1933	Aston Villa	H	League Division 1	1–0
1935	Blackburn Rovers	A	League Division 1	0–1
1936	Liverpool	H	League Division 1	2–0
1939	James Croal died in St Petherton, Somerset.			
1944	Crystal Palace	H	Football League South	8–2
1948	Charlton Athletic	H	League Division 1	2–2
1950	West Bromwich Albion	H	League Division 1	1–1
1959	Birmingham City	H	League Division 1	4–2
1961	West Ham United	A	League Division 1	1–2
1963	Blackburn Rovers	A	League Division 1	2–2
1964	Sheffield Wednesday	A	League Division 1	3–2
1967	Stoke City	H	League Division 1	2–2
1970	Aris Salonika, Greece	A	Cup-Winners' Cup 1st round	1–1
1972	Sheffield United	A	League Division 1	1–2
1978	Manchester City	H	League Division 1	1–4
1989	Tottenham Hotspur	A	League Division 1	4–1
1995	Southampton	H	Premier League	3–0

SEPTEMBER 17

| 1910 | Leicester Fosse | A | League Division 2 | 0–1 |
| 1921 | Manchester United | A | League Division 1 | 0–0 |

1927	Clapton Orient	A	League Division 2	1–2
1932	Wolverhampton Wanderers	A	League Division 1	2–1
1938	Birmingham City	H	League Division 1	2–2
1947	Sunderland	A	League Division 1	3–2

James Bowie made his debut three years after joining the club.

1949	Fulham	A	League Division 1	1–1
1955	Aston Villa	H	League Division 1	0–0
1958	Newcastle United	A	League Division 1	2–1
1960	Fulham	A	League Division 1	2–3
1966	Aston Villa	A	League Division 1	6–2

A day before his 25th birthday, Bobby Tambling cracked five of the six Chelsea goals. Although this was his best match tally, he also scored four goals on four other separate occasions.

1969	Burnley	H	League Division 1	2–0
1977	Manchester United	A	League Division 1	1–0
1979	Manchester United	H	Testimonial	5–3
1983	Sheffield Wednesday	A	League Division 2	1–2
1988	Barnsley	A	League Division 2	1–1

SEPTEMBER 18

1909	Sheffield United	H	League Division 1	2–2
1915	Watford	H	London Combination League (Part One)	1–0
1920	Manchester United	H	League Division 1	1–2

Chelsea debut of Frederick Barrett.

1926	Bradford City	A	League Division 2	1–0

First appearance made by Thomas Law.

1937	Middlesbrough	A	League Division 1	3–4

1941 Robert Victor Tambling was born in Storrington, Sussex. Without doubt one of the great names in Chelsea folklore, he joined the club as a fifteen-year-old and made his debut in the first team at the age of seventeen. He made 370 appearances for the Blues and scored 202 goals, a tally that established him as the most prolific goalscorer in Chelsea's history although, had he stayed longer, Jimmy Greaves may well have challenged this record. He was transferred to Crystal Palace in January 1970 for £40,000 and thereafter played for Cork Celtic, Waterford and Shamrock Rovers.

1942 Alex Stepney was born in Mitcham in Surrey. Signed by Millwall as an amateur from Tooting & Mitcham he spent three seasons at the Den before a £50,000 fee took him to Chelsea. It emerged that the Blues had only signed Stepney as there was a doubt over Peter Bonetti's future at the club but this was soon resolved. Four months and just one appearance later, Stepney was on the move again as Matt Busby paid £55,000, then a record for a goalkeeper, to take him to Old Trafford. At the end of his first season with Manchester United he won a championship medal, and in May 1968 appeared at Wembley twice within a week, collecting his one and only England cap on the 22nd and a European Cup winners' medal with the Reds on the 29th. He left United in February 1979 and played for a spell in America, returning briefly to Altrincham as player-coach before finishing his playing career back in America.

1943	Brentford	A	Football League South	1–3
1946	Manchester United	A	League Division 1	1–1
1948	Preston North End	A	League Division 1	2–3
1954	Everton	H	League Division 1	0–2
1957	West Bromwich Albion	A	League Division 1	1–1
1965	Manchester United	A	League Division 1	1–4
1968	Greenock Morton	H	Fairs Cup 1st round	5–0
1971	Derby County	H	League Division 1	1–1
1976	Bolton Wanderers	H	League Division 2	2–1
1982	Oldham Athletic	H	League Division 2	2–0

David Speedie played his first game for the club.

1991	Aston Villa	H	League Division 1	2–0
1993	Coventry City	A	Premier League	1–1
1994	Blackburn Rovers	H	Premier League	1–2
1996	Blackpool	A	League Cup 2nd round	1–1
1997	Slovan Bratislava	H	Cup-Winners' Cup 1st round	2–0

SEPTEMBER 19

1908	Sheffield United	A	League Division 1	3–1
1914	Middlesbrough	A	League Division 1	0–3
1925	Clapton Orient	A	League Division 2	2–1
1931	Aston Villa	H	League Division 1	3–6
1936	West Bromwich Albion	H	League Division 1	3–0
1942	Brentford	A	Football League South	2–0
1945	Derby County	H	Football League South	3–0
1953	Aston Villa	H	League Division 1	1–2
1956	Sheffield Wednesday	H	League Division 1	0–0
1959	West Ham United	H	League Division 1	2–4
1960	Blackburn Rovers	A	League Division 1	1–3

1960 Michael Fillery was born in Mitcham. Joined the club from school and graduated to the professional staff in August 1978. Made 181 appearances (scoring 41 goals) the majority of which were in the Second Division. He was transferred to Queens Park Rangers for £200,000 in August 1983 and subsequently played for Portsmouth, Oldham and Millwall.

1962	Southampton	A	League Division 2	1–2
1964	Leeds United	H	League Division 1	2–0
1970	Coventry City	A	League Division 1	1–0
1981	Shrewsbury Town	A	League Division 2	0–1
1987	Norwich City	A	League Division 1	0–3
1989	Scarborough	H	League Cup 2nd round	1–1

| 1995 | Stoke City | A | League Cup 2nd round | 0–0 |

SEPTEMBER 20

1913	Manchester United	H	League Division 1	0–2
1919	Newcastle United	A	League Division 1	0–3
1924	Clapton Orient	A	League Division 2	0–0
1930	Bolton Wanderers	H	League Division 1	0–1
1941	Aldershot	H	London War League	4–0
1947	Everton	H	League Division 1	3–1
1952	Sunderland	A	League Division 1	1–2
1954	Sheffield United	A	League Division 1	2–1
1958	West Ham United	A	League Division 1	2–4
1961	Cardiff City	H	League Division 1	2–3
1967	Clydebank	A	Friendly	4–1
1969	Leeds United	A	League Division 1	0–2
1975	Bristol City	H	League Division 2	1–1
1976	Huddersfield Town	H	League Cup 3rd round	2–0
1980	Preston North End	H	League Division 2	1–1
1986	Nottingham Forest	H	League Division 1	2–6
1988	Manchester City	H	League Division 2	1–3
1992	Manchester City	A	Premier League	1–0

SEPTEMBER 21

1907	Nottingham Forest	A	League Division 1	0–6
1908	Nottingham Forest	H	League Division 1	2–1
1912	Newcastle United	A	League Division 1	2–3
1929	Southampton	A	League Division 2	2–4
1931	Sheffield Wednesday	A	League Division 1	2–2
1935	West Bromwich Albion	A	League Division 1	2–1
1940	Tottenham Hotspur	H	Football League South	4–1
1946	Grimsby Town	A	League Division 1	1–2
1957	Burnley	H	League Division 1	6–1
1963	Tottenham Hotspur	H	League Division 1	0–3
1968	West Ham United	H	League Division 1	1–1
1974	Ipswich Town	A	League Division 1	0–2
1985	Arsenal	H	League Division 1	2–1

Mickey Hazard made his Chelsea debut.

1991	Queens Park Rangers	A	League Division 1	2–2
1994	Bournemouth	H	League Cup 2nd round	1–0
1996	Liverpool	A	Premier League	1–5
1997	Arsenal	H	Premier League	2–3

SEPTEMBER 22

| 1906 | West Bromwich Albion | A | League Division 2 | 2–1 |

1917	Brentford	H	London Combination League	3–1
1923	Sheffield United	H	League Division 1	1–1
1924	Stoke City	A	League Division 2	0–1
1928	Bristol City	A	League Division 2	0–0
1934	Preston North End	A	League Division 1	0–2

1942 Albert Murray was born in Shoreditch. He signed professional forms in May 1961 having served for three years in the Chelsea junior ranks. He amassed 183 appearances and scored 44 goals in the next five years then, in August 1966, moved to Birmingham City in a £25,000 deal. Later appeared for Brighton and Hove Albion and Peterborough United.

1945	Wolverhampton Wanderers	H	Football League South	1–1
1951	Wolverhampton Wanderers	A	League Division 1	3–5
1956	West Bromwich Albion	A	League Division 1	1–2
1962	Swansea Town	H	League Division 2	2–2
1965	AS Roma, Italy	H	Fairs Cup 1st round	4–1
1970	Sheffield Wednesday	H	League Cup 2nd round replay	2–1
1973	Manchester City	A	League Division 1	2–3
1979	Watford	H	League Division 2	2–0
1984	Luton Town	A	League Division 1	0–0
1990	Manchester City	H	League Division 1	1–1
1993	West Bromwich Albion	A	League Division 2	1–1

SEPTEMBER 23

1905	West Bromwich Albion	H	League Division 2	1–0
1907	Newcastle United	H	League Division 1	2–0

Goalkeeper Jack Whiteley played his first game for the club having been elected to take over from 'Pom-Pom' Whiting. He was an experienced custodian having spent time with Aston Villa, Everton, Stoke, Leeds City and Lincoln City before arriving at the Bridge in the summer of 1907. He retired from playing in 1914 after 138 games for Chelsea but remained on the staff and was trainer until 1939.

1911	Leicester Fosse	A	League Division 2	0–2
1916	Southampton	H	London Combination League	3–0
1922	Oldham Athletic	H	League Division 1	4–0
1929	Bury	H	League Division 2	5–3
1933	Leicester City	A	League Division 1	1–1

1934 John Mortimore was born in Farnborough. He was an amateur at Aldershot prior to joining Chelsea in August 1957 to carve a career that saw him make 279 appearances and score 10 goals over an eight year period. He moved on to Queens Park Rangers in September 1965 for £8,000 and later played for Sunderland.

1935 Ronald Albert Ernest Tindall was born in Streatham. He was a member of the Chelsea office staff when spotted by Ted Drake, turning professional in April 1953. He played 174 competitive senior games for the Blues and scored 69 times in a career that lasted until a part-exchange deal for Andy Malcolm took him to West Ham United in November 1961. Subsequently transferred to Reading and Portsmouth before emigrating to Australia.

1944	Charlton Athletic	A	Football League South	3–0
1950	Stoke City	A	League Division 1	1–2
1961	Blackburn Rovers	H	League Division 1	1–1
1964	Birmingham City	A	League Cup 2nd round	3–0
1967	Nottingham Forest	A	League Division 1	0–3

1970 Damian Matthew was born in Islington. Joined from trainee and played 27 games before moving to Crystal Palace for £150,000. Later with Bristol Rovers (on loan) and Burnley.

1972	Ipswich Town	H	League Division 1	2–0
1975	Portsmouth	A	League Division 2	1–1
1978	Birmingham City	A	League Division 1	1–1
1981	Charlton Athletic	H	League Division 2	2–2
1986	York City	A	League Cup 2nd round	0–1
1987	Reading	A	League Cup 2nd round	1–3
1989	Coventry City	H	League Division 1	1–0
1992	Walsall	A	League Cup 2nd round	3–0

SEPTEMBER 24

1910	Wolverhampton Wanderers	H	League Division 2	2–0
1921	Liverpool	H	League Division 1	0–1
1927	West Bromwich Albion	H	League Division 2	1–1
1932	Newcastle United	H	League Division 1	0–1
1938	Manchester United	A	League Division 1	1–5
1949	Stoke City	A	League Division 1	3–2
1955	Wolverhampton Wanderers	A	League Division 1	1–2
1960	Blackpool	A	League Division 1	4–1
1966	Arsenal	H	League Division 1	3–1
1969	Leeds United	A	League Cup 3rd round	1–1

1971 Craig Burley was born in Ayr. He joined Chelsea from school and graduated through the ranks making his first-team debut in April 1991. Strangely he seemed more assured of his place in the Scottish international side than in the Chelsea first team and this fact probably lead to his decision to return north of the border. He made just under 150 appearances at Stamford Bridge but was obviously looked upon primarily as a squad member. Discarded by Ruud Gullit, he joined Celtic with whom he won a League Championship medal in 1997–98.

1977	Queens Park Rangers	A	League Division 1	1–1
1983	Middlesbrough	H	League Division 2	0–0
1988	Leeds United	A	League Division 2	2–0
1994	Crystal Palace	A	Premier League	1–0

| 1995 | Newcastle United | A | Premier League | 0–2 |
| 1997 | Manchester United | A | Premier League | 2–2 |

SEPTEMBER 25

1909	Woolwich Arsenal	A	League Division 1	2–3
1915	Tottenham Hotspur	A	London Combination League (Part One)	3–1
1920	Burnley	A	League Division 1	0–4
1926	Fulham	H	League Division 2	2–2
1937	Stoke City	H	League Division 1	2–1
1943	Fulham	H	Football League South	3–0
1948	Burnley	H	League Division 1	1–0
1954	Newcastle United	A	League Division 1	3–1
1963	Swindon Town	A	League Division 2	0–3

Marvin Hinton and John Hollins made their debuts for the club.

1965	Newcastle United	H	League Division 1	1–1
1968	Derby County	H	League Cup 3rd round	0–0
1971	Sheffield United	A	League Division 1	0–1

Steve Kember's first appearance.

| 1974 | Derby County | A | League Division 1 | 1–4 |

John Hollins remarkable run of 167 consecutive appearances, which had begun in August 1971, came to an end. The run comprised 135 Football League, 10 FA Cup, 18 Football League Cup and 4 European Cup-Winners' Cup matches.

1976	Blackpool	A	League Division 2	1–0
1982	Sheffield Wednesday	A	League Division 2	2–3
1985	Mansfield Town	A	League Cup 2nd round	2–2
1991	Tranmere Rovers	H	League Cup 2nd round	1–1
1993	Liverpool	H	Premier League	1–0
1996	Blackpool	H	League Cup 2nd round	1–3

SEPTEMBER 26

1896 John Forsyth Crawford was born in Jarrow. After serving in the Navy during the First World War, Crawford spent a period of about three and a half years at Hull City before coming to London to join the Blues in a deal worth £3,000 in May 1923. Gave Chelsea great reward by emerging as one of the best wingers ever to play for the club, making over 300 appearances and scoring 26 goals. Finished his playing days at Queens Park Rangers to whom he was transferred in May 1934.

1908	Aston Villa	H	League Division 1	0–2
1914	Sheffield United	H	League Division 1	1–1
1925	Fulham	H	League Division 2	4–0
1931	Leicester City	A	League Division 1	0–1
1936	Manchester City	A	League Division 1	0–0

1939 Melvyn Scott was born in Claygate. A player who graduated through the youth system to make over 100 appearances at the heart of the Blues' defence during a seven-year period from 1956 to 1963, when he transferred to Brentford for £100,000. Finished his career playing in the USA.

1942	Fulham	H	Football League South	4–2
1953	Wolverhampton Wanderers	A	League Division 1	1–8

This was Chelsea's heaviest defeat in the top division (although the margin of seven goals has been equalled in two 0–7 defeats).

1955	Aberdeen	A	Friendly	3–4
1956	Luton Town	A	Southern Floodlight Cup 1st round	2–4

This was Chelsea's first and last appearance in a competition that proved popular with most professional teams in the south and south-east of England and continued (without the Blues) for several more years.

1959	Fulham	A	League Division 1	3–1
1964	Arsenal	A	League Division 1	3–1
1970	Ipswich Town	H	League Division 1	2–1
1978	New York Cosmos	H	Friendly	1–1
1981	Norwich City	H	League Division 2	2–1
1984	Millwall	H	League Cup 2nd round	3–1
1987	Watford	H	League Division 1	1–1
1990	Walsall	A	League Cup 2nd round	5–0
1992	Nottingham Forest	H	Premier League	0–0

SEPTEMBER 27

1913	Burnley	A	League Division 1	1–6
1919	Burnley	H	League Division 1	0–1
1924	Crystal Palace	H	League Division 2	2–2
1930	Liverpool	A	League Division 1	1–3
1941	Millwall	A	London War League	3–6

1941 Peter Phillip Bonetti was born in Putney. Brilliant goalkeeper dubbed 'the Cat' during his two periods at the club spanning over twenty years, in which he made 728 senior appearances. He won an FA Cup winners' medal in 1970, Football League Cup winners' medal in 1966 and a European Cup-Winners' Cup medal in 1971. He was also capped by England at full international level seven times. Sandwiched in between his two spells with the Blues was a brief interlude with the St Louis Stars in the USA and after his Chelsea career came to a close, he briefly played on with Dundee United. Eventually returned to the Bridge as goalkeeping coach.

1947	Wolverhampton Wanderers	A	League Division 1	0–1
1952	Wolverhampton Wanderers	H	League Division 1	1–2
1958	Nottingham Forest	H	League Division 1	4–1
1969	Arsenal	H	League Division 1	3–0
1975	Fulham	A	League Division 2	0–2
1980	Watford	A	League Division 2	3–2

| 1988 | Scunthorpe United | A | League Division 2 | 1–4 |
| 1997 | Newcastle United | H | Premier League | 1–0 |

SEPTEMBER 28

1907	Manchester United	H	League Division 1	1–4
1912	Oldham Athletic	H	League Division 1	1–1
1929	Tottenham Hotspur	H	League Division 2	3–0
1935	Sunderland	H	League Division 1	3–1
1946	Charlton Athletic	H	League Division 1	2–2
1957	Preston North End	A	League Division 1	2–5
1963	Wolverhampton Wanderers	A	League Division 1	1–4
1968	Burnley	A	League Division 1	1–2
1974	Wolverhampton Wanderers	H	League Division 1	0–1
1981	Orient	A	League Division 2	2–0
1985	Watford	A	League Division 1	1–3
1986	Manchester United	A	League Division 1	1–0
1991	Everton	H	League Division 1	2–2
1996	Nottingham Forest	H	Premier League	1–1

SEPTEMBER 29

1906	Leicester Fosse	H	League Division 2	1–0
1917	Arsenal	A	London Combination League	1–0
1923	Sheffield United	A	League Division 1	0–1
1928	Nottingham Forest	H	League Division 2	3–0
1934	Grimsby Town	H	League Division 1	2–0
1945	Wolverhampton Wanderers	A	Football League South	0–1
1951	Sunderland	H	League Division 1	2–1
1956	Portsmouth	H	League Division 1	3–3
1962	Portsmouth	A	League Division 2	2–0
1971	Jeunesse Hautcharage	H	Cup-Winners' Cup 1st round	13–0

Not surprisingly, Chelsea's biggest win in European competition. Peter Osgood helped himself to five goals, whilst Tommy Baldwin notched a hat-trick. The aggregate sore for the tie finished 21–0 in the Blues' favour!

1973	Wolverhampton Wanderers	H	League Division 1	2–2
1979	Cambridge United	A	League Division 2	1–0
1984	Leicester City	H	League Division 1	3–0
1990	Sheffield United	H	League Division 1	2–2
1994	Viktoria Zizkov	A	Cup-Winners' Cup 1st round	0–0

SEPTEMBER 30

1905	Leicester Fosse	A	League Division 2	1–0
1911	Gainsborough Trinity	H	League Division 2	1–0
1916	Arsenal	H	London Combination League	3–0
1922	Oldham Athletic	A	League Division 1	0–2
1933	Tottenham Hotspur	H	League Division 1	0–4

Albert Edward Thain played his first game for Chelsea.

1944	Clapton Orient	H	Football League South	5–0
1950	Everton	H	League Division 1	2–1
1958	Frem, Copenhagen	A	Fairs Cup 1st round	3–1
1961	Blackpool	A	League Division 1	0–4
1964	Manchester United	H	League Division 1	0–2
1967	Coventry City	H	League Division 1	1–1
1968	Greenock Morton	A	Fairs Cup 1st round	4–3
1970	Aris Salonika, Greece	H	Cup-Winners' Cup 1st round	5–1
1972	Coventry City	A	League Division 1	3–1

First appearance of Gary Locke.

1978	West Bromwich Albion	H	League Division 1	1–3
1989	Arsenal	H	League Division 1	1–1
1995	Arsenal	H	Premier League	1–0

OCTOBER 1

1910	Bolton Wanderers	H	League Division 2	3–0
1921	Liverpool	A	League Division 1	1–1
1927	Bristol City	A	League Division 2	1–1
1932	Aston Villa	A	League Division 1	1–3
1938	Stoke City	H	League Division 1	1–1
1949	Burnley	H	League Division 1	0–1
1955	Manchester City	H	League Division 1	2–1
1960	Everton	H	League Division 1	3–3
1966	Manchester City	A	League Division 1	4–1

Tommy Baldwin's Chelsea debut.

1968 Paul Furlong was born in Wood Green. He was picked up from non-League Enfield by Coventry City for £130,000 in July 1991 but despite making over 40 appearances in a year-long stay in the Midlands, moved to Watford for almost double the fee. Chelsea paid £2,300,000 to sign him in May 1994 but he was a disappointment at the Bridge and having made 84 outings in the Chelsea colours, the club cut their losses on him with a £1.5 million transfer to Birmingham City.

1977	Leeds United	H	League Division 1	1–2
1983	Huddersfield Town	A	League Division 2	3–2
1988	Leicester City	H	League Division 2	2–1

David Lee played his first game for the club.

OCTOBER 2

1909	Bolton Wanderers	H	League Division 1	3–2
1915	Millwall	H	London Combination League (Part One)	2–2
1920	Burnley	H	League Division 1	1–1
1926	Preston North End	H	League Division 2	2–1

Goalkeeper Simeon Millington made his League debut. In a career cut short by injury, he served between January 1926 and retirement in 1932, making 245 starts for the club.

1937	Portsmouth	A	League Division 1	4–2
1943	Charlton Athletic	A	Football League South	1–0
1948	Stoke City	A	League Division 1	3–4
1954	West Bromwich Albion	H	League Division 1	3–3
1963	Manchester United	H	League Division 1	1–1
1965	West Bromwich Albion	A	League Division 1	2–1
1968	Derby County	A	League Cup 3rd round replay	1–3

Ian Hutchinson played his first game for the club.

1971	Wolverhampton Wanderers	H	League Division 1	3–1
1976	Cardiff City	H	League Division 2	2–1
1982	Grimsby Town	H	League Division 2	5–2
1985	Portsmouth	H	Full Members Cup Group Match	3–0
1993	West Ham United	A	Premier League	0–1
1994	West Ham United	H	Premier League	1–2
1997	Slovan Bratislava	A	Cup-Winners' Cup 1st round	2–0

OCTOBER 3

1908	Nottingham Forest	A	League Division 1	1–2
1914	Aston Villa	A	League Division 1	1–2
1925	Hull City	H	League Division 2	4–0
1931	Liverpool	H	League Division 1	2–0
1936	Portsmouth	H	League Division 1	1–1
1942	West Ham United	A	Football League South	1–0
1953	Sunderland	H	League Division 1	2–2

1956 Stephen John Wicks was born in Reading. His Chelsea career came in two parts, the first commencing June 1974 when, after graduating through the junior ranks, he signed as a professional. He made his debut in March of the following year and went on to claim a regular first team place whilst still a teenager. He was transferred to Derby County for £275,000 in January 1979 and subsequently moved to Queens Park Rangers, Crystal Palace and QPR (for a second time) before returning to the Bridge in July 1986. It took £450,000 to bring him 'home' but his time was curtailed by a serious injury that forced his retirement in July 1988. His aggregate appearance record for Chelsea reached 172 games.

1959	West Bromwich Albion	A	League Division 1	3–1

1959 Michael William Nutton was born in St. Johns Wood. Another product of the youth set-up he signed as a professional in October 1977 and was in and out of the first team over six years without ever making a real breakthrough that would establish him as a regular. He made 83 appearances before being transferred to Millwall in March 1983.

1960	Guilford City	A	Friendly	4–2
1964	Blackburn Rovers	H	League Division 1	5–1
1970	Liverpool	A	League Division 1	0–1
1981	Cambridge United	A	League Division 2	0–1
1987	Newcastle United	A	League Division 1	1–3
1992	Arsenal	A	Premier League	1–2

OCTOBER 4

1913	Preston North End	H	League Division 1	2–0
1919	Burnley	A	League Division 1	3–2
1924	Southampton	A	League Division 2	0–0
1927	Notts County	A	League Division 2	1–0
1930	Middlesbrough	H	League Division 1	4–0
1941	Arsenal	A	London War League	0–3
1947	Aston Villa	H	League Division 1	4–2

Robert Inglis Campbell scored twice on his debut for the Blues.

| 1952 | Charlton Athletic | A | League Division 1 | 2–2 |

Debut of James Lewis.

1958	Burnley	A	League Division 1	0–4
1969	Sunderland	A	League Division 1	0–0
1972	Derby County	A	League Cup 3rd round	0–0
1975	York City	H	League Division 2	0–0
1980	Bolton Wanderers	A	League Division 2	3–2
1986	Charlton Athletic	H	League Division 1	0–1
1988	Walsall	H	League Division 2	2–0
1989	Scarborough	A	League Cup 2nd round	2–3
1994	Bournemouth	A	League Cup 2nd round	1–0
1995	Stoke City	H	League Cup 2nd round	0–1

OCTOBER 5

1907	Blackburn Rovers	A	League Division 1	0–2
1912	Sunderland	H	League Division 1	2–0
1918	Tottenham Hotspur	A	London Combination League	1–2
1929	West Bromwich Albion	A	League Division 2	0–2
1935	Birmingham City	A	League Division 1	1–2
1940	West Ham United	H	Football League South	1–1
1946	Middlesbrough	A	League Division 1	2–3
1954	Brentford	A	Friendly	4–0
1957	Sheffield Wednesday	H	League Division 1	1–0

1962 Kevin Hitchcock was born in Custom House, London. Began with non-League

Barking before joining Nottingham Forest and then Mansfield Town from where Chelsea signed him for £250,000 in March 1988. Although unable to command a regular first-team place, Hitch has remained at the club and proved a reliable deputy when called on to perform between the sticks. Season 1997–98 saw him given a testimonial match as reward for 10 years of service that have seen him make over 100 appearances.

1963	Stoke City	H	League Division 1	3–3
1966	Blackpool	A	League Cup 3rd round	1–1
1968	Ipswich Town	H	League Division 1	3–1
1974	Manchester City	A	League Division 1	1–1
1976	Bristol Rovers	A	League Division 2	1–2
1977	Leicester City	H	League Division 1	0–0
1983	Leicester City	A	League Cup 2nd round	2–0
1985	Manchester City	A	League Division 1	1–0
1991	Arsenal	A	League Division 1	2–3
1997	Liverpool	A	Premier League	2–4

OCTOBER 6

| 1906 | Nottingham Forest | A | League Division 2 | 1–3 |
| 1917 | West Ham United | H | London Combination League | 4–3 |

1919 Tommy Lawton was born in Bolton. One of the most famous names in English football, he signed for Chelsea at the end of the Second World War (November 1945) for £11,500 having already established his reputation with Bolton Wanderers, Sheffield Wednesday, Burnley and Everton. He managed to play just 53 matches and score 35 goals before departing, after a dispute with the Chelsea management, to Notts County in the Third Division for a then record £20,000 transfer fee. Later played for Brentford and Arsenal.

1923	Cardiff City	H	League Division 1	1–2
1928	West Bromwich Albion	A	League Division 2	0–3
1934	Everton	A	League Division 1	2–3

Richard Spence played the first game of his epic Chelsea career.

1945	West Ham United	A	Football League South	4–2
1951	Middlesbrough	A	League Division 1	2–2
1956	Tottenham Hotspur	H	League Division 1	2–4
1962	Cardiff City	H	League Division 2	6–0
1965	AS Roma, Italy	A	Fairs Cup 1st round	0–0
1969	Leeds United	H	League Cup 3rd round replay	2–0
1971	Nottingham Forest	A	League Cup 3rd round	1–1
1973	Queens Park Rangers	A	League Division 1	1–1
1979	Burnley	A	League Division 2	1–0
1981	Southampton	A	League Cup 2nd round	1–1

Steve Francis made his debut.

| 1982 | Tranmere Rovers | H | League Cup 2nd round | 3–1 |
| 1984 | Norwich City | A | League Division 1 | 0–0 |

| 1990 | Southampton | A | League Division 1 | 3–3 |
| 1993 | West Bromwich Albion | H | League Division 2 | 2–1 |

OCTOBER 7

1905	1st Grenadiers	H	FA Cup 1st Preliminary round	6–1
1911	Grimsby Town	A	League Division 2	1–2
1916	Luton Town	A	London Combination League	4–1
1922	Sheffield United	H	League Division 1	0–0
1933	Liverpool	A	League Division 1	0–3
1944	Portsmouth	A	Football League South	5–1
1950	Blackpool	A	League Division 1	2–3
1961	Sheffield Wednesday	A	League Division 1	3–5
1964	Benfica, Portugal	H	Friendly	2–4
1967	Leeds United	A	League Division 1	0–7

This defeat was by the heaviest margin inflicted upon the Blues (although a previous 1–8 reverse to Wolverhampton Wanderers in 1953 rates worse) in the top division of the Football League. It was later equalled at Nottingham Forest in April 1991.

1970	Middlesbrough	H	League Cup 3rd round	3–2
1972	Birmingham City	A	League Division 1	2–2
1978	Derby County	A	League Division 1	0–1
1985	Mansfield Town	H	League Cup 2nd round	2–0
1987	Reading	H	League Cup 2nd round	3–2
1992	Walsall	H	League Cup 2nd round	1–0

OCTOBER 8

1888 Jack Henry Harrow was born in Beddington. Came to Chelsea in March 1911 from Croydon Common for the sum of £50 and stayed until his retirement in 1926. He won two England international caps and made 333 appearances for the Blues, joining the training staff thereafter until 1938.

1910	Clapton Orient	A	League Division 2	0–0
1921	Newcastle United	H	League Division 1	1–1
1927	Stoke City	H	League Division 2	1–0
1932	Middlesbrough	H	League Division 1	2–1
1938	Blackpool	A	League Division 1	1–5
1949	Manchester City	H	League Division 1	3–0
1955	Charlton Athletic	A	League Division 1	2–1
1956	Reading	A	Friendly	2–2
1966	Burnley	H	League Division 1	1–3
1973	Stoke City	A	League Cup 2nd round	0–1
1977	Liverpool	A	League Division 1	0–2
1980	Bristol Rovers	H	League Division 2	2–0
1983	Fulham	A	League Division 2	5–3
1986	York City	H	League Cup 2nd round	3–0
1991	Tranmere Rovers	A	League Cup 2nd round	1–3

1994	Leicester City	H	Premier League	4–0

OCTOBER 9

1909	Middlesbrough	A	League Division 1	1–0
1915	Crystal Palace	A	London Combination League (Part One)	5–1
1920	Tottenham Hotspur	A	League Division 1	0–5
1926	South Shields	A	League Division 2	1–5
1937	Arsenal	H	League Division 1	2–2
1943	Aldershot	A	Football League South	3–1
1948	Liverpool	A	League Division 1	1–1
1954	Huddersfield Town	A	League Division 1	0–1
1965	Blackpool	H	League Division 1	0–1
1968	Sheffield Wednesday	A	League Division 1	1–1
1971	Liverpool	A	League Division 1	0–0
1972	Derby County	H	League Cup 3rd round replay	3–2
1974	Stoke City	H	League Cup 3rd round	2–2
1982	Leeds United	H	League Division 2	0–0
1984	Millwall	A	League Cup 2nd round	1–1
1988	Swindon Town	A	League Division 2	1–1

OCTOBER 10

1908	Sunderland	H	League Division 1	2–0
1914	Liverpool	H	League Division 1	3–1
1925	Darlington	A	League Division 2	1–1
1931	Grimsby Town	A	League Division 1	2–1

1934 Richard Whittaker was born in Dublin. Although he never made a breakthrough to a regular berth in the first team, Whittaker was nevertheless a dependable stand-in when called upon to perform as a deputy. He made 51 appearances over the course of eight years, arriving in May 1952 from junior football in Ireland and eventually departing to Peterborough United in July 1960. Later with Queens Park Rangers.

1936	Preston North End	A	League Division 1	0–1
1942	Aldershot	H	Football League South	1–3
1953	Sheffield Wednesday	A	League Division 1	0–2
1955	Leeds United	A	Friendly	1–1
1959	Bolton Wanderers	H	League Division 1	0–2
1960	Millwall	A	League Cup 1st round	7–1
1964	Nottingham Forest	A	League Division 1	2–2
1970	Manchester City	H	League Division 1	1–1
1981	Wrexham	H	League Division 2	2–0
1987	Everton	H	League Division 1	0–0
1990	Walsall	H	League Cup 2nd round	4–1

OCTOBER 11

1880 James Sharp was born in Jordanstone. Chelsea was the last club for the vastly experienced Sharp, the outbreak of the First World War putting the final nail in the coffin of a career that was winding down after time with Dundee, Fulham, Woolwich Arsenal and Glasgow Rangers. He notched up 64 games for Chelsea.

1913	Newcastle United	A	League Division 1	0–1
1919	Liverpool	H	League Division 1	1–0
1924	Fulham	H	League Division 2	0–0
1930	Huddersfield Town	A	League Division 1	1–1
1941	Queens Park Rangers	A	London War League	1–2
1947	Liverpool	A	League Division 1	0–3
1952	Preston North End	H	League Division 1	5–3
1954	Hull City	A	Friendly	3–0
1958	Bolton Wanderers	H	League Division 1	0–1
1969	Derby County	H	League Division 1	2–2
1971	Nottingham Forest	H	League Cup 3rd round replay	2–1
1975	Southampton	A	League Division 2	1–4
1980	Grimsby Town	H	League Division 2	3–0
1986	West Ham United	A	League Division 1	3–5
1992	Le Havre	H	Cross Channel Tournament	3–1

OCTOBER 12

1907	Bolton Wanderers	H	League Division 1	1–3

John Cameron made his debut for the Blues. He had signed just days before in a deal that cost Chelsea £900 from Blackburn Rovers (having previously played for St Mirren) and stayed for six years, during which time he amassed just under 200 appearances. He made a second and final appearance for Scotland against England in 1908–09 and departed for Burslem Port Vale in July 1931.

1912	Woolwich Arsenal	A	League Division 1	1–0
1918	Clapton Orient	H	London Combination League	6–0
1929	Bradford Park Avenue	H	League Division 2	1–2
1935	Arsenal	H	League Division 1	1–1
1940	Queens Park Rangers	A	Football League South	3–2
1946	Stoke City	H	League Division 1	2–5
1957	Aston Villa	H	League Division 1	4–2
1963	Ipswich Town	A	League Division 1	3–1
1968	Wolverhampton Wanderers	A	League Division 1	1–1
1970	Fulham	A	Testimonial	2–0
1974	Tottenham Hotspur	H	League Division 1	1–0
1985	Everton	H	League Division 1	2–1
1988	Scunthorpe United	H	League Division 2	2–2
1996	Leicester City	A	Premier League	3–1

OCTOBER 13

1906	Lincoln City	H	League Division 2	2–0

1917	Fulham	A	London Combination League	1–1
1923	Cardiff City	A	League Division 1	1–1
1928	Clapton Orient	H	League Division 2	2–2
1934	Huddersfield Town	H	League Division 1	2–1
1945	West Ham United	H	Football League South	1–2
1951	West Bromwich Albion	H	League Division 1	1–3
1956	Everton	A	League Division 1	3–0
1962	Huddersfield Town	A	League Division 2	0–1
1965	AC & Inter Milan XI	A	Friendly	1–2
1973	Ipswich Town	H	League Division 1	2–3
1979	Bristol Rovers	H	League Division 2	1–0
1984	Watford	H	League Division 1	2–3

OCTOBER 14

1905	Lincoln City	A	League Division 2	4–1
1911	Nottingham Forest	H	League Division 2	2–0
1916	Reading	H	London Combination League	6–0
1922	Sheffield United	A	League Division 1	2–0
1933	Middlesbrough	H	League Division 1	2–3

1942 The birth of a Chelsea legend, Charlie Cooke, who was born in St Monace, Fife. A mercurial winger who started his career at Aberdeen, moved to Dundee and finally arrived at Chelsea in April 1966 for a fee of £72,000. He was sold to Crystal Palace in 1972 for £85,000 but stayed only 16 months before returning to the Bridge for a second spell in a cut-price £17,000 deal. When he departed Chelsea for good it was to embark on a career in the USA which saw him play for Los Angeles Aztecs (1976), Memphis Rogues (1978) and California Surf (1981). Charlie won 16 full Scottish international caps, an FA Cup winners' medal in 1970 and a European Cup-Winners' Cup medal in 1971. He appeared 373 times in a Chelsea shirt and scored 30 goals.

1944	Tottenham Hotspur	A	Football League South	5–1
1950	Tottenham Hotspur	H	League Division 1	0–2
1951	Racing Club Paris	A	Friendly	2–1
1961	Leicester City	H	League Division 1	1–3

1965 Keith Jones was born in Dulwich. Signed professional forms in August 1983 several months after having made his first team debut. However, he failed to fulfil his early promise and despite gaining several spells of first team action departed for Brentford in September 1987, at a cost of £40,000, having made just 64 appearances with 10 goals to his credit. Later with Southend United and Charlton Athletic.

| 1967 | Everton | H | League Division 1 | 1–1 |
| 1972 | West Bromwich Albion | H | League Division 1 | 3–1 |

1975 Michael Wayne Duberry was born in Enfield. Signed as a professional from trainee in June 1993 and at one stage looked to be on his way out of the club when, after a loan spell with Bournemouth in September 1995 at a time he was seemingly surplus to Glenn Hoddle's requirements, a permanent deal did not materialise. On his return to Stamford Bridge he made rapid progress and was being hailed as a future England international. However, season 1997–98 was not his best and the close-season signing of World Cup star Marcel Desailly again appeared to cast doubt over the future of his Chelsea career.

1978	Bolton Wanderers	H	League Division 1	4–3
1989	Norwich City	A	League Division 1	0–2
1995	Aston Villa	A	Premier League	1–0

OCTOBER 15

| 1910 | Blackpool | H | League Division 2 | 0–0 |
| 1921 | Newcastle United | A | League Division 1 | 0–1 |

Debut of goalkeeper Benjamin Howard Baker.

1927	Southampton	A	League Division 2	4–2
1932	Bolton Wanderers	A	League Division 1	3–2
1938	Arsenal	H	League Division 1	4–2
1949	Charlton Athletic	A	League Division 1	0–1
1955	Tottenham Hotspur	H	League Division 1	2–0
1957	Fulham	H	Southern Floodlight Cup 1st round	1–2
1960	Birmingham City	A	League Division 1	0–1
1966	Manchester United	A	League Division 1	1–1
1969	Carlisle United	A	League Cup 4th round	0–1
1977	Middlesbrough	H	League Division 1	0–0
1983	Cardiff City	H	League Division 2	2–0
1988	Oldham Athletic	A	League Division 2	4–1
1994	Arsenal	A	Premier League	1–3
1997	Blackburn Rovers	H	League Cup 3rd round	1–1

OCTOBER 16

| 1909 | Blackburn Rovers | A | League Division 1 | 0–1 |

First game for Walter Bettridge who had been acquired from junior football playing for Burton United. He went on to make a total of 255 League and Cup appearances between this game and his departure to Gillingham in 1922, and was a member of Chelsea's first ever FA Cup final team in 1915.

1915	Croydon Common	H	London Combination League (Part One)	3–1
1920	Tottenham Hotspur	H	League Division 1	0–4
1926	Portsmouth	A	League Division 2	3–2
1937	Blackpool	A	League Division 1	2–0
1943	Luton Town	H	Football League South	6–0
1948	Blackpool	H	League Division 1	3–3
1954	Manchester United	H	League Division 1	5–6
1965	Blackburn Rovers	A	League Division 1	1–0
1971	Arsenal	H	League Division 1	1–2
1974	Stoke City	A	League Cup 3rd round replay	1–1
1976	Oldham Athletic	H	League Division 2	4–3

1981	Leicester City	A	League Division 2	1–1
1982	Blackburn Rovers	A	League Division 2	0–3
1993	Norwich City	H	Premier League	1–2

OCTOBER 17

1908	Sheffield Wednesday	H	League Division 1	2–2
1914	Bradford Park Avenue	A	League Division 1	0–3
1923	Sunderland	A	League Division 1	0–2
1925	South Shields	A	League Division 2	0–0
1931	Sunderland	A	League Division 1	1–2

1934 Frank Blunstone was born in Crewe. Joined Chelsea from his local club, Crewe Alexandra, for £7,000 in 1953 and played for the Blues until his retirement in June 1964, winning 5 full England international caps in the process. He was a member of the 1954–55 Football League Championship winning team as well as the 1962–63 Second Division promotion side and in total amassed nearly 350 appearances and over 50 goals.

1936	Sheffield Wednesday	H	League Division 1	1–1
1942	Southampton	A	Football League South	2–1
1953	Middlesbrough	H	League Division 1	1–1
1959	Luton Town	A	League Division 1	2–1
1964	Stoke City	H	League Division 1	4–0
1966	Blackpool	H	League Cup 3rd round replay	1–3

1968 Graham Pierre Le Saux was born in Jersey. Another whose Chelsea career has fallen in two parts, the first half commencing as at December 1988 when he signed professional forms some months after being spotted in Channel Islands football. He made his first-team debut within six months of joining the senior ranks and played some 100 plus games (10 goals) before departing to Blackburn Rovers in March 1993 where he was a regular in the side that won the Premier League title in 1995. However, a very public falling-out with one of his team mates during a match indicated that Le Saux was not entirely settled in the north and Chelsea swooped at the beginning of season 1997–98 with a cheque for £5,500,000 to bring him back to the Bridge. Suffered injury but still contributed to the Blues' double Cup winning season and returned to the England team for a tournament in Morocco and the World Cup finals in France.

1970	Derby County	A	League Division 1	2–1
1972	Bristol City	A	Testimonial	1–2
1979	Los Angeles Aztecs, USA	H	Friendly	2–0
1987	Coventry City	A	League Division 1	3–3
1992	Ipswich Town	H	Premier League	2–1

OCTOBER 18

| 1913 | Liverpool | H | League Division 1 | 3–0 |
| 1919 | Liverpool | A | League Division 1 | 1–0 |

1924	Stockport County	H	League Division 2	1–1
1930	Sheffield United	H	League Division 1	1–0

1934 Frank Upton was born in Ainsley Hill. Began at Northampton Town moving on to Derby County in June 1954 from where Chelsea bought him for £15,000 in August 1961, in time to take part in the promotion winning 1962–63 team. He amassed some 86 appearances for the Blues before returning to Derby County in 1965, followed by spells at Notts County, Worcester City and as player-manager at Workington. A full-time managerial post came his way at Northampton Town in 1969 and thereafter similar appointments at Aston Villa (1970–77), Chelsea (1977–78), Randers Freja, Dundee, Al-Arabi, and Wolverhampton Wanderers. He stayed in football at lower coaching levels after the more high-profile jobs eluded him.

1941	Reading	H	London War League	0–5
1947	Middlesbrough	H	League Division 1	4–2
1952	Burnley	A	League Division 1	1–1

Roy Bentley scored for the eighth match running but failed to find the net on his next outing and thus his run, which had commenced on 10 September, came to an end.

1954	Plymouth Argyle	A	Friendly	5–1
1955	Brentford	A	Friendly	4–0
1958	Luton Town	A	League Division 1	1–2
1969	West Bromwich Albion	H	League Division 1	2–0
1975	Blackpool	H	League Division 2	2–0
1980	Blackburn Rovers	A	League Division 2	1–1
1986	Manchester City	H	League Division 1	2–1
1997	Leicester City	H	Premier League	1–0

OCTOBER 19

1907	Birmingham City	A	League Division 1	1–1
1912	Bradford City	H	League Division 1	0–3
1918	Arsenal	H	London Combination League	4–1

1922 James Austin Russell Macaulay was born in Edinburgh. He joined Chelsea in October 1946 from Edinburgh City and over the course of five years made just under 100 appearances with 5 goals before transferring to Aldershot.

1929	Notts County	A	League Division 2	2–2
1935	Everton	A	League Division 1	1–5
1940	Queens Park Rangers	H	Football League South	3–1
1946	Portsmouth	A	League Division 1	2–0

Debut of the above-mentioned James Austin Russell Macaulay.

1957	Wolverhampton Wanderers	A	League Division 1	1–2
1959	Ashford	A	Friendly	7–2
1963	Sheffield Wednesday	H	League Division 1	1–2
1968	Leicester City	H	League Division 1	3–0

1985	Oxford United	A	League Division 1	1–2
1991	Liverpool	H	League Division 1	2–2
1996	Wimbledon	H	Premier League	2–4

OCTOBER 20

1906	Burton United	A	League Division 2	1–2
1917	Queens Park Rangers	H	London Combination League	1–2
1923	West Ham United	H	League Division 1	0–0
1928	Oldham Athletic	A	League Division 2	0–1
1934	Birmingham City	A	League Division 1	1–0
1945	West Bromwich Albion	H	Football League South	7–4
1951	Newcastle United	A	League Division 1	1–3
1956	Wolverhampton Wanderers	H	League Division 1	3–3
1962	Middlesbrough	H	League Division 2	3–2
1971	Atvidaberg, Sweden	A	Cup-Winners' Cup 2nd round	0–0
1973	Newcastle United	A	League Division 1	0–2
1979	Cardiff City	A	League Division 2	2–1
1984	Southampton	A	League Division 1	0–1
1990	Nottingham Forest	H	League Division 1	0–0
1994	Austria Memphis	H	Cup-Winners' Cup 2nd round	0–0

OCTOBER 21

1882 James Edwin Windridge was born in Sparkbrook, Birmingham. Started with Small Heath and joined the Blues in April 1905 for £190, making his debut in Chelsea's first ever league fixture and remaining at the club for six seasons before moving to Middlesbrough for £1,000 in November 1911, thus making a substantial profit for the club. The 'Wizard' as he was dubbed, made over 150 appearances and scored 58 goals in Chelsea's colours. After his time in the north-east he returned to see out his days at Birmingham.

| 1905 | Chesterfield | H | League Division 2 | 0–1 |
| 1911 | Burnley | A | League Division 2 | 2–2 |

Bob Thomson, who had only one eye, made his first appearance for the Blues.

1916	Millwall	A	London Combination League	0–0
1922	Sunderland	H	League Division 1	1–3
1933	Blackburn Rovers	A	League Division 1	2–4
1939	Brentford	A	Football League South B	2–2
1944	Millwall	H	Football League South	7–0
1950	Wolverhampton Wanderers	A	League Division 1	1–2
1961	Birmingham City	A	League Division 1	2–3

Bert Murray started his senior Chelsea career.

| 1970 | CSKA Sofia, Bulgaria | A | Cup-Winners' Cup 2nd round | 1–0 |
| 1972 | Tottenham Hotspur | A | League Division 1 | 1–0 |

1978	Liverpool	A	League Division 1	0–2
1980	Orient	A	League Division 2	1–0
1989	Derby County	A	League Division 1	1–0
1995	Manchester United	H	Premier League	1–4

OCTOBER 22

1910	Glossop North End	A	League Division 2	1–2
1921	Burnley	A	League Division 1	0–5
1927	Hull City	H	League Division 2	2–0
1932	Derby County	H	League Division 1	1–3
1938	Brentford	A	League Division 1	0–1
1949	Aston Villa	H	League Division 1	1–3
1955	Preston North End	A	League Division 1	3–2
1960	Burnley	H	League Division 1	2–6
1974	Stoke City	A	League Cup 3rd round 2nd replay	2–6

Chelsea went down to the heaviest defeat suffered in this competition.

| 1977 | Newcastle United | A | League Division 1 | 0–1 |

Debut of Trevor Aylott.

1983	Carlisle United	A	League Division 2	0–0
1988	Plymouth Argyle	H	League Division 2	5–0
1996	Bolton Wanderers	A	League Cup 3rd round	1–2

The tragic and premature death of vice-chairman Matthew Harding occurred when, returning to London from watching his beloved Chelsea in this match, his helicopter crashed out of the sky killing all those on board. Probably best remembered as a genuine fan (rather than generous benefactor) who tried by the use of the wealth, that he had been fortunate to accumulate, to accelerate the club that was a major part of his life toward the greatness he dreamed of. The sadness that remains for the family he left behind is also tinged with an irony that he was not able to see his vision of the club come to fruition. He would have celebrated the current status of the Blues in the most successful period in the club's history. The three Cup final victories, the crop of internationals on the playing staff and the development of Stamford Bridge into one of the best stadiums in Britain remain as tribute to the work he and Chairman Ken Bates undertook to transform the fortunes of Chelsea Football Club.

OCTOBER 23

1909	Nottingham Forest	H	League Division 1	0–1
1915	Queens Park Rangers	A	London Combination League (Part One)	0–1
1920	Oldham Athletic	H	League Division 1	1–1
1926	Oldham Athletic	H	League Division 2	1–0
1937	Brentford	H	League Division 1	2–1
1943	Crystal Palace	H	Football League South	2–1
1948	Derby County	A	League Division 1	1–2
1954	Blackpool	A	League Division 1	0–1

1965	Leicester City	H	League Division 1	0–2
1967	Derby County	A	Testimonial	1–2
1968	DWS Amsterdam	H	Fairs Cup 2nd round	0–0
1971	Southampton	H	League Division 1	3–0
1976	Blackburn Rovers	A	League Division 2	2–0
1982	Charlton Athletic	H	League Division 2	3–1
1985	Charlton Athletic	A	Full Members Cup Group Match	3–1
1991	Swindon Town	H	ZDS Cup 2nd round	1–0
1993	Aston Villa	A	Premier League	0–1
1994	Ipswich Town	H	Premier League	2–0
1997	Tromso	A	Cup-Winners' Cup 2nd round	2–3

OCTOBER 24

1908	Blackburn Rovers	A	League Division 1	0–2
1914	Oldham Athletic	H	League Division 1	2–2
1925	Preston North End	H	League Division 2	5–0
1931	Blackburn Rovers	H	League Division 1	1–2
1936	Manchester United	A	League Division 1	0–0
1942	Crystal Palace	H	Football League South	4–1
1959	Everton	H	League Division 1	1–0
1960	Workington Town	H	League Cup 2nd round	4–2

Allan Harris played his first senior game.

| 1964 | Tottenham Hotspur | A | League Division 1 | 1–1 |

1964 Frode Grodas was born in Sogndal, Norway. Joined from Lillestrom in September 1996 on a free transfer and whilst injury kept Dmitri Kharine out of the side, had a run as Chelsea's number one goalkeeper although he always faced competition from the ever reliable Kevin Hitchcock. The arrival of Ed De Goey put paid to his chances of regular first team action and, for a while before a transfer to Tottenham Hotspur in the second half of season 1997–98, he was in a situation where (with the World Cup finals fast approaching) he was regarded as his country's first choice keeper and only (at best) a reserve at club level.

| 1970 | Blackpool | A | League Division 1 | 4–3 |

John Phillips made his debut between the sticks. On the same day Graham Charles Stuart was born in Tooting. 'Bobby' signed as a professional in June 1989 and just topped 100 games when sold to Everton in August 1993 for £850,000.

1981	Barnsley	H	League Division 2	1–2
1987	Southampton	H	League Division 1	0–1
1992	Coventry City	A	Premier League	2–1

OCTOBER 25

1913	Aston Villa	A	League Division 1	2–1
1919	Bradford Park Avenue	A	League Division 1	0–1
1924	Portsmouth	A	League Division 2	0–0
1930	Birmingham City	A	League Division 1	2–6

1941	Brighton & Hove Albion	H	London War League	1–3
1947	Charlton Athletic	A	League Division 1	1–3
1952	Tottenham Hotspur	H	League Division 1	2–1

Ron Greenwood made his League debut for Chelsea.

1953	West Bromwich Albion	A	League Division 1	2–5
1958	Leicester City	H	League Division 1	5–2
1967	Leicester City	A	League Division 1	2–2
1969	Newcastle United	A	League Division 1	1–0
1975	Blackburn Rovers	A	League Division 2	1–1
1980	Newcastle United	H	League Division 2	6–0
1983	Leicester City	H	League Cup 2nd round	0–2
1986	Arsenal	A	League Division 1	1–3
1988	Hull City	A	League Division 2	0–3

OCTOBER 26

1907	Everton	H	League Division 1	2–1
1912	Manchester City	A	League Division 1	0–2
1918	Queens Park Rangers	A	London Combination League	2–2
1929	Reading	H	League Division 2	1–0
1935	Bolton Wanderers	H	League Division 1	2–1
1940	Millwall	A	Football League South	1–3
1946	Arsenal	H	League Division 1	2–1
1957	Arsenal	H	League Division 1	0–0
1963	Fulham	A	League Division 1	1–0
1964	Notts County	H	League Cup 3rd round	4–0
1966	Tottenham Hotspur	H	League Division 1	3–0
1968	Stoke City	A	League Division 1	0–2
1973	Norwich City	H	League Division 1	3–0
1974	Stoke City	H	League Division 1	3–3
1976	Arsenal	A	League Cup 4th round	1–2
1985	Manchester United	H	League Division 1	1–2
1991	Crystal Palace	A	League Division 1	0–0
1993	Manchester City	A	League Cup 3rd round	0–1
1994	West Ham United	A	League Cup 3rd round	0–1
1996	Tottenham Hotspur	H	Premier League	3–1
1997	Bolton Wanderers	A	Premier League	0–1

OCTOBER 27

1906	Grimsby Town	H	League Division 2	2–0
1909	Preston North End	H	League Division 1	2–0
1917	Millwall	A	London Combination League	0–0
1923	West Ham United	A	League Division 1	0–2
1928	Southampton	H	League Division 2	1–1

1934	Stoke City	H	League Division 1	0–2
1945	West Bromwich Albion	A	Football League South	1–8
1951	Bolton Wanderers	H	League Division 1	1–3
1956	Bolton Wanderers	A	League Division 1	2–2

1957 Glenn Hoddle was born in Hayes, Middlesex. One of the most naturally gifted players of his generation, he signed with Tottenham Hotspur as a youngster after a recommendation from Martin Chivers. He made his League debut in 1975 and was an established first team player by the end of the following year. He made his England debut in 1979 against Bulgaria at Wembley and marked the occasion by scoring. He remained with Spurs until 1987, during which time he won two FA Cup winners' medals and 44 England caps. Although it was felt by some that his work-rate was insufficient, he was not capped as often as his fans would have liked. He joined AS Monaco in 1987 and won a League Championship medal in his first season in France but was then troubled by injuries. Upon returning to England in 1990 he trained with Chelsea but then accepted an offer to become player-manager at Swindon, guiding them into the Premier League in 1993. He then left to hold a similar position with Chelsea and, after modest success, was subsequently appointed England manager in 1996.

1962	Derby County	A	League Division 2	3–1
1971	Bolton Wanderers	H	League Cup 4th round	1–1
1975	Italy Under-23	H	Friendly	0–0

Played for the Prince Philip Cup.

| 1979 | Fulham | H | League Division 2 | 0–2 |
| 1984 | Ipswich Town | H | League Division 1 | 2–0 |

Darren Wood made his Chelsea debut.

| 1990 | Liverpool | A | League Division 1 | 0–2 |

OCTOBER 28

1880 Norman Murray Fairgray was born in Dumfries. Joined Chelsea in September 1907 from Lincoln City at the start of a seven-year stay at the club in which he appeared 84 times, scoring five goals. Headed back north in May 1914 when he linked up with Motherwell before playing out his career with Queen of the South.

1905	Southern United	A	FA Cup 2nd preliminary round	1–0
1911	Clapton Orient	A	League Division 2	4–1
1916	Watford	H	London Combination League	3–2
1922	Sunderland	A	League Division 1	1–1
1933	Newcastle United	H	League Division 1	2–1
1939	Southampton	H	Football League South B	6–2
1944	Watford	A	Football League South	6–1
1950	Sunderland	H	League Division 1	3–0
1958	South Africa	H	Friendly	1–0
1961	Everton	H	League Division 1	1–1
1963	East Stirling	A	Friendly	2–2
1967	West Ham United	H	League Division 1	1–3

1970	Manchester United	A	League Cup 4th round	1–2
1972	Newcastle United	H	League Division 1	1–1
1978	Norwich City	H	League Division 1	3–3
1981	Southampton	H	League Cup 2nd round	2–1
1982	Tranmere Rovers	A	League Cup 2nd round	2–1
1986	Cardiff City	A	League Cup 3rd round	1–2
1989	Manchester City	H	League Division 1	1–1
1992	Newcastle United	H	League Cup 3rd round	2–1
1995	Blackburn Rovers	A	Premier League	0–3

OCTOBER 29

1910	Lincoln City	H	League Division 2	7–0
1921	Burnley	H	League Division 1	4–1
1927	Preston North End	A	League Division 2	3–0
1932	Blackpool	A	League Division 1	0–4

Debut of Leonard Hector Allum who had previously served Maidenhead United and Fulham (as an amateur). He managed 102 senior appearances, scoring just two goals in the League, over a period of seven years before moving on to Clapton Orient in May 1939.

1938	Derby County	H	League Division 1	0–2
1949	Wolverhampton Wanderers	A	League Division 1	2–2
1955	Burnley	H	League Division 1	0–0
1960	Preston North End	A	League Division 1	2–0
1962	Greenock Morton	H	Friendly	6–1
1966	Fulham	A	League Division 1	3–1
1977	Bristol City	H	League Division 1	1–0
1983	Charlton Athletic	H	League Division 2	3–2
1985	Fulham	H	League Cup 3rd round	1–1
1988	Brighton & Hove Albion	H	League Division 2	2–0

Chelsea began a run of 27 matches in the Second Division without tasting defeat. The longest sequence unbeaten home or away in the club's history.

| 1994 | Sheffield Wednesday | A | Premier League | 1–1 |

OCTOBER 30

1905	Burslem Port Vale	A	League Division 2	2–3
1909	Sunderland	A	League Division 1	0–4
1915	Arsenal	H	London Combination League (Part One)	3–1
1920	Oldham Athletic	A	League Division 1	2–1
1926	Grimsby Town	A	League Division 2	0–0
1937	Bolton Wanderers	A	League Division 1	5–5
1948	Arsenal	H	League Division 1	0–1
1954	Charlton Athletic	H	League Division 1	1–2

1965	Sheffield United	A	League Division 1	2–1
1968	DWS Amsterdam	A	Fairs Cup 2nd round	0–0
1971	Leicester City	A	League Division 1	1–1
1976	Southampton	H	League Division 2	3–1
1982	Carlisle United	A	League Division 2	1–2

Joey Jones made his debut for Chelsea.

| 1984 | Walsall | A | League Cup 3rd round | 2–2 |
| 1993 | Oldham Athletic | H | Premier League | 0–1 |

OCTOBER 31

1908	Bradford City	H	League Division 1	1–1
1914	Manchester United	A	League Division 1	2–2
1925	Oldham Athletic	A	League Division 2	1–1
1931	Portsmouth	A	League Division 1	0–1
1936	Derby County	H	League Division 1	1–1
1942	Tottenham Hotspur	A	Football League South	1–1
1953	Liverpool	H	League Division 1	5–2
1959	Nottingham Forest	A	League Division 1	1–3
1964	Burnley	H	League Division 1	0–1
1970	Southampton	H	League Division 1	2–2
1972	Bury	A	League Cup 4th round	1–0
1980	Cardiff City	A	League Division 2	1–0

Debut of Chris Hutchings.

| 1981 | Rotherham United | A | League Division 2 | 0–6 |

Although Chelsea have suffered heavier defeats, this ranks as their worst reverse in the (old) Second Division.

1987	Oxford United	A	League Division 1	4–4
1990	Portsmouth	H	League Cup 3rd round	0–0
1992	Sheffield United	H	Premier League	1–2

NOVEMBER 1

| 1913 | Middlesbrough | H | League Division 1 | 3–2 |
| 1919 | Bradford Park Avenue | H | League Division 1 | 4–0 |

Debut of John Cock.

1924	Hull City	H	League Division 2	1–0
1930	Blackpool	H	League Division 1	3–0
1941	Brentford	A	London War League	1–3
1947	Arsenal	H	League Division 1	0–0
1952	Sheffield Wednesday	A	League Division 1	0–1
1958	Preston North End	A	League Division 1	0–2

1963   Mark Hughes was born in Wrexham. Signed by Manchester United as a professional in June 1980, he soon developed a reputation as a feared striker, even though he had begun his career as a midfielder. First introduced to the side in 1983 he won an FA Cup winners' medal in 1985 and was sensationally sold to Barcelona for

£2.5 million in July 1986. The move was not a success and he was subsequently loaned to Bayern Munich before a £1.5 million return home to Old Trafford. In his second spell with the club he collected further FA Cup medals in 1990 and 1994, Premiership medals in 1993 and 1994, a League Cup medal in 1992 and scored both goals in the European Cup-Winners' Cup final victory over Barcelona in 1991. He was allowed to join Chelsea for £1.5 million in 1995, and, his medal collection continued to grow, with a further FA Cup medal in 1997 and a League Cup and European Cup-Winners' Cup medals in 1998. Increased competition for the striker role lead to rotation of players during season 1997–98 and Hughes was not always assured of his place in the starting line-up. When Pierluigi Casiraghi was signed for £5.4 million and the free transfer of Brian Laudrup was confirmed, Hughes was allowed to leave the club to join Southampton in July 1998 for £650,000.

1969	Coventry City	H	League Division 1	1–0
1975	Plymouth Argyle	H	League Division 2	2–2
1983	Arsenal	H	Friendly	2–1
1986	Watford	H	League Division 1	0–0
1997	Aston Villa	A	Premier League	2–0

NOVEMBER 2

1894 Buchanan Sharp was born in Alexandria. He joined Chelsea in November 1919, made72 appearances, scored 23 goals then left to play for Tottenham Hotspur, Leicester City, Nelson and Southport.

1907	Sunderland	A	League Division 1	0–3
1912	West Bromwich Albion	H	League Division 1	0–2
1918	Millwall	H	London Combination League	0–1
1929	Charlton Athletic	A	League Division 2	1–1
1935	Huddersfield Town	A	League Division 1	0–2
1940	Millwall	H	Football League South	2–2
1946	Blackpool	A	League Division 1	0–1
1957	Blackpool	A	League Division 1	1–2
1963	Birmingham City	H	League Division 1	2–3
1968	Manchester City	H	League Division 1	2–0
1974	Birmingham City	A	League Division 1	0–2
1985	Ipswich Town	A	League Division 1	2–0
1989	Bournemouth	A	ZDS Cup 2nd round	3–2
1991	Coventry City	A	League Division 1	1–0
1996	Manchester United	A	Premier League	2–1

NOVEMBER 3

| 1906 | Burslem Port Vale | A | League Division 2 | 0–2 |

1907 James Bambrick was born in Belfast where he began a promising junior career with local clubs before playing in senior football for Glentoran and Linfield from where he signed for Chelsea in 1934 for £2,000. 'Joe' made 66 appearances for the club in which he notched a tally of 37 goals. He played international football for Northern Ireland gaining 11 caps and, in February 1930, scored a record six goals in a game against Wales at Celtic Park, Belfast. He was sold to Walsall for £2,500 in March 1938.

1917	Tottenham Hotspur	H	London Combination League	0–0
1923	Bolton Wanderers	H	League Division 1	0–0
1934	Leeds United	A	League Division 1	2–5

William Barraclough made his debut.

1945	Birmingham City	A	Football League South	2–5
1951	Stoke City	A	League Division 1	2–1
1956	Charlton Athletic	H	League Division 1	1–3
1962	Newcastle United	H	League Division 2	4–2
1971	Atvidaberg, Sweden	H	Cup-Winners' Cup 2nd round	1–1
1973	Manchester United	A	League Division 1	2–2

1973 Andrew John Myers was born in Isleworth. A pupil at the FA National School at Lilleshall, Andy signed professional forms for the club in July 1990 and made his debut, at the age of just 17, in April 1991. Having played around 100 times for the club he is an established member of the squad but with the influx of foreign talent his chances of a regular first team place would appear limited.

1979	Sunderland	A	League Division 2	1–2
1984	Coventry City	H	League Division 1	6–2
1987	Arsenal	H	League Division 1	1–1

The start of a sequence that Chelsea fans would prefer to forget. Including this match the Blues went 21 games in Division 1 without a victory, up to April 1988.

1990	Aston Villa	H	League Division 1	1–0
1994	Austria Memphis	A	Cup-Winners' Cup 2nd round	1–1

NOVEMBER 4

1905	Barnsley	H	League Division 2	6–0
1911	Bristol City	H	League Division 2	2–2
1916	Clapton Orient	A	London Combination League	2–0
1922	Preston North End	A	League Division 1	0–2
1933	Sheffield Wednesday	A	League Division 1	1–2
1939	Brighton & Hove Albion	A	Football League South B	1–5
1944	Southampton	A	Football League South	3–3
1950	Charlton Athletic	A	League Division 1	2–1
1958	Frem, Copenhagen	H	Fairs Cup 1st round	4–1
1961	Arsenal	A	League Division 1	3–0
1967	Burnley	A	League Division 1	1–1
1970	CSKA Sofia, Bulgaria	H	Cup-Winners' Cup 2nd round	2–0
1972	Liverpool	A	League Division 1	1–3
1975	Celic, Yugoslavia	A	Friendly	3–2
1978	Queens Park Rangers	A	League Division 1	0–0

| 1989 | Millwall | H | League Division 1 | 4–0 |
| 1995 | Sheffield Wednesday | H | Premier League | 0–0 |

NOVEMBER 5

1921	Sheffield United	H	League Division 1	0–2
1927	Swansea Town	H	League Division 2	4–0
1932	Birmingham City	H	League Division 1	4–2
1938	Grimsby Town	A	League Division 1	1–2
1949	Portsmouth	H	League Division 1	1–4
1955	Birmingham City	A	League Division 1	0–3
1960	Newcastle United	H	League Division 1	4–2
1966	Manchester United	H	League Division 1	1–3
1977	Nottingham Forest	H	League Division 1	1–0
1983	Oldham Athletic	A	League Division 2	1–1
1988	Watford	A	League Division 2	2–1

This result began a sequence of 13 games played away from Stamford Bridge in which the Blues managed to remain unbeaten. It came to an end in April 1989. It was also incorporated in the record overall sequence of both home and away games which stretched to 27 games.

NOVEMBER 6

1909	Everton	H	League Division 1	0–1
1915	Fulham	A	London Combination League (Part One)	3–0
1920	Preston North End	H	League Division 1	1–1
1926	Blackpool	H	League Division 2	1–1
1937	Sunderland	H	League Division 1	0–0
1943	Arsenal	A	Football League South	0–6
1948	Huddersfield Town	A	League Division 1	4–3
1954	Sunderland	A	League Division 1	3–3
1965	Leeds United	H	League Division 1	1–0
1971	Nottingham Forest	H	League Division 1	2–0
1973	Fulham	H	Friendly	4–1
1974	Arsenal	H	Testimonial	1–1
1976	Hereford United	A	League Division 2	2–2
1982	Crystal Palace	H	League Division 2	0–0
1984	Walsall	H	League Cup 3rd round replay	3–0
1985	Fulham	A	League Cup 3rd round replay	1–0
1990	Portsmouth	A	League Cup 3rd round replay	3–2
1993	Leeds United	A	Premier League	1–4
1994	Coventry City	H	Premier League	2–2
1997	Tromso	H	Cup-Winners' Cup 2nd round	7–1

NOVEMBER 7

| 1908 | Manchester United | A | League Division 1 | 1–0 |

1914	Bolton Wanderers	H	League Division 1		2–1
1925	Stockport County	H	League Division 2		3–2
1931	Derby County	H	League Division 1		2–1
1936	Wolverhampton Wanderers	A	League Division 1		2–1
1942	Clapton Orient	H	Football League South		0–2
1953	Tottenham Hotspur	A	League Division 1		1–2
1955	Millwall	A	Friendly		2–3
1957	CDSA Moscow	H	Friendly		1–4
1959	Blackburn Rovers	H	League Division 1		3–1
1964	Sheffield United	A	League Division 1		2–0
1970	Huddersfield Town	A	League Division 1		1–0
1981	Newcastle United	H	League Division 2		2–1
1992	Crystal Palace	H	Premier League		3–1

NOVEMBER 8

1913	Sheffield United	A	League Division 1	2–3
1919	Preston North End	A	League Division 1	1–3
1924	Blackpool	A	League Division 2	2–1

Goalkeeper Peter Joseph McKenna played his first game for the club.

1930	Blackburn Rovers	A	League Division 1	0–2

1937 Peter Brabrook was born in Greenwich. Joined Chelsea as his first club in 1953 and signed professional forms two years later at which time he was given his full debut. Held his place on the wing for seven seasons before moving across London to join West Ham United in a deal that cost the Hammers £35,000. He appeared 270 times for the Blues and scored 57 goals.

1941	Crystal Palace	H	London War League	1–0
1947	Preston North End	A	League Division 1	0–2
1952	Cardiff City	H	League Division 1	0–2
1958	Leeds United	H	League Division 1	2–0

1962 Kevin McAllister was born in Falkirk. Signed from his local club in May 1985 at a cost of £34,000. Made close to 150 appearances but a high proportion came as substitute and as his Stamford Bridge career closed he returned north for spells with Falkirk, Hibernian and Falkirk (for a third time).

1969	Sheffield Wednesday	A	League Division 1	3–1
1971	Bolton Wanderers	A	League Cup 4th round replay	6–0
1975	Hull City	A	League Division 2	2–1
1980	Oldham Athletic	H	League Division 2	1–0
1986	Everton	A	League Division 1	2–2

NOVEMBER 9

1907	Woolwich Arsenal	H	League Division 1	2–1
1912	Everton	A	League Division 1	0–1
1918	Fulham	A	London Combination League	2–1

1923 Eric George Parsons was born in Worthing. 'The Rabbit' as he was dubbed started at West Ham United and was transferred to Chelsea in December 1950 for a fee of £23,000. He played 176 games for the Blues and scored 42 times. He was an ever present in the 1954–55 League Championship side. Left the Bridge in November 1956 on a free transfer to Brentford.

1928	Wolverhampton Wanderers	A	League Division 2	1–1
1929	Hull City	H	League Division 2	3–0
1935	Middlesbrough	H	League Division 1	2–1
1940	Aldershot	A	Football League South	3–5
1946	Brentford	H	League Division 1	3–2
1957	Luton Town	H	League Division 1	1–3
1963	West Bromwich Albion	A	League Division 1	1–1
1968	Liverpool	A	League Division 1	1–2
1974	Leicester City	H	League Division 1	0–0

Tommy Langley played his first senior game at the age of 16 years and 9 months.

1977	Chelmsford	A	Friendly	3–1
1982	Notts County	A	League Cup 3rd round	0–2
1983	West Bromwich Albion	H	League Cup 3rd round	0–1
1985	Nottingham Forest	H	League Division 1	4–2
1988	Plymouth Argyle	H	Simod Cup 1st round	6–2
1994	Liverpool	A	Premier League	1–3
1997	West Ham United	H	Premier League	2–1

NOVEMBER 10

1906	Burnley	H	League Division 2	2–0
1917	Crystal Palace	H	London Combination League	0–1
1923	Bolton Wanderers	A	League Division 1	0–4
1928	Preston North End	H	League Division 2	2–1
1934	West Bromwich Albion	H	League Division 1	2–3
1945	Birmingham City	H	Football League South	2–3
1951	Manchester United	H	League Division 1	4–2
1956	Sunderland	A	League Division 1	3–1

1959 Peter Nicholas was born in Newport, Gwent. He was 28 when he joined Chelsea and had already had two spells at Crystal Palace, and a time with Arsenal, Luton Town and Aberdeen who pocketed £350,000 when they sold him to the Blues in August 1988. Although he managed to approach 100 appearances before his departure to Watford in March 1991, his contribution to the team was not always obvious and it was no surprise when he left to ply his trade at a lower level.

1962	Walsall	A	League Division 2	5–1
1973	Everton	H	League Division 1	3–1
1976	Charlton Athletic	H	League Division 2	2–1
1979	Orient	A	League Division 2	7–3

Colin Pates made his first senior appearance.

| 1984 | Newcastle United | A | League Division 1 | 1–2 |
| 1990 | Norwich City | H | League Division 1 | 1–1 |

NOVEMBER 11

1905	Clapton Orient	A	League Division 2	3–0
1911	Birmingham City	A	League Division 2	4–1
1916	Fulham	H	London Combination League	4–0

1921 Ronald Greenwood was born in Burnley. First came to the club as a boy but was allowed to slip away to join Bradford where he spent three years before joining Brentford from where he was re-acquired in October 1952 for £5,000 in part exchange for Seamus D'Arcy. Played an important part in the League Championship winning team of 1955 and amassed 66 appearances before being granted a free transfer to Fulham later that year. Went on to manage West Ham United and England.

1922	Preston North End	H	League Division 1	0–1
1933	Derby County	H	League Division 1	0–2
1939	Reading	H	Football League South B	3–0
1944	Luton Town	H	Football League South	7–1
1950	Manchester United	H	League Division 1	1–0
1959	Entente Anversoise Antwerp	A	Friendly	4–1
1961	Bolton Wanderers	H	League Division 1	1–0
1964	Swansea Town	H	League Cup 4th round	3–2
1967	Sheffield Wednesday	H	League Division 1	3–0
1972	Leicester City	H	League Division 1	1–1
1978	Everton	A	League Division 1	2–3
1981	Wigan Athletic	A	League Cup 3rd round	2–4
1989	Everton	A	League Division 1	1–0
1995	West Ham United	A	Friendly	3–3

NOVEMBER 12

1910	Birmingham City	H	League Division 2	2–2
1921	Sheffield United	A	League Division 1	2–1
1927	Manchester City	A	League Division 2	1–0
1932	West Bromwich Albion	A	League Division 1	2–3
1938	Sunderland	H	League Division 1	4–0
1949	Huddersfield Town	A	League Division 1	2–1
1955	West Bromwich Albion	H	League Division 1	2–0

Ron Tindall made his debut.

1957	Beogradski Yugo	H	Friendly	2–1
1960	Arsenal	A	League Division 1	4–1
1966	West Bromwich Albion	A	League Division 1	1–0

1969 Jason Victor Cundy was born in Wimbledon. He joined Chelsea from school as a trainee, signed professional forms in August 1988, became captain of the reserve side and then made his first-team debut two years later. However, despite his early promise and fifty-odd first-team appearances the Blues management were obviously (rightly) not convinced about his ability at the highest level and shrewdly cashed in on him with a £750,000 sale to Tottenham Hotspur. At Spurs he was regarded as an expensive flop and having made less than 30 appearances was allowed out on loan to Crystal Palace and Bristol City before moving permanently to Ipswich Town in October 1996 for just £200,000.

1977	Norwich City	A	League Division 1	0–0
1980	Derby County	H	League Division 2	1–3
1983	Newcastle United	H	League Division 2	4–0
1988	Sunderland	H	League Division 2	1–1

NOVEMBER 13

1928 William Gibb Robertson was born in Glasgow. He joined from Arthurlie in July 1946 but, as understudy to goalkeeper Harry Medhurst, had to wait five years before making his first team debut. Incredibly when his chance finally came along, he was pitched into a team four points adrift at the foot of the First Division and without a win in 14 games. Chelsea, with Bill in goal, beat Liverpool and their next three opponents to end the season safe in 20th place on goal average. Not surprisingly Robertson was regarded as first choice after his heroic efforts had saved the club from relegation and he went on to make in excess of 200 appearances, winning a League Championship medal in 1955. He moved to Leyton Orient in September 1960 in a £1,000 transfer and completed 53 games for the O's before leaving first class football.

1909	Manchester United	A	League Division 1	0–2
1915	Clapton Orient	A	London Combination League (Part One)	6–1
1920	Preston North End	A	League Division 1	1–0
1926	Reading	A	League Division 2	1–2
1937	Everton	A	League Division 1	1–4
1943	Reading	A	Football League South	2–3

1944 Ronald 'Chopper' Harris was born in Hackney. Staked a big claim to be regarded as Chelsea's greatest ever servant. His reign began in November 1961 when he turned professional and continued until May 1980 when he was given a free transfer to Brentford to become player-coach. He made 655 League, 64 FA Cup, 48 League Cup and 27 European appearances to establish a Chelsea record for most games played. He also scored 14 goals whilst winning medals for the 1965 Football League Cup, 1970 FA Cup and 1971 European Cup-Winners' Cup.

1945	Moscow Dynamo	H	Friendly	3–3
1948	Manchester United	H	League Division 1	1–1
1954	Tottenham Hotspur	H	League Division 1	2–1

1961 Clive Wilson was born in Manchester. Clive began his career with Manchester City in 1979 and made his League debut in 1981. After a loan spell with Chester City he was transferred to Chelsea for £250,000 in 1987. Whilst at Stamford Bridge he made just over 100 appearances and scored 5 goals. Three years later he moved to Queens Park

Rangers for £450,000, eventually being released on a free transfer in June 1996 when he linked up with former QPR manager Gerry Francis at Tottenham Hotspur.

1965	West Ham United	A	League Division 1	1–2
1968	Portsmouth	A	Testimonial	0–1
1971	Stoke City	A	League Division 1	1–0
1974	Coventry City	H	League Division 1	3–3
1976	International XI	H	Testimonial	3–6
1982	Barnsley	A	League Division 2	1–1
1985	West Bromwich Albion	A	Full Members Cup semi-final	2–2

NOVEMBER 14

1908	Everton	H	League Division 1	3–3
1914	Blackburn Rovers	A	League Division 1	2–3

1919 John Gilbert Cock was born in Hayle, Cornwall. After several Junior clubs, a stint as an amateur with Brentford and a five-year spell at Huddersfield Town, Cock arrived at Stamford Bridge in October 1919 having cost £2,500. A powerful centre-forward who won two full English international caps, he made 110 appearances for Chelsea and scored 53 goals. He was sold to Everton in January 1923 and continued his career in League football through to the end of the decade with subsequent moves to Plymouth Argyle and Millwall.

1925	Wolverhampton Wanderers	A	League Division 2	0–0
1931	Everton	A	League Division 1	2–7

Debut of James Peter O'Dowd.

1936	Sunderland	H	League Division 1	1–3
1942	Reading	A	Football League South	4–1
1953	Burnley	H	League Division 1	2–1
1959	Manchester City	A	League Division 1	1–1
1970	Tottenham Hotspur	H	League Division 1	0–2
1979	West Ham United	H	League Division 2	2–1
1981	Oldham Athletic	A	League Division 2	0–1

NOVEMBER 15

1913	Derby County	H	League Division 1	2–1
1919	Preston North End	H	League Division 1	4–0
1924	Derby County	H	League Division 2	1–1
1930	Manchester City	H	League Division 1	2–0
1941	Fulham	A	London War League	4–1

1946 Alexander Skinner Jackson, the 'Gay Cavalier', was killed in a road accident in Cairo whilst serving as a Major in the Army.

1947	Stoke City	H	League Division 1	4–1
1950	Lille Olympique	H	Friendly	3–0
1952	Newcastle United	A	League Division 1	1–2

Debut of Leslie Stubbs.

1958	Manchester City	A	League Division 1	1–5
1964	Everton	H	League Division 1	5–1
1969	Everton	H	League Division 1	1–1
1975	Notts County	H	League Division 2	2–0
1978	Moscow Dynamo	H	Friendly	1–2
1980	Wrexham	A	League Division 2	4–0
1983	Charlton Athletic	A	League Division 2	1–1
1986	Aston Villa	A	League Division 1	0–0

NOVEMBER 16

1907	Sheffield Wednesday	A	League Division 1	1–3
1912	Sheffield Wednesday	H	League Division 1	0–4
1918	Brentford	H	London Combination League	2–2
1929	Stoke City	A	League Division 2	1–1
1935	Aston Villa	A	League Division 1	2–2
1940	Charlton Athletic	H	Football League South	2–2
1946	Sunderland	A	League Division 1	2–1
1957	Sunderland	A	League Division 1	2–2
1959	British Olympic XI	H	Friendly	4–1
1960	Doncaster Rovers	A	League Cup 3rd round	7–0

The victory established a record for a win in the Football League Cup and was established with a brace apiece for three players Brabrook, Blunstone and Tambling.

1963	Arsenal	H	League Division 1	3–1
1968	Southampton	H	League Division 1	2–3
1974	Newcastle United	A	League Division 1	0–5
1985	Newcastle United	A	League Division 1	3–1
1991	Norwich City	H	League Division 1	0–3
1993	Oxford United	Bisham	Friendly	1–1
1996	Blackburn Rovers	A	Premier League	1–1

NOVEMBER 17

1906	Leeds City	A	League Division 2	1–0
1917	Brentford	A	London Combination League	0–1
1923	Middlesbrough	H	League Division 1	0–2

John Crawford made his debut for the Blues.

1928	Millwall	A	League Division 2	1–2
1934	Blackburn Rovers	A	League Division 1	2–1
1945	Tottenham Hotspur	H	Football League South	1–2
1951	Tottenham Hotspur	A	League Division 1	2–3
1956	Luton Town	H	League Division 1	4–1

Reg Mattews played his first game in goal for the club after his record transfer from Coventry City.

1962	Norwich City	H	League Division 2	2–0

1965	Weiner SK, Austria	A	Fairs Cup 2nd round	0–1
1971	Norwich City	A	League Cup 5th round	1–0
1973	Arsenal	A	League Division 1	0–0
1979	Charlton Athletic	H	League Division 2	3–1
1984	West Bromwich Albion	H	League Division 1	3–1
1990	Wimbledon	A	League Division 1	0–1

NOVEMBER 18

| 1905 | Burnley | H | League Division 2 | 1–0 |
| 1905 | Crystal Palace | A | FA Cup 3rd Preliminary round | 1–7 |

Chelsea capitulated in their heaviest ever FA Cup defeat.

1911	Huddersfield Town	H	League Division 2	3–1
1916	Queens Park Rangers	A	London Combination League	2–1
1922	Burnley	A	League Division 1	0–1
1933	West Bromwich Albion	A	League Division 1	1–3
1939	Fulham	A	Football League South B	3–1
1944	Brighton & Hove Albion	A	Football League South	5–3
1949	Death of James Sharp.			
1950	Aston Villa	A	League Division 1	2–4
1961	Manchester City	A	League Division 1	2–2
1967	Tottenham Hotspur	A	League Division 1	0–2
1969	Ipswich Town	A	League Division 1	4–1
1972	Southampton	A	League Division 1	1–3
1978	Tottenham Hotspur	H	League Division 1	1–3
1987	Barnsley	H	Simod Cup 1st round	2–1
1989	Southampton	H	League Division 1	2–2
1995	Leeds United	A	Premier League	0–1

1995 Dan Petrescu joined from Sheffield Wednesday for £2,300,000.

NOVEMBER 19

1921	Bradford City	H	League Division 1	1–0
1927	Nottingham Forest	H	League Division 2	2–1
1932	Sheffield Wednesday	H	League Division 1	0–2
1938	Aston Villa	A	League Division 1	2–6
1949	Everton	H	League Division 1	3–2
1955	Manchester United	A	League Division 1	0–3
1960	Manchester City	H	League Division 1	6–3
1962	Greenock Morton	A	Friendly	1–1
1966	Sheffield United	H	League Division 1	1–1
1977	Aston Villa	H	League Division 1	0–0
1983	Crystal Palace	H	League Division 2	2–2
1988	Bradford City	A	League Division 2	2–2
1994	Nottingham Forest	A	Premier League	1–0

| 1997 | Southampton | H | League Cup 4th round | 2–1 |

NOVEMBER 20

1909	Bradford City	H	League Division 1	0–3
1915	West Ham United	H	London Combination League (Part One)	5–2
1920	Sheffield United	H	League Division 1	2–1
1926	Swansea Town	H	League Division 2	2–2
1937	Manchester City	H	League Division 1	2–2
1943	Millwall	H	Football League South	0–1
1948	Sheffield United	A	League Division 1	1–2
1954	Sheffield Wednesday	A	League Division 1	1–1
1971	Crystal Palace	A	League Division 1	3–2
1976	Nottingham Forest	A	League Division 2	1–1
1982	Shrewsbury Town	H	League Division 2	1–2
1993	Arsenal	H	Premier League	0–2

NOVEMBER 21

1908	Leicester Fosse	A	League Division 1	2–5
1914	Notts County	H	League Division 1	4–1
1925	Swansea Town	H	League Division 2	1–3
1931	Arsenal	H	League Division 1	2–1
1936	Huddersfield Town	A	League Division 1	2–4
1942	Millwall	H	Football League South	4–2
1953	Bolton Wanderers	A	League Division 1	2–2
1959	Arsenal	H	League Division 1	1–3
1970	Stoke City	H	League Division 1	2–1
1981	Grimsby Town	H	League Division 2	1–1
1984	Manchester City	H	League Cup 4th round	4–1
1992	Everton	A	Premier League	1–0

NOVEMBER 22

1910 William Mitchell was born in County Lurgan. Played in Ireland for Cliftonville and Distillery before joining Chelsea in June 1933 for a stay that took him up to the outbreak of the Second World War during which time he made over 100 starts for the Blues and scored 3 goals.

1913	Manchester City	A	League Division 1	1–2
1919	Middlesbrough	A	League Division 1	0–0
1924	South Shields	A	League Division 2	1–1
1930	Leeds United	A	League Division 1	3–2
1941	Tottenham Hotspur	H	London War League	1–1
1947	Sheffield United	A	League Division 1	1–3
1952	West Bromwich Albion	H	League Division 1	0–2
1958	Arsenal	H	League Division 1	0–3
1964	Birmingham City	A	League Division 1	6–1

1966	Real Madrid, Spain	H	Friendly	2–0
1969	Nottingham Forest	A	League Division 1	1–1
1972	Notts County	H	League Cup 5th round	3–1
1975	Blackpool	A	League Division 2	2–0
1978	Leeds United	A	League Division 1	1–2

John Bumstead made his debut.

1980	Sheffield Wednesday	H	League Division 2	2–0
1983	Swansea City	A	League Division 2	3–1
1986	Newcastle United	H	League Division 1	1–3
1987	Derby County	H	League Division 1	1–0
1993	Manchester City	H	Premier League	0–0
1995	Bolton	H	Premier League	3–2
1997	Blackburn Rovers	A	Premier League	0–1

NOVEMBER 23

1907	Bristol City	H	League Division 1	4–1

Chelsea debut of the much-travelled Billy Brawn.

1912	Blackburn Rovers	A	League Division 1	1–1

James Sharp played his first game for the club.

1918	West Ham United	A	London Combination League	1–3
1929	Wolverhampton Wanderers	H	League Division 2	1–1

1934 Sylvan James Anderton was born in Reading. Broke into senior football with his local club, Reading, with whom he made nearly 200 appearances before joining Chelsea for £10,000 in March 1959. He quickly established a place in the first team and completed 82 games in which he scored 2 goals over a period of a little more than three years at the Bridge. Left for Queens Park Rangers in January 1962 in a deal that cost the R's £5,000.

1935	Brentford	H	League Division 1	2–1
1940	Portsmouth	A	Football League South	2–4
1946	Aston Villa	H	League Division 1	1–3
1957	Leicester City	H	League Division 1	4–0
1963	Leicester City	A	League Division 1	4–2
1968	Arsenal	A	League Division 1	1–0
1971	Glasgow Rangers	H	Testimonial	0–1
1985	Aston Villa	H	League Division 1	2–1
1991	Southampton	A	League Division 1	0–1
1994	Tottenham Hotspur	A	Premier League	0–0
1996	Newcastle United	H	Premier League	1–1

NOVEMBER 24

1906	Barnsley	H	League Division 2	2–1
1917	Arsenal	H	London Combination League	4–3
1923	Middlesbrough	A	League Division 1	2–0

1928	Port Vale	H	League Division 2	3–3
1934	Arsenal	H	League Division 1	2–5
1945	Tottenham Hotspur	A	Football League South	2–3
1951	Preston North End	H	League Division 1	0–0
1956	Aston Villa	A	League Division 1	1–1
1962	Grimsby Town	A	League Division 2	3–0
1973	Southampton	H	League Division 1	4–0
1975	Chelsea Past XI	H	Testimonial	4–3
1979	Notts County	A	League Division 2	3–2
1981	Charlton Athletic	A	League Division 2	4–3
1984	Tottenham Hotspur	A	League Division 1	1–1

NOVEMBER 25

1905	Leeds City	A	League Division 2	0–0
1911	Blackpool	A	League Division 2	0–1
1916	Tottenham Hotspur	H	London Combination League	2–4
1922	Burnley	H	League Division 1	0–1
1933	Birmingham City	H	League Division 1	1–1
1939	Portsmouth	H	Football League South B	1–0
1944	Arsenal	H	Football League South	2–1
1950	Derby County	H	League Division 1	1–2
1961	West Bromwich Albion	H	League Division 1	4–1
1967	Manchester United	H	League Division 1	1–1
1971	Halmstad, Sweden	A	Friendly	6–0
1972	Crystal Palace	H	League Division 1	0–0
1978	Manchester United	H	League Division 1	0–1
1986	West Ham United	A	Full Members Cup 2nd round	2–1
1989	Manchester United	A	League Division 1	0–0
1990	Manchester United	A	League Division 1	3–2
1995	Tottenham Hotspur	H	Premier League	0–0

NOVEMBER 26

| 1910 | Hull City | H | League Division 2 | 2–0 |

1911 James Argue was born in Glasgow. He played firstly for St Roch's Juniors in Glasgow before making his way to Birmingham City at the end of 1931 where he was managed by Leslie Knighton who, on becoming the boss of the Blues, made Argue his first signing for the club (on a free transfer in May 1933). He played 125 games for Chelsea in which he scored a total 35 League and Cup goals before being released to join Shrewsbury Town in 1947.

1921	Bradford City	A	League Division 1	1–0
1927	Port Vale	A	League Division 2	1–1
1932	Leeds United	A	League Division 1	0–2
1938	Wolverhampton Wanderers	H	League Division 1	1–3

1949	Middlesbrough	A	League Division 1	1–2
1955	Sheffield United	H	League Division 1	1–0

1957 Birth of Trevor Aylott in Bermondsey. Graduated from the junior ranks to the First team where, after 30 games in which he managed just 2 goals, it was judged he had failed to make the grade. After a spell on loan at Queens Park Rangers he was sold to Barnsley for £50,000 but quickly moved to a succession of clubs and never looked likely to prove the Blues' management wrong for releasing him.

1960	Nottingham Forest	A	League Division 1	1–2
1964	Workington Town	A	League Cup 5th round	2–2
1966	Stoke City	A	League Division 1	1–1

1969 David John Lee was born in Bristol. From being a trainee he signed professional forms in July 1988 and, apart from loan spells, has been with the club ever since making close on 200 appearances in the first team. He has suffered more than his fair share of injuries and this has set his career back.

1977	Manchester City	A	League Division 1	2–6
1983	Leeds United	A	League Division 2	1–1
1985	Everton	H	League Cup 4th round	2–2
1988	Shrewsbury Town	H	League Division 2	2–0
1991	Ipswich Town	H	ZDS Cup quarter-final	2–2
1994	Everton	H	Premier League	0–1
1997	Everton	H	Premier League	2–0

NOVEMBER 27

1909	Sheffield Wednesday	A	League Division 1	1–4
1915	Watford	A	London Combination League (Part One)	3–0
1920	Sheffield United	A	League Division 1	1–0
1926	Nottingham Forest	A	League Division 2	1–4
1937	Leicester City	A	League Division 1	0–1
1943	Queens Park Rangers	A	Football League South	11–2
1948	Aston Villa	H	League Division 1	2–1
1954	Portsmouth	H	League Division 1	4–1

1958 John Bumstead was born in Rotherhithe. Signed professional forms in December 1976 after being on the club's books from the age of 13. He made over 400 appearances and scored 44 goals, being a prominent member of the sides that won the Second Division Championship in 1984 and 1989. Also picked up Full Members' Cup winners' medals in 1986 and 1990. He was released in April 1991 and joined Charlton Athletic where injury finished his career.

1965	Aston Villa	A	League Division 1	4–2
1971	Tottenham Hotspur	H	League Division 1	1–0
1976	Burnley	H	League Division 2	2–1
1978	Queens Park Rangers	H	Testimonial	2–2
1982	Rotherham United	A	League Division 2	0–1
1983	'Joe' Bambrick died.			
1993	Sheffield United	A	Premier League	0–1

NOVEMBER 28

1908	Woolwich Arsenal	H	League Division 1	1–2
1914	Sunderland	A	League Division 1	1–2
1925	Sheffield Wednesday	A	League Division 2	1–4
1931	Sheffield United	A	League Division 1	2–4
1936	Everton	H	League Division 1	4–0
1942	Queens Park Rangers	A	Football League South	1–4
1949	AIK Stockholm	H	Friendly	2–1
1953	Preston North End	H	League Division 1	1–0
1959	Wolverhampton Wanderers	A	League Division 1	1–3
1964	West Ham United	H	League Division 1	0–3
1970	West Bromwich Albion	A	League Division 1	2–2
1981	Derby County	A	League Division 2	1–1
1987	Wimbledon	A	League Division 1	2–2
1990	Oxford United	A	League Cup 4th round	2–1

NOVEMBER 29

1906 Goalkeeper John Jackson was born in Glasgow. Came from Partick Thistle in the close season of 1926 and stayed for 12 years, making just 51 appearances but gaining four full Scottish international caps whilst playing predominantly for Chelsea's reserves. He was transferred to Guilford City in 1945.

1913	Bradford City	H	League Division 1	2–1
1919	Middlesbrough	H	League Division 1	3–1
1924	Bradford City	H	League Division 2	3–0
1930	Arsenal	H	League Division 1	1–5
1941	Portsmouth	A	London War League	3–2
1947	Manchester United	H	League Division 1	0–4

Benny Jones played his first game for the club.

1952	Middlesbrough	A	League Division 1	0–4
1958	Everton	A	League Division 1	1–3

1964 Kenneth John Monkou was born in Necare, Surinam. He was signed from Dutch club Feyenoord in March 1989 at a cost of £100,000 and played over 100 games before accepting a transfer to Southampton in August 1992 in a deal that cost the Saints £750,000. Whilst with the Blues he was a part of the team that won the Full Members Cup in 1990.

1966	London XI	H	Friendly	9–7
1975	Bristol Rovers	A	League Division 2	2–1
1986	Leicester City	A	League Division 1	2–2
1992	Leeds United	H	Premier League	1–0
1997	Derby County	H	Premier League	4–0

NOVEMBER 30

1907	Notts County	A	League Division 1	0–2

1912	Derby County	H	League Division 1	3–1
1918	Tottenham Hotspur	H	London Combination League	3–1
1929	Bradford City	A	League Division 2	1–0
1935	Sheffield Wednesday	A	League Division 1	1–4
1940	Portsmouth	A	Football League South	0–5
1943	Tottenham Hotspur	A	Football League South	1–5

1944 George Graham was born in Bargeddie. Chelsea paid Aston Villa £5,000 for his services in June 1964 and he quickly established a rapport with striking partner Barry Bridges. Although he spent just a little over two years at Stamford Bridge his 46 goals in 102 games was an impressive return, and it took a £50,000 cash adjustment and Tommy Baldwin in exchange for Arsenal to lure him away. Later played for Manchester United, Portsmouth and Crystal Palace before moving into a management career with Millwall, Arsenal and Leeds United.

1946	Derby County	A	League Division 1	1–3

1954 Steven James Finnieston was born in Edinburgh. He joined straight from school becoming a professional in December 1971 and making his debut a couple of months later. Restricted by injuries he totalled 90 appearances with 37 goals before being transferred to Sheffield United for £90,000 in June 1978.

1957	Bolton Wanderers	A	League Division 1	3–3
1963	Bolton Wanderers	H	League Division 1	4–0
1968	Leeds United	H	League Division 1	1–1
1974	Leeds United	A	League Division 1	0–2
1980	Notts County	A	League Division 2	1–1
1985	Liverpool	A	League Division 1	1–1
1988	Bradford City	A	Simod Cup 2nd round	3–2
1991	Nottingham Forest	H	League Division 1	1–0

DECEMBER 1

1906	Chesterfield	A	League Division 2	0–0

Debut of William Bridgeman.

1917	West Ham United	A	London Combination League	1–1
1923	Preston North End	A	League Division 1	1–1

Andrew Nesbit Wilson played his first game for the Blues.

1928	Hull City	A	League Division 2	2–2
1934	Portsmouth	A	League Division 1	1–1
1945	Brentford	A	Football League South	4–4
1951	Burnley	A	League Division 1	1–1
1956	Blackpool	H	League Division 1	2–2
1962	Plymouth Argyle	H	League Division 2	1–1
1965	Weiner SK, Austria	H	Fairs Cup 2nd round	2–0
1979	Preston North End	H	League Division 2	2–0
1984	Liverpool	H	League Division 1	3–1
1990	Tottenham Hotspur	H	League Division 1	3–2
1996	Leeds United	A	Premier League	0–2

DECEMBER 2

1905	Burton United	H	League Division 2	3–0
1907	Blackburn Rovers	H	League Division 1	1–0

Ben Whitehouse scored in just 13 seconds, the fastest ever goal by a Chelsea player.

1911	Glossop North End	H	League Division 2	1–0
1916	Crystal Palace	A	London Combination League	1–1
1922	Huddersfield Town	H	League Division 1	2–2
1933	Everton	A	League Division 1	1–2
1939	Queens Park Rangers	A	Football League South B	2–3
1944	Fulham	H	Football League South	2–0
1950	Liverpool	A	League Division 1	0–1

Eric George Parsons, 'The Rabbit', played his first game for the club.

1959	Athletic Bilbao	H	Friendly	5–3

1960 Nigel Spackman was born in Romsey. He was signed from AFC Bournemouth in June 1983 for £40,000, sold to Liverpool in February 1987 for £400,000 and then, via Queens Park Rangers, was purchased for a second time from Glasgow Rangers in September 1992 for £485,000. He finally quit the Bridge for good in July 1996 on a free transfer to Sheffield United where he eventually became manager for a short period before resigning during the 1997–98 season. His combined record over his two spells finished just above 250 appearances.

1961	Ipswich Town	A	League Division 1	2–5
1967	Sunderland	A	League Division 1	3–2
1972	Stoke City	A	League Division 1	1–1
1989	Wimbledon	H	League Division 1	2–5
1992	Everton	A	League Cup 4th round	2–2
1995	Manchester United	A	Premier League	1–1

DECEMBER 3

1910	Fulham	A	League Division 2	0–1
1921	Preston North End	H	League Division 1	0–0
1927	South Shields	H	League Division 2	6–0
1932	Everton	H	League Division 1	1–0
1938	Everton	A	League Division 1	1–4
1949	Blackpool	H	League Division 1	1–1
1955	Everton	A	League Division 1	3–3
1960	West Bromwich Albion	H	League Division 1	7–1

The Blues equalled the record First Division victory they had set against Leeds United a quarter of a century before. Jimmy Greaves contributed five goals to the tally that in turn helped him to compile a record 43 goals for the season.

1966	Everton	H	League Division 1	1–1

1971 Frank Mohammed Sinclair was born in Lambeth although by parentage he qualified to play for the 'Reggae Boyz', Jamaica, and took part in their first ever World Cup final campaign in the France 1998 tournament which failed to get beyond the initial group stages. He signed professional forms for Chelsea in May 1990 and has made around 200 appearances in a career that has seen him play a part in all the recent cup successes, the FA Cup in 1997, the Coca-Cola League Cup and the European Cup-Winners' Cup in 1998. He was transferred after the World Cup to Leicester City.

1976	Sheffield United	A	League Division 2	0–1
1977	Everton	H	League Division 1	0–1
1983	Manchester City	H	League Division 2	0–1
1988	Stoke City	A	League Division 2	3–0
1994	Southampton	A	Premier League	1–0

DECEMBER 4

1909	Bristol City	H	League Division 1	4–1
1915	Tottenham Hotspur	H	London Combination League (Part One)	8–1
1920	Arsenal	H	League Division 1	1–2
1926	Barnsley	H	League Division 2	4–2
1937	Huddersfield Town	H	League Division 1	3–1
1943	Brighton & Hove Albion	H	Football League South	0–1
1948	Sunderland	A	League Division 1	0–3
1954	Wolverhampton Wanderers	A	League Division 1	4–3
1965	Liverpool	H	League Division 1	0–1
1971	Newcastle United	A	League Division 1	0–0
1979	Weymouth	A	Testimonial	1–2
1982	Burnley	H	League Division 2	2–1
1985	Oxford United	A	Full Members Cup Southern final	4–1

DECEMBER 5

1908	Notts County	A	League Division 1	0–3
1914	Sheffield Wednesday	H	League Division 1	0–0
1925	Stoke City	H	League Division 2	1–1
1931	Manchester City	H	League Division 1	3–2
1936	Bolton Wanderers	A	League Division 1	1–2
1942	Brighton & Hove Albion	H	Football League South	0–0
1953	Newcastle United	A	League Division 1	1–1
1959	Sheffield Wednesday	H	League Division 1	0–4
1964	West Bromwich Albion	A	League Division 1	2–0
1970	Newcastle United	H	League Division 1	1–0
1973	Lincoln City	A	Friendly	4–2
1981	Sheffield Wednesday	H	League Division 2	2–1
1992	Tottenham Hotspur	A	Premier League	2–1
1993	Blackburn Rovers	A	Premier League	0–2

DECEMBER 6

1913	Blackburn Rovers	A	League Division 1	1–3
1919	Arsenal	A	League Division 1	1–1
1924	Port Vale	A	League Division 2	1–1
1930	Derby County	A	League Division 1	2–6
1941	Clapton Orient	H	London War League	1–2
1947	Burnley	A	League Division 1	0–1
1958	Birmingham City	H	League Division 1	1–0

1965 Gordon Scott Durie was born in Paisley. A Scottish international who joined the Blues from Hibernian in April 1986 for a fee of £381,000. He was a member of the Second Division Championship winning side in 1989 and the team that won the Full Members' Cup in 1990. Moved to Tottenham Hotspur, later to return to his native Scotland where he enjoyed success with Glasgow Rangers.

1969	Manchester United	A	League Division 1	2–0
1975	Bolton Wanderers	H	League Division 2	0–1
1980	Swansea City	H	League Division 2	0–0
1983	Swansea City	H	League Division 2	6–1
1986	Wimbledon	H	League Division 1	0–4
1987	Liverpool	H	League Division 1	1–1
1997	Tottenham Hotspur	A	Premier League	6–1

DECEMBER 7

1907	Manchester City	H	League Division 1	2–2
1912	Tottenham Hotspur	A	League Division 1	0–1
1918	Clapton Orient	A	London Combination League	5–0
1929	Swansea Town	H	League Division 2	1–0
1935	Portsmouth	H	League Division 1 (Abandoned)	1–2
1940	West Ham United	A	Football League South	2–6
1946	Everton	H	League Division 1	1–1
1957	Leeds United	H	League Division 1	2–1
1963	Everton	A	League Division 1	1–1
1968	Sunderland	A	League Division 1	2–3
1974	Luton Town	H	League Division 1	2–0
1976	Southampton	A	League Division 2	1–1
1985	Coventry City	A	League Division 1	1–1
1991	Sheffield Wednesday	A	League Division 1	0–3
1996	Everton	H	Premier League	2–2

DECEMBER 8

1901 Peter Joseph McKenna was born in Toxteth Park, Liverpool. A goalkeeper who spent seven years at the Bridge but made only 66 appearances in the first team.

1906	Wolverhampton Wanderers	A	League Division 2	2–1

1917	Fulham	H	London Combination League	2–2
1923	Preston North End	H	League Division 1	1–2
1928	Tottenham Hotspur	H	League Division 2	1–1
1934	Liverpool	H	League Division 1	4–1
1945	Brentford	H	Football League South	4–2

1948 Stephen Dennis Kember was born in Croydon. He had spent six years with local club Crystal Palace before Chelsea picked him up for £170,000 in September 1971 to bolster a somewhat depleted squad. He made 150 appearances and scored 15 goals before departing to Leicester City in July 1975 for £80,000 and later returned to Crystal Palace.

1951	Charlton Athletic	H	League Division 1	1–0
1956	Manchester City	A	League Division 1	4–5
1959	Athletic Bilbao	A	Friendly	0–1
1962	Preston North End	A	League Division 2	3–1
1973	Leicester City	H	League Division 1	3–2
1979	Oldham Athletic	A	League Division 2	0–1
1984	Sheffield Wednesday	A	League Division 1	1–1
1990	Crystal Palace	H	League Division 1	2–1

DECEMBER 9

1905	Grimsby Town	H	League Division 2	2–0
1911	Hull City	A	League Division 2	0–1
1916	Brentford	H	London Combination League	7–2
1922	Huddersfield Town	A	League Division 1	0–3
1933	Manchester City	H	League Division 1	1–2

Debut for James Argue.

1939	Aldershot	H	Football League South B	2–2
1944	Aldershot	A	Football League South	4–3
1950	Fulham	H	League Division 1	2–1
1961	Burnley	H	League Division 1	1–2
1972	Norwich City	H	League Division 1	1–1
1978	Aston Villa	H	League Division 1	0–1
1989	Queens Park Rangers	A	League Division 1	2–4
1995	Newcastle United	H	Premier League	1–0

DECEMBER 10

1910	Bradford Park Avenue	H	League Division 2	3–0
1921	Preston North End	A	League Division 1	0–2
1927	Leeds United	A	League Division 2	0–5
1932	Arsenal	A	League Division 1	1–4
1938	Huddersfield Town	H	League Division 1	3–0
1949	Newcastle United	A	League Division 1	2–2

Francis John Saunders made his first appearance after his arrival from Darlington in May 1948. Although his stay at the club extended to six years, his time was mostly spent in reserve and he made only 60 first team starts before moving on to Crystal Palace.

1955	Newcastle United	H	League Division 1	2–1
1960	Cardiff City	A	League Division 1	1–2
1966	Newcastle United	A	League Division 1	2–2
1977	Wolverhampton Wanderers	A	League Division 1	3–1
1983	Barnsley	A	League Division 2	0–0
1988	Portsmouth	H	League Division 2	3–3
1991	Crystal Palace	A	ZDS Cup Southern semi-final	1–0
1994	Norwich City	A	Premier League	0–3

DECEMBER 11

1909	Bury	A	League Division 1	2–4
1915	Millwall	A	London Combination League (Part One)	0–1
1920	Arsenal	A	League Division 1	1–1
1926	Manchester City	A	League Division 2	1–1
1937	Derby County	A	League Division 1	0–4
1943	Portsmouth	A	Football League South	5–1
1948	Wolverhampton Wanderers	H	League Division 1	4–1

1953 Alan Mayes was born in Edmonton. He was acquired from Northampton Town at a cost of £200,000 in December 1980 after time spent at Queens Park Rangers and Watford. Although he managed a respectable goals-to-games ratio of 24 in 76 appearances, he was given a free transfer to Swindon Town by manager John Neal in July 1983. He later played for Carlisle United, Blackpool and Newport County.

1954	Aston Villa	H	League Division 1	4–0
1963	MTK Hungary	A	Friendly	2–0
1965	Tottenham Hotspur	A	League Division 1	2–4
1971	Leeds United	H	League Division 1	0–0
1973	Crystal Palace	A	Friendly	3–1
1976	Wolverhampton Wanderers	H	League Division 2	3–3
1982	Middlesbrough	A	League Division 2	1–3
1985	Everton	A	League Cup 4th round replay	2–1
1992	Middlesbrough	A	Premier League	0–0
1993	Ipswich Town	H	Premier League	1–1

DECEMBER 12

1883 William Walter Bridgeman was born in Bromley, Kent. Joined Chelsea in 1906 from West Ham United and remained at the Bridge for the best part of 13 years making 160 appearances and scoring 22 goals. Finished his career with Southend United.

| 1908 | Newcastle United | H | League Division 1 | 1–2 |

1914	West Bromwich Albion	A	League Division 1	0–2
1925	Middlesbrough	A	League Division 2	2–1
1931	West Bromwich Albion	A	League Division 1	0–4
1936	Brentford	H	League Division 1	2–1
1942	Portsmouth	A	Football League South	0–3
1953	Manchester United	H	League Division 1	3–1
1959	Blackpool	A	League Division 1	1–3

John Brooks played his first game in Chelsea's colours.

1964	Wolverhampton Wanderers	H	League Division 1	2–1
1970	Nottingham Forest	A	League Division 1	1–1
1978	Crystal Palace	H	Testimonial	2–0
1987	West Ham United	A	League Division 1	1–4
1990	Swindon Town	H	ZDS Cup 2nd round	1–0

DECEMBER 13

1913	Sunderland	H	League Division 1	1–1
1919	Arsenal	H	League Division 1	3–1
1924	Middlesbrough	H	League Division 2	2–0
1930	Sunderland	H	League Division 1	5–0
1941	Charlton Athletic	H	London War League	2–4
1947	Portsmouth	H	League Division 1	1–0
1952	Manchester City	A	League Division 1	0–4
1958	West Bromwich Albion	A	League Division 1	0–4
1969	Wolverhampton Wanderers	A	League Division 1	0–3

1971   Edward (Eddie) Newton was born in Hammersmith. Upgraded from trainee to full professional in May 1990, he has since played nearly 200 games for the senior team, the highlight of which was the FA Cup final in 1997 against Middlesbrough in which he scored the second goal.

1972	Norwich City	H	League Cup semi-final	0–2
1975	Carlisle United	A	League Division 2	1–2
1980	Grimsby Town	A	League Division 2	0–2
1997	Leeds United	H	Premier League	0–0

DECEMBER 14

1907	Preston North End	A	League Division 1	4–2
1912	Middlesbrough	H	League Division 1	2–3
1918	Arsenal	A	London Combination League	0–3

1918   Angus Douglas died of influenza.

1929	Cardiff City	A	League Division 2	0–1
1935	Preston North End	A	League Division 1	0–2
1940	Crystal Palace	H	Football League South	1–3
1946	Huddersfield Town	A	League Division 1	4–1

1947	William Garner was born in Leicester. Signed from Southend United in September 1972 for £80,000 and, over the course of six years, made over 100 appearances and scored 36 goals. Was given a free transfer to Cambridge United in November 1978 where he played for five years before winding down his career at Brentford.			
1957	Manchester United	A	League Division 1	1–0
1960	Portsmouth	A	League Cup 4th round	0–1
1963	West Ham United	A	League Division 1	2–2
1968	Wolverhampton Wanderers	H	League Division 1	1–1
1974	Carlisle United	A	League Division 1	2–1
1985	Sheffield Wednesday	H	League Division 1	2–1
1986	Liverpool	A	League Division 1	0–3

DECEMBER 15

1906	Clapton Orient	H	League Division 2	2–1
1917	Queens Park Rangers	A	London Combination League	1–0
1923	Burnley	A	League Division 1	0–2
1928	Reading	A	League Division 2	3–3
1934	Manchester City	A	League Division 1	0–2
1945	Swansea Town	A	Football League South	3–5
1951	Blackpool	H	League Division 1	2–1
1954	Red Banner, Hungary	H	Friendly	2–2
1956	Burnley	H	League Division 1	2–0
1962	Rotherham United	H	League Division 2	3–0

1966	Dennis Frank Wise was born in Kensington. Started as an amateur with Southampton but it was with Wimbledon that he came to the fore. He joined Chelsea in July 1990 for a then club record fee of £1,600,000 and quickly established himself as a favourite with the crowd. An England international with over 300 games for the club, and a contract into the next millennium. He is one of a select band of Chelsea heroes and one of the few Englishmen at the club who can expect to hold their place in the first team in the face of stiff competition from the Blues' foreign imports. Has been at the heart of the three recent cup successes, and has won FA Cup (1997), Coca-Cola League Cup and European Cup-Winners' Cup (1998) medals.			
1973	Leeds United	H	League Division 1	1–2
1979	Swansea City	H	League Division 2	3–0
1984	Stoke City	H	League Division 1	1–1
1990	Derby County	A	League Division 1	6–4
1991	Manchester United	H	League Division 1	1–3
1996	Sunderland	A	Premier League	0–3

DECEMBER 16

1905	Gainsborough Trinity	A	League Division 2	2–0
1911	Barnsley	H	League Division 2	2–1
1916	Southampton	A	London Combination League	0–2

1922	Tottenham Hotspur	H	League Division 1	0–0
1933	Arsenal	A	League Division 1	1–2
1939	Bournemouth	A	Football League South B	2–2
1944	Brentford	H	Football League South	0–2
1961	Nottingham Forest	A	League Division 1	0–3
1964	Workington Town	H	League Cup 5th round replay	2–0

1964 Peter Osgood made his first appearance for the Blues' senior side and scored both goals.

1967	West Bromwich Albion	H	League Division 1	0–3
1972	Wolverhampton Wanderers	A	League Division 1	0–1
1978	Middlesbrough	A	League Division 1	2–7
1987	Manchester City	A	Simod Cup 2nd round	2–0
1988	Birmingham City	A	League Division 2	4–1
1989	Liverpool	H	League Division 1	2–5
1992	Everton	H	League Cup 4th round replay	1–0
1995	Arsenal	A	Premier League	1–1

DECEMBER 17

1910	Burnley	A	League Division 2	1–1
1921	Tottenham Hotspur	A	League Division 1	0–0
1927	Wolverhampton Wanderers	H	League Division 2	2–0
1932	Manchester City	H	League Division 1	3–1
1938	Portsmouth	A	League Division 1	1–2

1939 Joe Kirkup was born in Hexham. Joined late in his career after spending nine years at West Ham United from where he was purchased in March 1966 for £35,000. Lasted only two years before being used in part exchange in the deal that brought Dave Webb to Chelsea from Southampton in February 1968. He made 70 appearances whilst at the Bridge and scored 2 goals.

1949	Birmingham City	H	League Division 1	3–0
1955	Bolton Wanderers	A	League Division 1	0–4
1960	Aston Villa	H	League Division 1	2–4
1966	West Ham United	H	League Division 1	5–5
1971	Coventry City	A	League Division 1	1–1
1977	Norwich City	H	League Division 1	1–1
1983	Grimsby Town	H	League Division 2	2–3
1985	Oxford United	H	Full Members Cup Southern final	0–1

DECEMBER 18

1909	Tottenham Hotspur	H	League Division 1	2–1
1915	Crystal Palace	H	London Combination League (Part One)	6–1
1920	Bradford Park Avenue	H	League Division 1	4–1
1926	Darlington	H	League Division 2	2–2

1937	Wolverhampton Wanderers	H	League Division 1	0–2
1943	Watford	A	Football League South	0–1
1948	Middlesbrough	A	League Division 1	1–1
1954	Leicester City	H	League Division 1	3–1
1976	Hull City	A	League Division 2	1–1
1979	Queens Park Rangers	A	League Division 2	2–2
1982	Bolton Wanderers	H	League Division 2	2–1
1994	Liverpool	H	Premier League	0–0

DECEMBER 19

1908	Bristol City	A	League Division 1	0–1
1910	West Bromwich Albion	A	League Division 2	3–1
1914	Everton	H	League Division 1	2–0
1925	Portsmouth	H	League Division 2	0–0
1931	Birmingham City	H	League Division 1	2–1
1936	Arsenal	A	League Division 1	1–4
1942	Brentford	H	Football League South	2–4
1953	Blackpool	H	League Division 1	5–1
1959	Preston North End	A	League Division 1	5–4
1964	Sunderland	A	League Division 1	0–3
1970	West Ham United	H	League Division 1	2–1
1974	Everton	H	League Division 1	1–1
1981	Blackburn Rovers	H	League Division 2	1–1
1992	Manchester United	H	Premier League	1–1

DECEMBER 20

1913	Everton	A	League Division 1	0–0
1919	Sheffield United	A	League Division 1	1–3

1919 Sydney Bathgate was born in Aberdeen. His career was delayed by the Second World War and it was only after being demobbed from the RAF in 1946 that he was able to take up full time football at Stamford Bridge. Even so he amassed 147 appearances before heading back to Scotland to play for Hamilton Academical in July 1953.

1924	Barnsley	A	League Division 2	3–3

Leslie Frank Odell made his first start for the club as an amateur (a month later he turned professional) to commence a career that would stretch for 13 years at the Bridge. In this time he amassed just over 100 games in the first team and spent the majority of his time in the reserves. He departed for Bedford Town where he took up the post of player-manager in September 1937.

1930	Portsmouth	A	League Division 1	1–1

1933 Goalkeeper Reginald Derrick Matthews was born in Coventry. He was signed from his local club, Coventry City, for what was at the time a record British fee for a goalkeeper (£20,000) in December 1956 by which time he had already won his five English international caps. He had made 148 appearances 'between the sticks' for

Chelsea when, having lost his place in the side to Peter Bonetti, he was transferred to Derby County in October 1961 for £10,000.

1941	West Ham United	A	London War League	0–5
1947	Blackpool	H	League Division 1	2–2
1952	Manchester United	H	League Division 1	2–3
1958	Manchester United	H	League Division 1	2–3

Debut of Stanley Crowther.

1969	Manchester City	H	League Division 1	3–1

Paddy Mulligan played his first game for Chelsea.

1972	Norwich City	A	League Cup semi-final (Abandoned)	2–3
1975	Sunderland	H	League Division 2	1–0
1980	Orient	H	League Division 2	0–1
1986	Tottenham Hotspur	H	League Division 1	0–2
1987	Charlton Athletic	H	League Division 1	1–1
1995	Gareth Hall was transferred to Sunderland for £300,000.			
1997	Sheffield Wednesday	A	Premier League	4–1

DECEMBER 21

1907	Bury	H	League Division 1	3–4
1912	Notts County	A	League Division 1	0–0
1918	Queens Park Rangers	H	London Combination League	2–0
1929	Preston North End	H	League Division 2	5–0

George Robert Mills played his first game in senior football.

1935	Wolverhampton Wanderers	H	League Division 1	2–2
1935	Ted Birnie died in Southend.			
1940	Charlton Athletic	A	Football League South	3–1
1946	Wolverhampton Wanderers	H	League Division 1	1–2
1957	Tottenham Hotspur	H	League Division 1	2–4
1963	Sheffield United	H	League Division 1	3–2

Peter Houseman made his debut for the club.

1968	Leicester City	A	League Division 1	4–1
1974	West Ham United	H	League Division 1	1–1
1985	Birmingham City	A	League Division 1	2–1
1991	Oldham Athletic	H	League Division 1	4–2
1996	West Ham United	H	Premier League	3–1

DECEMBER 22

1906	Gainsborough Trinity	A	League Division 2	1–1
1917	Millwall	H	London Combination League	6–2
1923	Burnley	H	League Division 1	3–2
1928	Notts County	H	League Division 2	1–1
1934	Middlesbrough	H	League Division 1	2–1

1945	Swansea Town	H	Football League South	3–4
1951	Liverpool	A	League Division 1	1–1
1962	Charlton Athletic	A	League Division 2	4–1

1967 Daniel Vasile Petrescu was born in Bucharest, Romania. He had played for two clubs in Italy, Foggia and Genoa, before coming to England to play for Sheffield Wednesday who paid £1,250,000 for his signature in August 1994. He joined Chelsea in November 1995 for £2.3 million and has been a regular fixture in the side ever since being to the fore in Chelsea's three winning cup campaigns in 1997 and 1998.

| 1971 | Tottenham Hotspur | H | League Cup semi-final | 3–2 |
| 1973 | Wolverhampton Wanderers | A | League Division 1 | 0–2 |

1978 Jody Morris was born in Hammersmith. A highly promising graduate of the youth set-up, he signed professional forms in January 1996 and although still in the early stages of his career and not yet a first-team regular, he could achieve a great deal.

1984	Everton	A	League Division 1	4–3
1989	West Ham United	H	ZDS Cup 3rd round	4–3
1990	Coventry City	H	League Division 1	2–1

1992 Goalkeeper Dmitri Kharine joined the club from CSKA Moscow in a £200,000 deal.

DECEMBER 23

1905	Bristol City	H	League Division 2	0–0
1911	Bradford Park Avenue	A	League Division 2	1–1
1916	Arsenal	A	London Combination League	1–2
1922	Tottenham Hotspur	A	League Division 1	1–3

1931 Walter Bettridge died in Measham, Leicestershire.
John Brooks was born in Reading. After a start at local club Reading and then six years with Tottenham Hotspur, Brooks came to Stamford Bridge in exchange for Les Allen in December 1959 but never really justified his reputation playing just 52 games (with 7 goals). Lasted for two years before signing for Brentford then Crystal Palace.

1933	Leeds United	H	League Division 1	1–1
1950	Middlesbrough	H	League Division 1	1–1
1961	Aston Villa	H	League Division 1	1–0

Graham Moore, at the time a club record signing from Cardiff City at £35,000, made his debut.

1967	Fulham	A	League Division 1	2–2
1972	Everton	H	League Division 1	1–1
1978	Bristol City	H	League Division 1	0–0

Mickey Nutton played his first senior game.

| 1995 | Manchester City | A | Premier League | 1–0 |

DECEMBER 24

| 1910 | Gainsborough Trinity | H | League Division 2 | 3–0 |

1921	Tottenham Hotspur	H	League Division 1	1–2
1927	Barnsley	A	League Division 2	1–3
1932	Sunderland	A	League Division 1	1–2
1938	Liverpool	H	League Division 1	4–1

1945   Peter Houseman was born in Battersea. Rose through the youth and reserve ranks to make his club debut in December 1963 from which time, until May 1975 when he joined Oxford United in a £30,000 deal, he was a constant member of the first team squad. As such he picked up winners' medals for the 1970 FA Cup and 1971 European Cup-Winners' Cup. He played a total of 343 games and scored 39 goals for the Blues. Tragically, he died within two years of leaving the club when he and his wife were involved in a fatal car crash.

1949	Derby County	A	League Division 1	2–2
1955	Arsenal	H	League Division 1	2–0
1960	Manchester United	H	League Division 1	1–2
1966	Liverpool	H	League Division 1	1–2

DECEMBER 25

1905	Manchester United	A	League Division 2	0–0
1906	Hull City	A	League Division 2	1–0
1907	Liverpool	A	League Division 1	4–1
1908	Manchester City	A	League Division 1	2–1
1909	Notts County	A	League Division 1	1–2

Frederick Taylor made his debut for the Blues. He joined earlier in the month from Gainsborough Trinity and remained an integral part of the defence until his career was interrupted by the outbreak of the First World War. He was a part of the side that lost in the final of the 1915 FA Cup and in total played 171 games for the club. In 1919 he switched to Brentford then moved on soon after to non-League football with Maidstone United.

1911	Fulham	A	League Division 2	1–0
1912	Manchester United	H	League Division 1	1–4
1913	Sheffield Wednesday	H	League Division 1	2–1
1914	Manchester City	H	League Division 1	0–0
1915	Brentford	A	London Combination League (Part One)	2–1
1916	West Ham United	H	London Combination League	1–1
1917	Clapton Orient	A	London Combination League	4–1
1918	Crystal Palace	H	London Combination League	0–2
1919	Aston Villa	A	League Division 1	2–5
1920	Liverpool	H	League Division 1	1–1
1922	Nottingham Forest	H	League Division 1	2–2
1923	Nottingham Forest	A	League Division 1	0–2
1924	Wolverhampton Wanderers	H	League Division 2	1–0
1925	Blackpool	A	League Division 2	0–0
1926	Hull City	H	League Division 2	1–0

1928	Stoke City	A	League Division 2	1–0
1929	Blackpool	A	League Division 2	1–1
1930	Aston Villa	H	League Division 1	0–2
1931	Blackpool	A	League Division 1	4–2
1934	Aston Villa	H	League Division 1	2–0

'Joe' Bambrick made his Chelsea debut.

1935	Manchester City	A	League Division 1	0–0
1936	Stoke City	A	League Division 1	0–2
1937	Charlton Athletic	H	League Division 1 (Abandoned)	1–1
1939	Southampton	A	Football League South B	3–5
1940	Fulham	H	Football League South	5–2
1941	Watford	H	London War League	2–2
1942	Arsenal	H	Football League South	5–2
1943	West Ham United	H	Football League South	3–3
1945	Millwall	H	Football League South	3–0
1946	Preston North End	H	League Division 1	1–2

Goalkeeper Harry Medhurst played his first game for the Blues.

1946   John Boyle was born in Motherwell. Chelsea was his first club, he joined in August 1964, and he served nearly ten years before being sold for a nominal fee to Brighton and Hove Albion. He was a member of all three Cup winning teams of the period and amassed over 250 appearances in which he scored a dozen goals.

1947	Grimsby Town	A	League Division 1	0–0
1948	Portsmouth	H	League Division 1	1–2
1950	Portsmouth	A	League Division 1	3–1
1951	Manchester City	H	League Division 1	0–3
1954	Arsenal	A	League Division 1	0–1
1956	Arsenal	H	League Division 1	1–1
1957	Portsmouth	H	League Division 1	7–4
1958	Blackburn Rovers	A	League Division 1	3–0

DECEMBER 26

1905	Glossop North End	A	League Division 2	4–2
1907	Middlesbrough	H	League Division 1	1–0
1908	Manchester City	H	League Division 1	1–2
1910	Leeds City	A	League Division 2	3–3
1911	Fulham	H	League Division 2	1–0
1912	Manchester United	A	League Division 1	2–4
1913	Sheffield Wednesday	A	League Division 1	0–3
1914	Manchester City	A	League Division 1	1–2
1916	West Ham United	A	London Combination League	0–2
1917	Clapton Orient	H	London Combination League	0–2
1918	Crystal Palace	A	London Combination League	0–0
1919	Oldham Athletic	H	League Division 1	1–0
1921	Middlesbrough	H	League Division 1	1–0

1922	Nottingham Forest	A	League Division 1	4–0
1923	Nottingham Forest	H	League Division 1	1–1
1924	Wolverhampton Wanderers	A	League Division 2	1–0
1925	Blackpool	H	League Division 2	2–3
1927	Grimsby Town	A	League Division 2	1–1
1928	Stoke City	H	League Division 2	3–1
1929	Blackpool	H	League Division 2	4–0
1930	Aston Villa	A	League Division 1	3–3

George Barber made his debut.

1931	Blackpool	H	League Division 1	4–1
1932	Liverpool	A	League Division 1	0–3
1933	Sunderland	H	League Division 1	4–0
1934	Aston Villa	A	League Division 1	3–0
1935	Manchester City	H	League Division 1	2–1
1936	Leeds United	H	League Division 1	2–1
1938	Leeds United	A	League Division 1	1–1
1939	Brighton & Hove Albion	H	Football League South B	3–2
1942	Arsenal	A	Football League South	5–1
1945	Millwall	A	Football League South	8–0
1946	Preston North End	A	League Division 1	1–1
1949	Liverpool	H	League Division 1	1–1
1950	Portsmouth	H	League Division 1	1–4
1951	Manchester City	A	League Division 1	1–3
1952	Stoke City	A	League Division 1	1–1

Goalkeeper Chick Thomson played his first game for Chelsea.

1953	Cardiff City	H	League Division 1	2–0
1955	Cardiff City	A	League Division 1	1–1
1956	Arsenal	A	League Division 1	0–2
1957	Portsmouth	A	League Division 1	0–3
1959	Newcastle United	H	League Division 1	2–2
1960	Manchester United	A	League Division 1	0–6
1961	Tottenham Hotspur	H	League Division 1	0–2
1962	Luton Town	A	League Division 2	2–0
1963	Blackpool	A	League Division 1	5–1
1964	Blackpool	H	League Division 1	2–0
1966	Liverpool	A	League Division 1	1–2
1967	Arsenal	H	League Division 1	2–1
1968	Ipswich Town	A	League Division 1	3–1
1969	Southampton	H	League Division 1	3–0
1972	Ipswich Town	A	League Division 1	0–3

Graham Wilkins made his debut for Chelsea.

1973	West Ham United	H	League Division 1	2–4

1974	Arsenal	A	League Division 1	2–1
1975	Orient	A	League Division 2	1–3
1977	Arsenal	A	League Division 1	0–3
1978	Southampton	A	League Division 1	0–0
1979	Leicester City	H	League Division 2	1–0
1980	Luton Town	A	League Division 2	0–2

Alan Mayes played his first game for the Blues.

1981	Queens Park Rangers	A	League Division 2	2–0
1983	Shrewsbury Town	A	League Division 2	4–2
1984	Queens Park Rangers	A	League Division 1	2–2
1986	Southampton	A	League Division 1	2–1
1987	Queens Park Rangers	A	League Division 1	1–3
1988	Ipswich Town	H	League Division 2	3–0
1989	Crystal Palace	A	League Division 1	2–2
1990	Leeds United	A	League Division 1	1–4
1991	Notts County	A	League Division 1	0–2
1992	Southampton	H	Premier League	1–1
1994	Manchester United	H	Premier League	2–3
1995	Wimbledon	H	Premier League	1–2
1996	Aston Villa	A	Premier League	2–0
1997	Wimbledon	H	Premier League	1–1

DECEMBER 27

1909	Newcastle United	H	League Division 1	2–1
1910	Stockport County	H	League Division 2	2–0
1913	Tottenham Hotspur	A	League Division 1	2–1
1915	Brentford	H	London Combination League (Part One)	4–1
1919	Sheffield United	H	League Division 1	1–0
1920	Liverpool	A	League Division 1	1–2

Thomas Meehan who had been signed from Manchester United for £3,300 earlier in the month, made his debut. He made 133 starts for the club and scored 4 goals but died prematurely from a bout of sleeping sickness in August 1924. Shortly before his death he had made his international debut for England, against Ireland in Belfast, but this was to be his only cap.

1921	Middlesbrough	A	League Division 1	1–1
1924	Coventry City	A	League Division 2	3–0
1926	Hull City	A	League Division 2	1–0
1930	Grimsby Town	H	League Division 1	5–0
1932	Liverpool	H	League Division 1	0–2
1937	Charlton Athletic	A	League Division 1	1–3
1938	Leeds United	H	League Division 1	2–2
1941	Aldershot	A	London War League	3–2
1943	West Ham United	A	Football League South	0–3
1947	Grimsby Town	H	League Division 1	2–3

1948	Portsmouth	A	League Division 1	2–5
1949	Liverpool	A	League Division 1	2–2
1952	Stoke City	H	League Division 1	0–0
1954	Arsenal	H	League Division 1	1–1
1955	Cardiff City	H	League Division 1	2–1
1958	Blackburn Rovers	H	League Division 1	0–2
1965	Northampton Town	A	League Division 1	3–2
1969	Crystal Palace	A	League Division 1	5–1
1971	Ipswich Town	H	League Division 1	2–0

A goalkeeping crisis left the Blues with no alternative but to call on outfielder, Dave Webb, to perform between the sticks. He responded to the challenge by keeping a clean sheet!

1975	Charlton Athletic	H	League Division 2	2–3
1976	Fulham	H	League Division 2	2–0
1977	West Ham United	H	League Division 1	2–1
1980	Bristol City	H	League Division 2	0–0
1982	Queens Park Rangers	A	League Division 2	2–1
1983	Portsmouth	H	League Division 2	2–2
1986	Aston Villa	H	League Division 1	4–1
1993	Southampton	A	Premier League	1–0

DECEMBER 28

1906 Albert Eric Oakton was born in Kiveton Park. A tricky winger who had spells with Grimsby Town, Rotherham United, Worksop Town, Sheffield United, Scunthorpe United and Bristol Rovers prior to joining Chelsea in May 1932. He played 112 times and scored 28 goals in a five-year stay at the Bridge then departed for Nottingham Forest.

1907	Aston Villa	A	League Division 1	0–0
1912	Bolton Wanderers	H	League Division 1	2–3
1914	Burnley	H	League Division 1	1–4
1918	Millwall	A	London Combination League	1–1
1925	Derby County	A	League Division 2	2–4
1929	Nottingham Forest	A	League Division 2	0–0
1935	Liverpool	A	League Division 1	3–2
1936	Stoke City	H	League Division 1	1–0
1940	Aldershot	H	Football League South	3–5

1942 Allan Harris was born in Hackney. He had two spells at Chelsea the first of which commenced straight from school in June 1960 and the second when he was re-signed from Coventry City to whom he had been sold for £35,000 in November 1964. The Blues had to pay £45,000 to get him back in May 1966 and eventually he managed a cumulative total of just over 100 appearances in a Chelsea shirt with a single goal to his credit. The older brother of Ron 'Chopper' Harris departed the club again, this time to join Queens Park Rangers, in July 1967 for a transfer fee of £30,000. Later played for Plymouth Argyle and Cambridge United before carving a successful career in football management, the pinnacle of which was a spell in charge of Barcelona in Spain.

1946	Bolton Wanderers	A	League Division 1	1–1
1953	Cardiff City	A	League Division 1	0–0
1957	Birmingham City	A	League Division 1	3–3
1959	Newcastle United	A	League Division 1	1–1
1963	Blackpool	H	League Division 1	1–0
1965	Northampton Town	H	League Division 1	1–0
1974	Queens Park Rangers	H	League Division 1	0–3
1982	Fulham	H	League Division 2	0–0
1985	Tottenham Hotspur	H	League Division 1	2–0
1987	Norwich City	H	League Division 1	1–0
1991	Luton Town	A	League Division 1	0–2
1992	Wimbledon	A	Premier League	0–0
1993	Newcastle United	H	Premier League	1–0
1994	Aston Villa	A	Premier League	0–3
1996	Sheffield Wednesday	H	Premier League	2–2

DECEMBER 29

1890 Robert John Thomson was born in Croydon. Bob was signed from his local side, Croydon Common, in September 1911 as a centre-forward of some repute. However, he found it difficult to adjust to life at Chelsea and struggled to retain a regular place in the starting line-up. Nevertheless he did manage to accumulate 95 appearances and score some 29 goals in an 11-year spell that was interrupted by the First World War. He is best known as the man who played in place of Vivian Woodward in the 1915 FA Cup final, when the famous amateur who was unexpectedly given leave from the Army, declined to take the place of Thomson who had been instrumental in getting Chelsea there. He moved to Charlton Athletic in March 1922.

| 1906 | Glossop North End | A | League Division 2 | 1–0 |

1908 George Robert Mills was born in Depford. He cost Chelsea £10 when signed from local amateur club Bromley in December 1929 but won three England international caps and became the first Chelsea player to top 100 goals for the club on his way to a total of 124 in 239 appearances. He retired in 1943 and coached the A team after the war.

1917	Tottenham Hotspur	A	London Combination League	0–2
1923	Arsenal	A	League Division 1	0–1
1928	Swansea Town	A	League Division 2	1–0
1934	Derby County	H	League Division 1	1–1
1945	Southampton	A	Football League South	0–7
1951	Portsmouth	H	League Division 1	1–1
1956	Leeds United	H	League Division 1	1–1
1973	Liverpool	H	League Division 1	0–1
1976	Luton Town	A	League Division 2	0–4
1979	Wrexham	A	League Division 2	0–2

Peter Rhoades-Brown made his debut for Chelsea.

1984	Manchester United	H	League Division 1	1–3
1990	Luton Town	A	League Division 1	0–2
1997	Southampton	A	Premier League	0–1

DECEMBER 30

1905	Stockport County	H	League Division 2	4–2
1911	Stockport County	A	League Division 2	1–0
1916	Luton Town	H	London Combination League	1–4
1922	Liverpool	H	League Division 1	0–0
1933	Stoke City	H	League Division 1	2–0
1939	Reading	A	Football League South B	5–1
1944	Crystal Palace	A	Football League South	3–3
1961	Tottenham Hotspur	A	League Division 1	2–5
1967	Arsenal	A	League Division 1	1–1
1972	Derby County	H	League Division 1	1–1

Ian Britton's first game for Chelsea.

1978	Ipswich Town	A	League Division 1	1–5
1989	Luton Town	A	League Division 1	3–0
1995	Liverpool	H	Premier League	2–2

DECEMBER 31

1910	Derby County	H	League Division 2	3–2
1921	Arsenal	H	League Division 1	0–2
1927	Reading	H	League Division 2	0–0
1932	Blackburn Rovers	A	League Division 1	3–1
1938	Leicester City	A	League Division 1	2–3
1949	West Bromwich Albion	H	League Division 1	2–1
1955	Portsmouth	A	League Division 1	4–4
1960	Wolverhampton Wanderers	A	League Division 1	1–6

1965   Anthony Robert Dorigo was born in Melbourne, Australia, but despite his place of birth, he qualified and gained full international caps for England. His first English club was Aston Villa where he played over 100 games and from where Chelsea signed him for £475,000 in July 1987. He made 180 appearances for the club scoring a dozen goals before moving to Leeds in May 1991 for £1 million. There he won a League Championship medal before injury forced him out of the side and he took the opportunity of a further move, this time to Torino in Italy to play in Serie B.

1966	Sheffield Wednesday	A	League Division 1	1–6
1977	Birmingham City	A	League Division 1	5–4
1983	Brighton & Hove Albion	H	League Division 2	1–0
1988	West Bromwich Albion	H	League Division 2	1–1
1994	Wimbledon	H	Premier League	1–1